LATERAL WINE-TASTING

To 2elma

Hope this leads you

to some good bottles

& thank you for

a friendly visit to

Simi.

Rosemary

11. 6. 93

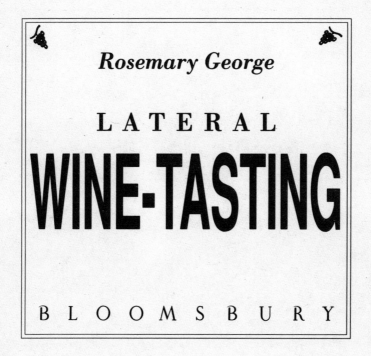

Rosemary George

LATERAL

WINE-TASTING

BLOOMSBURY

First published 1991

This updated paperback edition first published 1992.

© Rosemary George 1991, 1992

Bloomsbury Publishing Ltd.,
2 Soho Square, London W1V 5DE

British Library Cataloguing in Publication Data
A CIP record for this book is available from the British Library

ISBN 0 7475 1227 2

Designed by Geoff Green
Typeset by Florencetype Ltd, Kewstoke, Avon
Printed by Clays Ltd, St Ives plc

CONTENTS

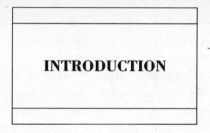

INTRODUCTION

Most of us gravitate towards the familiar. It seems to be a basic characteristic of human nature that we are reassured by what we know and recognise, be it a mood-catching tune, a favourite novel or poem, an evocative painting, or indeed the taste of a favourite wine or food. We know what we enjoy, and often we are reluctant to change and experiment. But that is what this book sets out to achieve; to encourage, persuade, even cajole you to look at less well-known wines, by linking them with more familiar names.

The British have one big advantage above the wine drinkers and wine lovers of just about every other country. The choice of wines on offer in the wine shops is far greater than virtually anywhere else in the world. The reason for that is quite simple. Britain is not a serious wine-producing country in its own right. With apologies to the stalwart but growing band of English and Welsh wine producers, locally produced wine has not been the subject of seriously chauvinistic claims. This has resulted in a far broader view and objective appreciation of the world's wines, compared with most other countries. Wine lists in restaurants in the heart of vineyard areas are inevitably dominated by the local wines. It would be a brave person who would ask for fine Burgundy in the best restaurant in Bordeaux. A wine list in Florence will inevitably be filled with Chiantis and other Tuscan wines. But go to a restaurant anywhere in Britain and you are likely to find a choice of wines from several countries, if not from two or more continents.

The same is true of wine shops in Britain. The smallest wine shop, with any pretensions to discernment in its choice of wines, will not only offer a wide selection of bottles from France, Germany, Spain, Italy and several other European countries, but also include wines from California, Australia, Chile, New Zealand – and that list is by no means complete. In fact it is possible to find wines from over fifty different

1

countries on sale somewhere in Britain. New York is probably the only other place in the world that attempts to rival that claim.

In any wine-producing countries, London is seen as the shop window of the world. The smallest boutique winery in California or New Zealand is proud and eager to send its wine to London, even though it may not produce enough wine to satisfy the demand at home. And yet, ironically, even with this enormous advantage, the vast majority of us are very conservative in our taste. We keep to the familiar. We continue to buy ▷Piat d'Or, ▷Liebfraumilch, ▷Lutomer Laski Riesling and ▷Lambrusco.

That is why the object of this book is to encourage an extension of our vinous horizons. If ▷Muscadet is your favourite wine, try an ▷Apremont or ▷Côtes de Gascogne; if you thought you only liked ▷Liebfraumilch, you can find other enjoyable bottles in Austria, Alsace, Portugal and Spain; if you are hooked on ▷Rioja, there is so much more on offer from northern Spain. It is such a waste that only a very small minority of us take advantage of the phenomenal choice of wines available to us. And to benefit from them, you do not need to live in a large city. Some of the best wine merchants offer an excellent mail-order service, without any significant addition to the cost of a bottle. I am not encouraging you to drink more, but just to drink more imaginatively. Do not desert the familiar completely, but consider the alternatives as well.

Taste is very subjective. Professional wine-tasters do not always agree about a wine, but this is not to say that one of them is wrong. Essentially there are no wrong answers in wine tasting. It is what you enjoy that matters and your own opinion that counts. The problem is that there are very few basic yardsticks to describe a precise flavour and very few specific words in the English language to determine a taste. Consequently wine writers' tasting notes tend to invoke comparisons with flowers, fruits and other associations of smell and taste. Sometimes these are very far-fetched and sometimes very down-to-earth. Even though two people are tasting the identical wine, they may not necessarily agree in their descriptions, although they may come to the same conclusions about its quality, for the taste and smell will bring different associations to each of them. The smell of a particular grape variety may remind one person of blackcurrants and the other of the cedarwood of cigar boxes. Both are perfectly acceptable ways of describing the bouquet of a fine claret.

There is no mystique about wine tasting. It is true that some people are better tasters than others, in the way that some are born with a musical ear or an artistic eye. But if you can tell the difference between lamb and pork or sage and chives, there is no reason why you cannot develop your tastebuds to recognise the difference between ▷Chardonnay and ▷Riesling, or ▷Sauvignon and ▷Gewürztraminer. Wine tasting is a skill which you can learn. All that is required is frequent practice and a good memory.

In fact memory is the key. For most of us our senses of smell and taste are undeveloped. As children we were taught to consider what we see and hear, to enjoy art or music, but it was considered almost self-indulgent to discuss what we were putting in our mouths. Consequently we tend to take our tastebuds for granted. However if you are prepared to say that this is a good piece of beef, or a deliciously flavoured sauce, you are equally capable of appreciating the quality of a bottle of ▷claret or ▷Bulgarian Cabernet Sauvignon.

Sometimes in an effort to pin down an elusive, fleeting smell or taste, imagery may become far-fetched and imaginative. The taste components in a mouthful of wine are numerous. The descriptions in this book are inevitably very personal and I have tried not to be too poetic, favouring a more down-to-earth approach. You may well disagree with me, but that is not the point. By giving some guidelines and pointing out similarities, I hope that I will have encouraged you to experiment and try an unfamiliar name.

Each time you taste a wine, write down what you think it tastes like, with the details of its name, vintage, the winemaker and anything else that is relevant on the label. This is the way you develop your own taste memory and your own yardsticks of smell and flavour. Remember that there are no wrong answers. It is what your tastebuds tell you that matters.

Again, as with the smell, think of what the taste reminds you. Is it old or young, undeveloped for its vintage, or prematurely aged? Do you recognise a grape variety? Has it spent some time in oak barrels? Is there fruit; is there acidity, tannin? Think of the weight of the wine? Does it feel light and ethereal or is it heavy and full-bodied? Is it balanced? Does the flavour linger in your mouth (this is called the *finish* of a wine), even after you have swallowed it, or is the finish disappointingly short. With experience these are some of the things that your tastebuds may register. But you must never lose sight of the fact that what really matters is: do you like it? And if so, why?

3

HOW TO TASTE

When we taste a wine, we are using not just one, but three of our senses; not just our tastebuds but also our eyes and nose, and of the three the nose is probably the most important of all.

But first look at the wine in your glass. Before that though, ensure that the glass is clean, with no smears or lingering smells from a cupboard, tea towel or traces of detergent. The glass should also be large enough to contain a reasonable amount of wine without being over-full and the bowl should be tapered, curving inwards towards the rim. This helps to concentrate the smell or bouquet of the wine.

A close scrutiny of the appearance of your wine will give you certain clues about it. First check its clarity. The wine should be clear and bright. There should not be any haze or cloudiness, which would indicate a possible fault. If you tilt your glass at an angle, against a white background, table cloth or piece of paper, you will be able to see the gradation of shades of colour. The variations of colour are more marked with red than with white wine. However even a deep red wine will be almost watery on the rim.

The depth of colour in both red and white wine is significant. Take white first. The spectrum of colours can range from the very palest straw yellow, that may be almost watery in appearance, through shades of yellow to deep gold and from there to the brown amber tones of old sherry. A white wine that is pale in colour is likely to be young and also dry. White wines take on a deeper colour as they age. Sweet wines, like ⊳Sauternes or German ⊳Beerenauslese are always deeper in colour than dry wines, maturing into a wonderful golden hue. White wines that are too old, take on a tell-tale tarnished tinge. They lose their brightness and become dull and faded.

The colour of a red wine is also a significant indicator of its maturity, but with a much more noticeable variation in colour. A very young wine, such as a newly released ▷Beaujolais Nouveau will be brilliant purple red, while a ▷claret of several years age will have developed shades of orange brick around the rim. Between purple and orange comes a ruby red. Depth and intensity of colour is significant. Someone once said that the first duty of a red wine is to be red and sometimes you do find so-called red wines that are more dark pink in colour than a positive red. The deeper the colour of the wine, the more body, substance and weight it will have, while a paler red will accordingly be lighter and less substantial.

You will also see streaks of glycerine running down the sides of the glass. More poetically, these are called tears, legs, and even church windows and are an indication of the alcohol content of the wine. A wine that is low in alcohol will have negligible legs, while a hefty alcoholic number will, in contrast, have very noticeable legs.

The next thing is to smell your wine. Hold your glass by the base, not by the bowl, and rotate it gently. This gentle movement encourages the wine to give off more of its aroma, and if the wine is particularly unforthcoming, you could even put your hand over the glass and shake it vigorously a couple of times. Even more aroma will be released. Then take a short, sharp sniff. Do you like what you smell? That is the most important thing. The wine should smell appealing and appetising. It should not smell dirty, corky, musty or of vinegar. If it does, then there is something wrong with it.

But given that the smell is attractive, you may try to identify it. The expert taster learns to recognise grape varieties, for these are the yardsticks of positive identification in wine appreciation. Less experienced tasters draw comparisons with other smells. You will learn to recognise and appreciate the aroma of blackcurrants, pencil shavings, eucalpytus, Nivea cream, gooseberries, vanilla and so on. The possibilities are endless. Some of these are commonly associated with one particular grape variety, but it cannot be emphasised enough that our sense of smell is very subjective, and the smell that makes one person think of strawberries, will remind someone else of raspberries. Neither are wrong. The important thing is to build up your own taste vocabulary with all its different associations and develop your own sense of smell, which helps you to appreciate and enjoy a wine.

The smell of a wine may be pronounced and obvious, leaping out from the glass, or it may be fleeting and elusive. It gives you your first impression as to how the wine will taste. Does it smell young and fruity or is it old and tired? Has it developed the subtle bouquet of a mature

5

wine or does it have the youthful freshness of a young wine? Does it give you an uncomfortable prickling sensation at the back of your nose, which is an indication that the winemaker has been heavy-handed with sulphur dioxide in the cellar. Sulphur dioxide is commonly used in winemaking as an antiseptic that eliminates mild yeasts, destroys harmful bacteria and prevents the grape juice from oxidation. Maximum levels are strictly controlled.

And finally you come to taste the wine. By smelling it first, you will already have some idea of what to expect, as most wines taste remarkably as they smell. Here again our appreciation is purely subjective and hampered by the fact that our tongue registers only four primary tastes, namely sweetness, saltiness, bitterness and sourness. Sugar comes on the tip of the tongue, sourness on the sides, bitterness on the back and saltiness in the middle. What we taste is so very much more, a combination of all the numerous components in the wine.

When you taste, take a small mouthful. Swill it round your mouth, sucking in a little air at the same time and make sure that the wine covers every part of your tongue and palate. This sounds a little inelegant, but by exposing the wine to a little air, you are enabling it to give off yet more flavour and since different parts of the tongue register different tastes, it is essential that the wine comes into contact with every part of the tongue. A professional taster, confronted with a long row of wines to assess, will then spit it out. This is often decried as being a waste. In fact all you are missing out on is the impact of the alcohol in the wine, which you will certainly want if you are enjoying a bottle with friends around a convivial dinner table.

Four basic factors make a wine taste the way it does. They are, quite simply, grape variety, soil, climate and winemaker.

Take grape variety first. There are many thousands of different grape varieties or varietals that can be used for making wine, but fewer than fifty that are of international importance and of those only a handful actually appear on a wine label as a varietal wine. The most popular and eye-catching are ▷Chardonnay and ▷Cabernet Sauvignon, but ▷Merlot, ▷Shiraz, ▷Sauvignon, ▷Chenin Blanc, ▷Riesling and ▷Gewürztraminer are amongst the others.

The grape variety (or blend of grape varieties) determines the basic flavour of a wine, but what the grape variety gives is then influenced by soil and climate. For example, Chardonnay grown in the cooler northern climate of ▷Chablis will have some similarity with a Chardonnay produced in hot southern California, but there will also be a fundamental difference originating from the climatic conditions. Quite simply, grapes from cooler climes have much more acidity and less sugar than those grown in a hot, sunny region. The same grape variety grown in different soil will also differ in taste. Some grape varieties are better suited to some soils than others. In the traditional wine-producing countries of Europe, what grows best where has been established by long experience over the centuries, while in the New World there is considerable experimentation as to what is most suited to what terrain, with much less respect for the concept of appellations and defined areas of origin.

Generally, vines like poor, stony soil and do not produce good results from rich, fertile land. Many of the world's great vineyards are in places where nothing else but vines will grow. Consider the granite slopes of the Douro valley, or the steep hillsides of the Mosel. Compare the results from vines grown on the rugged foothills of the Massif Central in the south of France, with the dull, insipid wine that comes from the coastal plains of the Midi.

Climate determines where the vines can grow. The weather must be neither too hot, nor too cold, so that there is broad band across Europe, roughly between latitudes 50° and 35°, between the Rhineland of Germany and the north African coast, with a similar band in the southern hemisphere which takes in central Chile and Argentina, the Cape lands of South Africa, a small part of Western Australia as well as the south-east corner of that continent and much of New Zealand. Of course there are exceptions to every rule, and so vines seem to thrive in other unlikely places, such as the foothills of the Peruvian Andes or in the Sahyadri mountains near Bombay. Altitude and aspect are the key factors here, tempering otherwise blistering heat.

However, like most agricultural products, vines do best in the northern hemisphere, towards the northern edge of that climatic band. That is to say, they give much better results, with wines that attain greater depth of flavour and heights of quality in regions where the climate is verging on the marginal. For the same reason English strawberries and apples have much more flavour than those grown in Italy, and Tuscan olive oil is better than Greek. That is why Bordeaux is one of the world's greatest red wine areas, northern Burgundy the star for dry white wine, and the sweet wines of the Mosel and Rhineland of Germany some of the best. It is as though vines that are assured of endless days of sunshine become bored; they are not stressed in any way, so that the wine they produce is consequently bland, insipid and over-alcoholic. In contrast where they are subjected to climatic vagaries, great wines can be made, but not every year.

It is weather therefore that determines the annual variations of the vintage. In regions where there are considerable differences from year to year, this is all-important. Sunshine and rain at the right time are crucial for a great vintage. Spring frosts can affect the size of the crop, as can cool weather or rain at the flowering. Rain at the harvest may swell the grapes, but to the detriment of their quality, diluting their flavour. A fine summer generally means a good vintage, with ripe, healthy grapes. Other climatic problems include hail, which can cause considerable localised damage. A drought, or any prolonged period without rain, can also prevent the grapes from ripening properly.

The winemaker has the final decision as to what is done with the grapes and consequently plays an enormous part in determining the ultimate taste of the wine. A good winemaker will be able to redeem an unpromising vintage, while a bad winemaker has the ability to spoil perfect grapes. As with cooks, the diversity between winemakers is infinite. Take an area like ▷Chablis, where the only grape variety is ▷Chardonnay, the soil is a mixture of clay and limestone and the vineyard area is small enough for there not to be a significant variation in the weather from one hillside to another. And yet there are as many different nuances of flavour in Chablis as there are producers of Chablis, and while it is true that there is an underlying similarity in the wines, no one Chablis (or any other wine for that matter) will be exactly like another. The reason is the winemaker, whose identity, usually in the form of an estate name, is given on the label of the bottle. They may be talented or careless, experimental or conservative in outlook, favour new oak barrels for their wine, adhere firmly to stainless steel vats, bottle their wine as early as possible or leave it in barrel or vat for several months or even years. The permutations are endless.

In the more traditional parts of Europe, the winemaker has to follow what the French appellation laws call 'les usages, locaux, loyaux et constants' which basically means that local viticultural practices must be firmly adhered to. For instance if you own a château in Bordeaux, you may not plant ▷Pinot Noir instead of ▷Cabernet Sauvignon. If you have an estate in ▷Sancerre, you cannot begin experimenting with ▷Riesling to replace ▷Sauvignon. However, if you have vineyards in Australia or California, there is nothing to prevent you planting exactly what you like. The only restriction on choice of grape variety would be any quarantine laws. Some parts of Europe also have a more flexible approach. The south of France and Tuscany are currently two of the most experimental vineyard areas of Europe, with some exciting results, as winemakers work outside the appellation laws to question the established practices of centuries. These wines can come into the category of ▷vin de pays or vino de tavola, rather than appellation contrôlée or Denominazione di Origine Controlata.

The same grape vinified in different ways will give different results. You will never completely lose the underlying characteristics of the grape, which may be enhanced or overwhelmed, depending on what the winemaker has done to them. Sometimes you can be more aware of how a wine is made, rather than of the flavour of the grape variety or of any regional characteristics. The use of ▷oak is a particular example of how wine flavours can be determined. The fermentation technique of carbonic maceration, whereby you put whole bunches of grapes into a vat

9

of carbon dioxide, produces an eminently fruity red wine that smells very much of that process, rather than of its origins.

As will be seen, it is certainly not implicit that the same grape variety will produce a similar wine all over the world. This is far from being the case. Some similarities of taste originate from winemakers' methods or maybe from climatic conditions, or just from the sheer coincidence that two wines from contrasting regions do have an underlying similarity. While it is likely that if you like the taste of Cabernet Sauvignon in Bordeaux, you will also favour Cabernet Sauvignon in Australia, it is not a foregone conclusion. You may be more likely to enjoy a ▷Brunello di Montalcino that has the similar bite of tannin, and has also been aged in oak barrels, although it does not contain a single drop of Cabernet Sauvignon.

There are inevitably good and bad bottles of the same wine, with the variations coming from the vintage as well as the winemaker. In the suggestions that follow, I have based my tasting notes on what I consider to be good, characteristic examples and have substantiated them with the names of other reputable producers. However, as a caveat, not all ▷Barolo, for example, may taste exactly like one I have described, and the suggestions for tasting on, may vary accordingly. While I think Barolo has an affinity with ▷Cahors, you may find it has more to do with ▷Dão. And we will both be right. The suggestions that follow are intended as guidelines. You may disagree with me, but the essential thing is that you are encouraged to 'taste on' in the first place.

Key to wine quality
   Ÿ   good value for money, but not necessarily cheap.
   ŸŸ   worth seeking out as a curiosity.
   ŸŸŸ expensive and a treat.

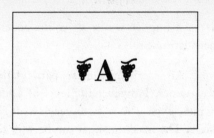

🐂 Acidity

Acidity is a vital component for without it any wine, be it red, white or pink, would taste dull, flabby and lifeless. However the effects of acidity are much more noticeable to the tastebuds in some wines than in others, namely in dry whites and pinks, and particularly those produced in a cool climate. That is not to say that red wines do not contain acidity, but its presence in red wine is usually much less obvious to the palate. Acidity gives ▷Muscadet, for example, a dry, crisp, fresh bite. But there should not be too much acidity either or the taste will be sour, green and unripe. Acidity can be described in different ways, such as crisp, stoney, flinty, mouthwatering, lemony or citric and it should always be balanced with ▷fruit.

Wines in which the acidity is particularly noticeable include:

FRANCE: ▷Muscadet, ▷Sancerre, ▷Pouilly Fumé, ▷Sauvignon de Touraine, Menetou-Salon, ▷Chablis, ▷Bordeaux Blanc, ▷Vin de Pays des Côtes de Gascogne, ▷Apremont, ▷Champagne, ▷Vouvray Sec and other dry ▷Chenin Blanc from the Loire Valley, ▷Riesling d'Alsace.

ITALY: The white wines of north east Italy from the Alto Adige and Friuli, made from ▷Pinot Bianco and ▷Pinot Grigio; white wines from Sicily, such as Corvo Bianco, Terre di Ginestra, Cellaro.

PORTUGAL: ▷Vinho Verde, both red and white.

SPAIN: ▷Rueda and whites from Galicia, such as ▷Rias Baixas.

NEW ZEALAND: ▷Sauvignon.

11

ENGLAND: All English wines, given the generally cool climate and northern latitude.

GERMANY: All German wines, particularly ▷*trocken* and ▷*halbtrocken* wines. However the level of acidity is high in all German wines, even if they taste very sweet like a ▷Trockenbeerenauslese. The mask of sugar can be very deceptive.

Alcohol

Alcohol is an essential ingredient in any wine. It comes from the natural process of fermentation, whereby the yeast converts the sugar in the grapes into carbon dioxide and alcohol. The amount of alcohol in a wine can vary considerably, depending on how much sugar there is in the grapes in the first place, and also whether the juice was chaptalised, with the addition of extra sugar, which is permitted in the cooler vineyards of Europe. Take two extreme examples, a Chardonnay from sunsoaked California could reach 16° while a Mosel from one of Germany's cooler vineyard regions may barely scrape 9°. It is now compulsory for the alcohol level of a wine to appear on the label, given as a percentage by volume, or in degrees, for example 12% or 12°, which is average for most table wines. A ▷fortified wine, which has had grape brandy added during the vinification process, may be as much as 20°.

Alcohol as such does not really taste of anything very much, apart from a faint sweetness, but you can detect its presence by the feel of the wine in your mouth. Tears of glycerine on the side of the glass also indicate the presence of alcohol. A wine that is low in alcohol tastes light and ethereal, while one that is high in alcohol tastes full-bodied and heavy. Without any alcohol at all, wine is completely out of balance and tastes very thin and skeletal, as in a ▷dealcoholised wine. Sometimes you can detect a slight burn on the finish of a wine from a very hot region, such as southern Spain, which is an indication that the wine is over-alcoholic, and also out of balance. The presence of alcohol should not jar.

Taste on:
Wines with high alcohol levels:
▷Fortified wines; ▷Châteauneuf-du-Pape; ▷California Cabernet Sauvignon; ▷Zinfandel; ▷Australian Shiraz; ▷Jumilla.

Low in alcohol:
▷English wines; ▷Bernkastel and other German wines; ▷Asti Spumante; ▷Vinho Verde; ▷dealcoholised wines.

🍇 Aligoté

Aligoté, which grows all over Burgundy for the appellation Bourgogne Aligoté, is considered there to be something of a poor relation to Chardonnay. The problem is that it is usually planted on less favourable sites, so that inevitably the resulting wine is less successful. The one exception to this is Bourgogne Aligoté de Bouzeron from a village in the Côte Chalonnaise that makes something of a speciality of Aligoté. In St Bris-le-Vineux, in the Yonne, they also plant Aligoté in some of the better vineyard sites. Aligoté is crisp and dry, sometimes tear-jerkingly so, with a dry, firm, stoney flavour, that very occasionally, in the ripest years, may be laced with a little honey. Usually it is firmly acidic with an underlying leanness. In Burgundy it is often drunk with a drop of blackcurrant liqueur to make a Kir Cassis.

- **Vintages:** Drink the youngest and freshest available.

- **Recommended producers:** Domaine Thévenot le Brun, Robert Defrance, de Villaine, Pierre Cogny.

 Taste on:
FRANCE: ▷Muscadet and Gros Plant du Pays Nantais. Occasionally you find Bourgogne Aligoté that has been bottled *sur lie* (on the fine lees or sediment left from the fermentation), like good Muscadet; ▷Apremont and Abymes; ▷Côtes de Gascogne.

PORTUGAL: ▷Vinho Verde.

AUSTRIA: ▷Grüner Veltliner.

▷English wine.

🍇 Anjou

The appellation of Anjou comes from vineyards all over that province of the Loire valley, around the town of Angers. It can be red, white or pink,

13

and occasionally sparkling or slightly sparkling, described as *mousseux* and *pétillant* respectively.

Anjou Rouge is usually made with the Cabernet Franc grape, though sometimes includes a drop of Cabernet Sauvignon and has the earthy flavours of ▷Chinon, with a mixture of potato peelings and ripe berry fruit. Alternatively it can be made from the Gamay grape, in which case it is called Anjou Gamay, and has more in common with ▷Beaujolais. The newer designation of Anjou Villages ▼ covers fuller-flavoured wine from some of the better villages of the province.

▷Chenin Blanc is the grape variety for Anjou Blanc, making a wine that is usually slightly sweet, or off dry, but always with some underly-ing firm acidity, typical of the grape variety. In cooler years it can be quite green, if not so sour as to bring tears to the eyes. The nose of most dry Chenin Blanc from the Loire Valley reminds me of wet wool or of a dog that has just plunged into the village duckpond, or maybe of damp hay. However if the winemaker knows what he is doing, there will also be a redeeming hint of honey on both nose and palate, and maybe a touch of apricots. Nonetheless it is a wine I could happily live without.

I could say the same too for Anjou Rosé which tends to be a slightly sweet, pale pink wine, made from the Groslot grape which grows only in the Loire valley.

● **Vintages:** For white and pink wines, drink the youngest avail-able and certainly nothing more than a couple of years old. Reds do not usually merit much keeping, but there are sometimes exceptions: 1990, 1989, 1988, 1985.

● **Recommended producers:** Moulin Touchais for exceptional sweet white wines; Domaine Chauvigné, Château du Breuil, Domaine de Montgilet, Domaine de Dreuille; Domaine de Bablut.

 Taste on:

RED:

FRANCE: ▷Chinon, Bourgeuil, St-Nicolas de Bourgueil, Saumur, Touraine, Vin de Pays des Marches de Bretagne, Cabernet du Haut Poitou, all of which are made from the Cabernet Franc grape.

Côtes du Fronton.

Vins de Pays des Côtes de Murveil. (In a blind tasting, I thought this came from Anjou!)

ITALY: Cabernet from Trentino and Friuli, where Cabernet on the label tends to mean Franc rather than Sauvignon, or a mixture of both.

NEW ZEALAND: Cabernet Sauvignon which sometimes has a slightly earthy, herbal quality, reminiscent of the Loire Valley.

WHITE:
FRANCE: ▷Vouvray, Montlouis, which is on the opposite side of the river; other dry white Loire wines made from Chenin Blanc like Coteaux de l'Aubance, Jasnières, Saumur.
Côtes de St Mont from the foothills of the Pyrenees has some of the honey and acidity of Chenin Blanc, although the grape varieties are quite different.

SOUTH AFRICA: Chenin Blanc which is sometimes labelled ▷Steen.

GERMANY: ▷*Halbtrocken* wines, though not from the same grape variety, for Chenin Blanc is not grown in Germany at all, have a similar balance of acidity and sweetness.

PINK:
FRANCE: ▷Cabernet d'Anjou and other pink Loires, such as Saumur Rosé, Rosé de la Loire.

PORTUGAL: ▷Mateus Rosé, which is synonymous with pink wine from Portugal.

▷English wine.

♈ Aphrodite

The white wines of the island of Cyprus tend to go under a variety of brand names like Aphrodite, Thisbe, Arsinoe, Bellapais. Mythical legend has it that Aphrodite, the goddess of love, emerged from the sea off the shores of Cyprus. It is mainly large cooperatives of grape growers that control the wine production of Cyprus. Aphrodite belongs to the one called Keo. It is a dry, rather flat white wine, with an almost salty tang on the finish, the sort of white wine that is perfect with seafood, in warm sunshine by the sea, but may not have quite the same appeal under a grey winter sky.

- **Vintages:** Drink the youngest available.

 Taste on:

CYPRUS: Other island whites, which all tend to taste very similar, although maybe slightly sweeter like Thisbe, or slightly sparkling like Bellapais.

GREECE: The most popular Greek brand is ▷Demestica from Achaia Clauss, which is similarly flat and dry. Robola of Cephalonia is dry, and slightly nutty, as is the white wine of Patras.

FRANCE: Dry whites from the warm south, like ▷Corbières, ▷Minervois, and Côtes du Roussillon, though they usually have a little more fruit and acidity.

PORTUGAL: Dry whites like ▷Douro, ▷Dão and ▷Bairrada.

ITALY: Wines from Campania and Molise, like Fiano di Avellino and Greco di Tufo.

Apremont ♥♥

Apremont is one of the better-known *crus* or vineyard areas of the all-embracing appellation, Vin de Savoie, which covers most of the Savoie region of France, with scattered vineyards around the towns of Chambéry, Aix-les-Bain and Annecy. The principal grape variety in the vineyards close to Chambéry is Jacquère, which makes light, rather dry, stoney white wines that are popular on the ski slopes and with the Savoie cheese dishes, fondue and raclette. They are relatively low in alcohol, with some firm acidity and a refreshing bite.

With its light, somewhat ethereal flavours, Apremont is best drunk as young as possible, and while each vintage varies slightly, it is still best to seek out the most recent.

- **Recommended growers:** Le Vigneron Savoyard, Pierre Boniface at Domaine des Rocailles.

Taste on:

FRANCE: Other white *crus* of Vin de Savoie, notably nearby Abymes ♥♥ and Chignin; Vin du Bugey, from just the other side of the Rhône valley, but only if it says Jacquère on the label; ▷Muscadet; ▷Vin de Pays des Côtes de Gascogne.

AUSTRIA: ▷Grüner Veltliner, a grape variety, with a slightly neutral, but dry, flinty flavour.

Arbois ♥♥

Arbois is one of the four appellations of the Jura. It can be red, white or pink, not to mention sparkling as well as yellow, as in ▷Vin Jaune. White Arbois strongly resembles ▷Côtes du Jura, as indeed do the red and pink, but it is for its red wine that Arbois is known. You might say that red and pink Arbois are indistinguishable in that the pink wine is deep in colour and the red unusually light. The grape varieties include two that are peculiar to the Jura, namely Trousseau and Poulsard, while a third, Pinot Noir, is known as the mainstay of fine red Burgundy. There is a soft raspberry fruit in red Arbois, with occasional vegetal overtones and a hint of sweetness.

• **Vintages:** 1990, 1989, 1988, 1986, 1985.

• **Recommended producers:** Rollet Frères, Lucien Aviet, Henri Maire (the largest producer of the Jura who has four estates in Arbois), Domaine de Montfort, Domaine de la Croix d'Argis, Domaine de Sorbief, Domaine de Grange Grillard.

Taste on:

FRANCE: ▷Côtes du Jura Rouge which is made from the same grape varieties.
▷Bourgogne Rouge. This is the basic appellation for red burgundy and there are affinities between Trousseau and the Pinot Noir in young red burgundy, not in the great names but with village wines, such as a good Beaune or Pommard, which have a similar soft raspberry perfume and chewy, almost sweet fruit.
▷Irancy.

Pinot Noir d'Alsace for a red wine that is almost pink in colour, and soft and fruity.

SWITZERLAND: The red wines of Dôle, from across the border are made from Pinot Noir.

GERMANY: Wines labelled Spätburgunder, are made from Pinot Noir and have a soft fruitiness.

NEW ZEALAND: ▷Pinot Noir from a cool climate such as Canterbury and Martinborough.

🍇 Arruda 🍷

Arruda is one of the small wine areas of the large Torres Vedras region of Portugal, which lies north of the river Tagus and covers vineyards up as far as the southern edge of Bairrada. Arruda itself owes its reputation to the fact that the regional cooperative sells most of its wine to one large supermarket. It has thus provided a wonderful value-for-money introduction to Portuguese wines for discerning shoppers at Sainsburys.

Arruda is a dry red wine, made from a blend of different grape varieties. The colour is quite deep, with no signs of ageing. On the nose there is some full berry fruit and just a hint of the redcurrant greenness you can find on some Loire wines, as well as some liquorice and prunes, not unlike young ▷port. On the palate there is just enough tannin, with plenty of soft, ripe plummy fruit and a hint of spice and liquorice to fill the mouth.

● **Vintages:** Sold without a vintage date.

● **Recommended producers:** The local cooperative, Adega Cooperative de Arruda dos Vinhos.

 Taste on:
PORTUGAL: ▷Douro, ▷Bairrada.
Other Portuguese wines, such Quinta da Bacalhõa, Periquita and Camarate, without any regional delimitation, from two notable producers, João Pires and J. M. da Fonseca.

SPAIN: ▷Jumilla.

FRANCE: ▷Coteaux du Languedoc, with St Chinian and Faugères; ▷Minervois; ▷Corbières.

Red Loire wines, such as ▷Chinon and Bourgueil, but only in exceptionally ripe years, when they have lots of rich, spicey berry fruit and less acidity.

▼ Asti Spumante

Asti Spumante is one of those rare wines that does actually taste of grapes. Think of the taste of sweet, ripe Muscatel table grapes; add some bubbles and you have Italy's most individual sparkling wine, coming from vineyards around the town of Asti, near Turin. Unlike other Italian sparklers, it has no aspirations to emulate Champagne, but is unashamedly sweet, and quite lusciously so. However, good Asti Spumante should never be cloying. It is also low in alcohol, as no extra sugar or yeast are added to induce the second fermentation. Instead the bubbles and sweetness are what is left after the first fermentation has been stopped in midstream. You either love Asti Spumante or hate it. I love it. I find its fresh, grapey flavour irresistible and it goes a lot better with wedding cake than many a dry Champagne.

• **Vintages:** Drink the youngest available. Asti Spumante simply does not age and must be absolutely fresh to be really enjoyable.

• **Recommended producers:** Viticoltori dell'Acquese, Fontanafredda, Riccadonna, as well as some of the big vermouth producers who also make quite respectable Asti Spumante such as Gancia, Martini & Rossi, Cinzano.

 Taste on:

ITALY: Moscato d'Asti, which is not quite as fizzy as Asti Spumante; also Moscato Naturale di Asti, in other words a still wine from the Muscat, with the same sweet taste, but no bubbles; Moscato di Strevi, a neighbouring DOC; Moscadello di Montalcino, which is lightly rather than fully sparkling, but still deliciously grapey.

FRANCE: Clairette de Die Tradition ▼▼. The word Tradition is the key here, indicating the traditional use of the Muscat grape, alongside the drier, less flavoursome Clairette grape.

Some of the best low-alcohol wines are based on the Muscat grape. As Asti Spumante or Moscato d'Asti are naturally fairly low in alcohol, a degree or two less deforms the taste somewhat less than with dry, low-alcohol wines, while the authentic ripe sweetness compensates more than adequately for the body lost because of the lower alcohol.

Auslese

Auslese is a key word on a German wine label as it tells you how sweet the wine is likely to be. It comes third in the hierarchy of German Prädikat wines (and second in Austria), between Spätlese and Beerenauslese, and literally means 'selected harvest'. The grapes are not necessarily late picked but are a choice of the best bunches that are especially ripe or more affected than average with noble rot. The resulting wine will be deliciously honeyed, not opulently luscious, but delicately sweet or, more prosaically, medium sweet.

The finest Auslese wines are made in both Germany and Austria from the Riesling grape. Those from the Mosel valley have a subtle balance of honey and acidity that is never cloying. From the cooler vineyards of the Mosel, an Auslese may be mistaken for a Spätlese from the Rheingau, while an Auslese from the Rheingau will be fuller in the mouth than one from the Mosel. From Austria it will be riper still. The flavour varies according to the grape variety. Whereas Riesling can be steely and honeyed, Scheurebe or Optima are less elegant and more blowsy.

The New World equivalent of Auslese on the label is Individual Bunch Selection, which indicates a picking of the best bunches of grapes that are probably affected by noble rot. Words like 'late harvest' or 'botrytis-affected' also imply a similar degree of sweetness. You can find some lovely honeyed wines from California and Australia, but they will be heavier in taste, and more alcoholic than their German counterparts.

Taste on:

GERMANY: Any producer worth his salt produces Auslese wines in good vintages like 1990, 1989, 1988, 1985, 1983. This is the quality of wine they aspire to in what can be difficult climatic conditions and certainly a Mosel Auslese would be one of my desert island wines.

Auslese from ▷Bernkastel, ▷Johannisberg, ▷Nierstein, ▷Nahe-Schlossböckelheim.

Try also any ▷Spätlese or ▷Beerenauslese for a similar level of sweetness.

AUSTRIA: Again Auslese is an indication of quality, with wines that are fuller and higher in alcohol than Auslesen from Germany.

USA: California, Oregon and Washington State all produce sweet wines, with a comparable level of sweetness, from Riesling and occasionally Gewürztraminer.

AUSTRALIA: Gewürztraminer, Riesling, Muscat and Sémillon may all be late harvested.

NEW ZEALAND: Look for Late Harvest Riesling.

FRANCE: The term *moelleux* implies a wine that is delicately sweet rather than lusciously honeyed, as in ▷Jurançon *moelleux*, ▷Vouvray *moelleux*, Montlouis *moelleux*.

Vendange Tardive wines from Alsace made from Riesling, Gewürztraminer, Muscat or Pinot Gris will also be comparable in richness to Auslese in Germany, though fuller-bodied, with more alcohol and weight.

▷Barsac.

ITALY: *Abboccato* as in ▷Orvieto is an indication of sweetness, but probably not quite as ripe as an Auslese.

Ψ Australian Cabernet Sauvignon

Cabernet Sauvignon has adapted easily to Australia, growing successfully all over the continent, from the Hunter Valley and Mudgee in New South Wales to the Margaret and Swan rivers of Western Australia, and even in the vineyards of Château Hornsby in the semi-desert of Alice Springs. However, it is Coonawarra in South Australia, with its famous terra rossa, red iron-packed soil, that is generally considered to produce the most exciting examples of Cabernet Sauvignon from Australia, with rich blackcurrant flavours. These are wines that are full and ripe, with hints of minty eucalyptus making a rounded mouthful of cassis fruit, backed with some soft tannins to allow for bottle ageing. Cabernet Sauvignon from Australia has the weight of Cabernet Sauvignon from elsewhere in the New World, but often lacks the elegance of Bordeaux. However, there is a richness of fruit that may compare with a good Pomerol or ▷St-Emilion.

● **Vintages:** There is considerable variation all over the continent. Take Coonawarra as the best source of Cabernet Sauvignon: 1991, 1990, 1986, 1984, 1982, 1980.

● **Recommended producers:** Montrose Wines, Rouge Homme, Tim Knappstein, Hungerford Hill, Cape Mentelle, Vasse Felix, Cullen Wines, Redgate, Lindemans, Wynns, Balgownie Estate, Penfolds, Coldstream Hills, Chittering Estate, Geoff Merril and Mount Hurtle, Tisdall Wines.

 Taste on:

AUSTRALIA: Australia blends Cabernet Sauvignon, not only with Merlot, but also Shiraz. Blends with Merlot of which Yarra Yering No. 1 is one of the best, are most Bordelais in character, while Shiraz can add a spiciness reminiscent of the Rhône Valley.

USA: ▷California Cabernet Sauvignon, and also examples from Oregon, Washington State and Long Island.

FRANCE: ▷Claret; Pomerol and ▷St-Emilion rather than the ▷Médoc and ▷Graves.

SPAIN: Jean Léon Cabernet Sauvignon; Raimat Cabernet Sauvignon, Marqués de Griñon Cabernet Sauvignon and wines from ▷Ribera del Duero.

PORTUGAL: Quinta da Bacalhôa, a Portuguese example of Cabernet Sauvignon.

ITALY: Cabernet Sauvignon from Tuscany, sometimes labelled Predicato del Biturica, such as Tavernelle from Banfi.

🐂 Australian Chardonnay

Chardonnay is grown all over the vineyards of Australia, following the current fashion for this eminently adaptable grape variety. Australia produces good examples of Chardonnay, with a bit of oak ageing, making for a buttery taste, with overtones of tropical fruit, lychees, pineapples and peaches. There is a ripeness and richness about Australian Chardonnay, often with some flavours that are foreign to the classic Chardonnay of Burgundy. Sometimes the flavours are a little overblown and lacking in elegance; sometimes the taste finishes with a firm citric ▷acidity. However, in cooler regions such as the Yarra Valley in Victoria, Chardonnay becomes more elegant and subtle, with some understated toasted nuances and good ageing potential. Probably the closest that any Australian Chardonnay comes to fine Meursault is in that of Yarra Yering. Coldstream Hills and Tarrawarra are close behind.

● **Vintages:** Yarra Valley, as the source of some of Australia's finest Chardonnay: 1991, 1990, 1988, 1986, 1984, 1982, 1980.

● **Recommended producers:** Lake's Folly, Yarra Yering, Coldstream Hills, Tarrawarra, Schinus Molle, Geoff Merrill, Moss Wood, Cullen Wines, Petaluma, Chittering, Penfolds, Lindemans, David Wynn, Rothbury Estate, Plantagenet Wines, Giants Creek and Roxburgh, both single vineyards from the Rosemount Estate, Smith and Shaw.

Taste on:

AUSTRALIA: Sémillon Chardonnay blends and also pure Australian ▷Sémillon.

NEW ZEALAND: ▷Chardonnay.

USA: ▷California Chardonnay, and also Oregon, Washington State and Long Island.

▷CHILE: Chardonnay.

FRANCE: ▷Burgundy from the Côte d'Or; so choose ▷Meursault rather than ▷Chablis or ▷Mâcon.

ITALY: Chardonnay from Tuscany, sometimes under the Predicato del Muschio label.

SPAIN: Chardonnay from Penedés, such as Jean Léon, Raimat and Torres' Milmanda.

Australian Sémillon

It is the Sémillon grape that makes the most distinctive and individual white wines of Australia. Even in Bordeaux it is rare to find a pure Sémillon – one exception is Château de Landiras; normally it is blended with Sauvignon. The Hunter Valley is where Sémillon shows its best, enjoying the warm climate. These are wines that do require some bottle age, needing at least five years to develop into something not unlike Chardonnay, but with an indefinably different tang. Indeed, if you ever come across a bottle of Lindemans Hunter Valley Chablis, it is pure Sémillon and quite delicious. There is a dry, toasted quality about mature Hunter Valley Sémillon, with a hint of oily richness. It benefits from a bit of oak ageing, not too much, while in contrast young Sémillon can be rather thin and lacking in appeal.

Other parts of Australia are looking at Sémillon too, or sometimes you find Sémillon/Chardonnay blends or more traditionally a Sémillon/Sauvignon mix. This may work well in Bordeaux, but pure Sémillon is what Australia is really good at.

Exciting too are the botrytis-affected Sémillons of the Murrumbidgee Irrigation Area of New South Wales, which have some of the roasted, sweet character of ▷Sauternes, with honey and toffee apples.

• **Vintages:** In the Hunter Valley: 1991, 1990, 1987, 1986, 1985, 1983, 1981, 1980.

• **Recommended producers:** De Bortoli are best of all for sweet Sémillon; for dry wines: Rothbury, Rosemount, Lindemans, Penfolds.

Taste on:
▷AUSTRALIA: ▷Chardonnay.

USA: Washington State: Cascade Estate Sémillon has some of the characteristics of the Hunter Valley wines.
▷California: Chardonnay.

FRANCE: ▷Graves, or rather the better estates of the new appellation of Pessac-Léognan.

The dry wines of Sauternes, notably Y (pronounced 'Ygrec'), G de Guiraud, R de Rieussec.

▷Meursault.

♛ Australian Shiraz ♛

The best Australian Shiraz is virtually identical in taste with the best ▷Syrah of the Rhône valley. Shiraz grows in the warm Hunter Valley of New South Wales, as well as in the cooler regions of Victoria and South Australia. Penfolds Grange, previously called Grange Hermitage, is the supreme example of just how great Australian Shiraz can be, with rich complex flavours of spice and pepper, especially when it has some bottle age. Younger wines have the typical nose and taste of blackcurrant gums that are the benchmark of good Shiraz or Syrah, and sometimes an almost sweet, mint and eucalyptus taste that is characteristic of some New World Shiraz. They are always deep in colour, chunky, meaty, mouthfilling wines, with some tannin and a rich, fruity impact and a long finish. Shiraz can be blended with Cabernet Sauvignon which makes for a little more elegance and more subtle blackcurrant fruit. Much however depends upon the producer, so that you can find Shiraz that is light and fruity, more like a young ▷Beaujolais in style, or blended with Mataro, otherwise known as Mourvèdre in France, when it tastes more like red table wine from the ▷Douro valley, which could be described as unfortified port.

• **Vintages:** 1991, 1990, 1988, 1987, 1986, 1985, 1983, 1981, 1980.

• **Recommended producers:** Penfolds with Grange ♛♛♛ and wines such as Kalimna Bin 28, Coonawarra Shiraz Bin 128, David Wynn, Bannockburn Vineyards, Henschke, Peppertree Vineyard, Plantagenet, Rouge Homme, Rothbury, Montrose, Wynns Kies Estate.

Taste on:
FRANCE: ▷Hermitage, ▷Côte Rôtie, ▷Cornas, ▷Crozes Hermitage, ▷Bandol.

ITALY: Sagrantino di Montefalco 🦋🦋 from Umbria, with some sweet and dry berry fruit. Syrah 🦋🦋 from Isole e Olena in Tuscany.

CALIFORNIA: ▷Zinfandel, as well as Syrah from the Golden State.

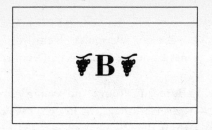

Bairrada ▼

Bairrada is the rising star amongst Portuguese wines. Coming from vineyards in central Portugal, south of the town of Oporto, it can be red, white or sparkling. However red is most common outside Portugal.

The main grape variety for red Bairrada is Baga, a tough-skinned variety that can make ungiving, tannic, astringent red wines, which require several years ageing in both barrel and bottle. However, a move amongst the leading producers to soften the taste of Bairrada is making it drinkable younger, with experiments in stalk-free fermentations and new oak contributing to a gradual change, and indeed improvement, in the taste of Bairrada.

Bairrada has a richness of flavour that is something of a cross between good ▷claret and a ▷Côtes du Rhône with a high proportion of Syrah. There is the spicey pepperiness associated with the Rhône valley, combined with some of the blackcurrant fruit and tannin that you find in Bordeaux. Young Bairrada may have stalky flavour of young ▷claret, but will age gracefully, developing some rich, mellow flavours.

White Bairrada on the other hand seems to have little identity. I have had wines that smell of dry apricots, with a hint of ▷Muscat, while others are dry and dusty like Vermentino from ▷Corsica, or they have the heavy, almost oxidised flavour of old-fashioned winemaking.

• **Vintages:** 1991, 1990, 1989, 1988, 1987, 1985, 1983, 1980.

• **Recommended producers:** Caves São João, Caves Aliança, Luis Pato, Sogrape. Garrafeira on the label means that the producer considers it one of their better wines.

27

Taste on:

PORTUGAL: ▷Dão, Periquita from J. M. da Fonseca, ▷Arruda, wines from the Alentejo region of southern Portugal.

FRANCE: ▷Bordeaux Rouge and young claret of *petit château* quality; ▷Crozes Hermitage, St Joseph, ▷Côtes du Rhône and other wines from the Rhône Valley based on Syrah; ▷Fitou, Faugères in the ▷Coteaux du Languedoc; ▷Corbières.

ITALY: Rosso di Montalcino, the second string of ▷Brunello di Montalcino and Rosso di Montepulciano, a younger ▷Vino Nobile di Montepulciano.

Balance

Balance describes the relationship between all the component parts of a wine, notably ▷fruit, ▷tannin, ▷acidity, ▷alcohol and maybe ▷sweetness. They should present a harmonious whole, with no jarring, obtrusive edges. When this is not the case, a wine can be described as unbalanced, when it has, for example, too much acidity or alcohol. Any wine with any pretensions to quality should be well balanced.

The possible exceptions are very young wines, especially class-growth ▷claret and vintage ▷port, that are destined for a long life. Here the tannin will dominate the fruit, but as the wine matures, the tannin will soften so that it comes into balance with the fruit.

Baden ❦

Baden is Germany's southernmost vineyard area and therefore also the warmest. It is only separated from the vineyards of Alsace by the river Rhine, so that there are affinities between the two regions that cross both frontier and river. Müller-Thurgau is grown in the bulk of the vineyards, along with some Riesling, Silvaner, Weissburgunder or Pinot Blanc, Spätburgunder or Pinot Noir, Gewürztraminer and Ruländer, which is also called Pinot Gris. All of them except Müller-Thurgau are also to be found in Alsace.

Bottles from Baden have only recently begun to appear on our wine merchants' shelves, often labelled quite simply as Baden Dry, without any more specific indication of provenance. However Ortenau, Kaiserstuhl and Markgräflerland are among the better vineyard sites. The majority of wine from Baden is dry, or ▷*trocken*, rather than retaining some of the characteristic sweetness of wines from northern Germany. A typical Baden Dry has a firm stoney or softer grassy flavour, with some pithy, spicey fruit, maybe with hints of apricots. These are heavier wines than those from further north, so they are quite full in the mouth and maybe a little earthy on the finish. The depth of flavour depends on the dominant grape variety. A Riesling may be quite steely; Ruländer a bit mushroomy, while Silvaner is grassy and Spätburgunder a light red, with soft vegetal fruit.

● **Vintages:** 1990, 1989, 1988, 1985, 1983; drink youngest available.

● **Recommended producers:** The region is dominated by growers' cooperatives, most of which in turn belong to an enormous central cooperative, the ZBW or Zentralkellerei Badischer Winzer-genossenschaft, which does a sound job for the region. Amongst independent growers look for Weingut Karl H. Johner, Freiherr von Göler'sche Verwaltung.

 Taste on:
GERMANY: Wine from Franconia and ▷*trocken* and ▷*halb-trocken* styles from elsewhere in the country.

FRANCE: ▷Pinot Blanc d'Alsace, Sylvaner (spelt with a y in France) d'Alsace, ▷Edelszwicker and basic house wines such as Hugel's Flambeau d'Alsace, ▷Pinot Gris d'Alsace, Pinot Noir or simply Rouge d'Alsace.

AUSTRIA: ▷Grüner Veltliner.

ITALY: ▷Pinot Bianco and ▷Pinot Grigio from the Alto Adige, Friuli and Trentino in north east Italy.

Bandol

Bandol is a rich, meaty wine from steeply terraced vineyards behind the Mediterranean port of the same name. Serious Bandol is red; there is white and pink too, but of less significance and interest. Mourvèdre is the principal grape variety, accounting for at least half the blend, with a minimum of 18 month's ageing in large oak barrels. This makes for a pretty hefty, solid red wine, with meaty flavours, which the French call *viandé*. There is a leathery, animal quality about the nose, while the taste is full-bodied, with some tannin and warm southern flavours. You can find some of the herbal scents of the south, with smokey bacon, cherries and raspberries, and an underlying firm backbone. These are wines that develop with further bottle age.

- **Vintages:** 1990, 1989, 1988, 1986, 1985, 1983, 1982, 1981.

- **Recommended producers:** Domaine Tempier, Château Vannières, Domaine de Pibarnon, Domaine de Terrebrune, Moulin des Costes, Mas de la Rouvière, Domaine de l'Hermitage, Domaine de la Laidière.

Taste on:

FRANCE: ▷Châteauneuf-du-Pape, and other southern Rhône wines, like Gigondas and Vacqueyras.

🍷🍷 Palette, a tiny appellation just outside the town of Aix-en-Provence, where the Rougier family at Château Simone, the only estate of note, maintain traditional methods of vinification with delicious results; the wines are rich, meaty and long-lived. ▷Côtes de Provence, ▷Coteaux d'Aix-en-Provence.

ITALY: Tanca Farrà from Sardinia, a dry, meat-flavoured wine. Rosso Cònero, from the Marche, with its meaty, spicey flavours and an underlying rustic quality.

CANADA: Wines from the Maréchal Foch grape variety have a meaty flavour, making a solid, spicey mouthful of wine.

CALIFORNIA: Wines from Mourvèdre, like Jade Mountain Mourvèdre, Taurus Mourvèdre, Domaine de la Terre Rouge (yes, it really is in California!). ▷Zinfandel.

AUSTRALIA: Shiraz – Cabernet Sauvignon blends.

Barbaresco

Barbaresco is one of the great red wines of Piedmont, coming like
▷Barolo, from the Nebbiolo grape. It too takes its name from the
village. Under the DOCG regulations it must be aged for a minimum of
two years in barrel and bottle, while three years makes a *riserva* and four a
riserva speciale. However, compared with Barolo, Barbaresco is light,
elegant and charming. The reason lies with the soil, which in turn is
lighter than that of the vineyards of Barolo, resulting in a less substantial
wine.

Some people say that violets are the key theme of the Nebbiolo grape
but I have never found that so. Good Nebbiolo and particularly
Barbaresco, remind me of lovely rich Christmas fruitcake, a combination of nuts and dried fruit, and a touch of brandy. Chocolate, prunes,
liquorice and raspberries are possible other descriptions. Barbaresco is
always tannic, but less aggressively so than Barolo, and there is acidity
too. Like Barolo, Barbaresco is a wine to age for ten, or even twenty
years. As it matures and the youthful tannins fade, it can develop almost
vegetal, Burgundian overtones, with some underlying sweetness.

• **Vintages:** 1990, 1989, 1988, 1987, 1986, 1985, 1982, 1979, 1978,
1974, 1971, 1970.

• **Recommended producers:** Gaja, Ceretto, Bruno Giacosa, Pio
Cesare, Marchesi di Gresy, Vietti, Castello di Neive, Produttori del
Barbaresco, Prunotto, Contratto, Franco Fiorina, Fratelli Oddero.

 Taste on:
ITALY: ▷Barolo, and other Piedmontese wines made from
Nebbiolo, such as Donnaz, Spanna, Carema, Sizzano,
Gattinara, Ghemme, Fara and Bramaterra.

FRANCE: ▷Cahors; mature fine red burgundy; ▷Gevrey-
Chambertin, ▷Volnay.

PORTUGAL: ▷Dão.

Barbera

Barbera is a red grape variety that is grown over large parts of Italy, in
both the south and the north, but really comes into its own in Piedmont,

in wines such as Barbera d'Alba, Barbera d'Asti and Barbera di Montferrato. The dominant characteristic of Barbera is acidity. It has a very Italian, bittersweet flavour, with lots of sour cherries and plum-flavoured fruit, a little spiciness and a refreshingly astringent finish. Barbera d'Alba is the most solid of the three, while Barbera di Montferrato is the lightest and most frivolous.

- **Vintages:** 1990, 1989, 1988, 1987. Drink Barbera when it is young and fresh, and no more than four years old.

- **Recommended producers:** Often it is part of the repertoire of Barolo and Barbaresco producers, such as Pio Cesare, Gaja, Ratti, Prunotto, Guiseppe Mascarello, Vietti, Conterno, both Aldo and Giacomo, and Ascheri.

Taste on:

ITALY: ▷Dolcetto, ▷Chianti.
Other wines from elsewhere in Italy with a high proportion of Barbera, such as Oltrepò Pavese Rosso and Oltrepò Barbera in Lombardy and Gutturnio dei Colli Piacentini in Emilia Romagna.

FRANCE: ▷Coteaux du Languedoc.

PORTUGAL: Some Portuguese wines have the astringency of Barbera combined with some ripe fruit like ▷Arruda and ▷Douro.

USA: California: young lightweight ▷Zinfandel. Barbera is also grown in California, but gets lost in a blend for anonymous jug wine.

Bardolino

Bardolino takes its name from a pretty little village on the shores of Lake Garda. If the label says *Classico*, the wine originates from vineyards in the immediate vicinity of the village, while *Superiore* denotes a year's ageing. However Bardolino is at its best when it is young, fresh and fruity. It does not age well, but should have a deliciously youthful ripe cherry flavour, which makes it immediately appealing.

Bardolino is light red in colour, and light in body too, while Bardolino Chiaretto is a pink version, that is crisp and fresh, with light cherry fruit. Finally there is Bardolino Novello, a pure imitation of ▷Beaujolais Nouveau.

● **Vintages:** Drink the youngest possible, and never anything more than two or three years old.

● **Recommended producers:** Boscaini, Masi, Guerrieri–Rizzardi Bolla, Bertani, Zenato, Tedeschi, Santa Sofia.

Taste on:

ITALY: Young ▷Valpolicella, but not the *recioto* and *amarone* styles.
▷Dolcetto.
Vin Ruspo, the pink wine of Carmignano.

FRANCE: ▷Beaujolais and other Gamay-based wines like Gamay de Touraine, Côtes du Forez and Gamay de l'Ardèche, with the same weight and fruity drinkability.

Barolo

Barolo is THE great red wine of northern Italy, coming solely from the Nebbiolo grape, which is the most characteristic variety of Piedmont, and rarely grown elsewhere. The vineyards of Barolo are centred on the village of the same name, in the Langhe hills south east of the town of Alba.

In its youth, Barolo is tough and ungiving, for Nebbiolo gives wines with deep colour and masses of tannin, acidity and extract. Lengthy contact with the grape skins during fermentation also makes for tough, sturdy wine. Traditionally, Barolo needs several years of ageing in large oak casks, that may be as much as a hundred years old, to soften it. The DOCG regulations dictate at least a minimum of two years in wood plus another year in vat before sale. *Riserva* on the label indicates four years ageing and *Riserva Speciale* five years. However, there is currently a move amongst less traditionally minded producers to make somewhat softer, more accessible wine, with subtle changes in vinification methods and by giving it more bottle than barrel ageing.

Nonetheless Barolo remains a serious, solid mouthful, demanding food to assist its appreciation. Young Barolo is severely tannic, with acidity as well, and also fruit, liquorice and prunes, with an underlying austerity, leaving a dry, tarry finish in the mouth. There is an unyielding quality about Barolo, but that is what turns it into great wine when it is ten, if not 20 years old. With age Barolo develops a rich nose that is reminiscent of Christmas fruitcake, with a similar fruity, mixed spice taste on the palate. Some also associate it with truffles, for Piedmont happens to be the home of some of the world's finest truffles. Barolo is always a serious, substantial mouthful of wine. The best will be rich in flavour and the less good somewhat lean, if not mean in the mouth.

●   **Vintages:** 1990, 1989, 1988, 1985, 1982, 1978, 1974, 1971, 1970, 1967, 1964, 1962, 1961.

●   **Recommended producers:** Noted modernists: Ceretto, Ratti, Giuseppe Mascarello, Angelo Gaja. Traditionalists: Bruno Giacosa, Giacomo Conterno. Others: Altare, Pio Cesare, Aldo Conterno, Prunotto, Cavallotto, Vietti.

    Taste on:
ITALY: Other wines from the Nebbiolo grape: ▷Barbaresco, Barolo's more elegant neighbour.
Lighter Nebbiolo wines from Piedmont, called Nebbiolo d'Alba, Roero, or the non-DOC, Spanna.
Gattinara, Ghemme, Sassella.
The DOC of the Valtellina, up towards the Swiss border, with the evocatively named Inferno, as well as Sassella, Grumello and Valgella, not to mention plain Valtellina Rosso.
Donnaz from the Valle d'Aosta.
Aglianico del Vulture, for Aglianico is sometimes called the Nebbiolo of southern Italy, with tannin and spice.
Ronco di Mompiano, made mainly from the Marzemino grape near Brescia, is similarly austere, with some underlying fruit.
Taurasi, made with Aglianico by Mastroberardino in Campania.

FRANCE: ▷Cahors, with its inherent austerity and ability to age.

PORTUGAL: ▷Dão.

❦ Barsac

Barsac is the adjacent appellation to ▷Sauternes and there is a basic similarity between the two wines, to the extent that a Barsac may be called Sauternes, while a Sauternes from outside the village of Barsac may not be called Barsac. However, there is a difference between the two wines. Barsac has a delicacy that Sauternes lacks. While Sauternes is rich, Barsac is elegant, with a certain honeyed, lemony character. In the best years it too will have the slightly roasted quality that comes from grapes that have been affected by noble rot, which is so essential to its quality and prevents it from being too cloyingly sweet.

● **Vintages:** The 1980s were a lucky run for Barsac and Sauternes. The only years in which the wines were not very successful were 1984 and 1987. 1983, 1986, 1988 and 1989 are outstanding, and so is 1990. Also try 1976 and 1967.

● **Recommended producers:** Coutet and Climens vie with each other as to which is best. Also try Broustet, Caillou, Doisy-Daëne, Doisy-Védrines, Suau.

Taste on:

FRANCE: ▷Sauternes and nearby appellations like Ste-Croix du Mont, Cadillac, Cérons and Loupiac; ▷Monbazillac.

The sweet wines of the Loire Valley, such as ▷Coteaux du Layon, ▷Vouvray, Bonnezeaux and Quarts de Chaume. They are made from ▷Chenin Blanc which is as susceptible to noble rot as Sauvignon and Sémillon. They too mature into splendid bottles in their old age.

Occasionally you find a ▷Muscat *vin doux naturel* that seems to have more in common with Barsac than other Muscats. One such example is the deliciously delicate Muscat de Rivesaltes produced by the Sarda-Malet family.

▷Jurançon *moelleux*.

▷Auslese wines from Germany and Austria.

ITALY: ▷Orvieto *abboccato*; Recioto di ▷Soave; Picolit, an obscurity from Friuli, made from the grape variety of the same name that is also susceptible to noble rot; Torcolato, made by Maculan in Breganze ❦❦❦.

Late Harvest wines from California, Oregon, Australia and New Zealand.

❦ Beaujolais

Essentially there are three styles of Beaujolais, namely the basic appellation of Beaujolais or Beaujolais Villages, ▷Beaujolais Nouveau and then the more substantial wines of the ten *crus*, such as Fleurie, Morgon and ▷Moulin à Vent. You occasionally see Beaujolais Supérieur, which simply denotes an extra degree of alcohol, but nothing more. Although Beaujolais can be also white or pink, a bottle of Beaujolais usually means a red wine, for which the grape variety is always Gamay.

Beaujolais is the southernmost wine area of ▷Burgundy, coming from stunningly beautiful hillsides north of the city of Lyon. The Gamay grape is vinified in a particular way (called carbonic maceration, whereby whole bunches of grapes are put into vats full of carbon dioxide) to bring out all its youthful, fruity, lively charm; or an adaption of this method, called *semi maceration carbonique* whereby no extra carbon dioxide is added, but that produced from the fermentation is retained in the vat. ▷Acidity rather than ▷tannin is the dominant characteristic of this light, easy-to-drink red wine. The flavour is reminiscent of slightly sour but very fruity cherries. Basic Beaujolais, or Beaujolais Villages, from some of the better villages is not a wine to age and should be drunk within a year or two of the vintage. More long-lasting wines come from some of its *crus*, like ▷Moulin à Vent.

● **Vintages:** 1991, 1990, 1989, 1988, 1987, 1986, 1985.

● **Recommended producers:** Georges Duboeuf, Loron, Sarrau, Jean-Charles Pivot, André Depardon, Eventail des Producteurs, Pierre Ferraud, Pasquier-Desvignes, Chanut Frères, Caveau de Fleurie, Dépagneux, Jean Descombes.

 Taste on:
FRANCE: The nearby wines of the Côte Roannaise, Côtes du Forez ❦❦ , Coteaux Lyonnais ❦ all come from the Gamay grape

and are very similar in taste, and not quite as expensive as Beaujolais is now. Red St-Pourçain can include Pinot Noir in its blend but has a comparable fruity acidity and lack of body, as do some of the red wines of the Côtes d'Auvergne. Consider too some of the red wines of Savoie and Bugey, where they also grow Gamay. Nearby red ▷Mâcon, which is less common than white, has a similar light, fruity character.

Gamay also grows in the Loire Valley, in the form of Gamay de Touraine and the occasional Gamay-based Vin de Pays du Jardin de la France, as well as Vin de Pays des Fiefs Vendéens.

Red wines from the Loire Valley: ▷Anjou rouge, ▷Chinon and Bourgueil have a similar weight and fruitiness, as well as lack of tannin, but not an identical flavour.

In the Rhône Valley there is Gamay de l'Ardèche, while the Coteaux de Tricastin have some peppery fruit, not dissimilar to Beaujolais. In the Midi too some of the lighter wines have a comparable fruity character. If you like Beaujolais, you would also enjoy the immediately appealing flavour of a Côtes du Lubéron such as Château Val Joanis.

ITALY: ▷Dolcetto from Piedmont.

A newcomer from Tuscany, Sarmento is also very similar in style. This is a wine that is intended, like a lot of Beaujolais, for drinking the summer after the harvest. Fruity acidity, little body and no tannin are its chief characteristics.

The lighter styles of ▷Bardolino and ▷Valpolicella.

Terre di Ginestra *rosso*, from a leading Sicilian estate, making an uncharacteristically light, red wine for the island, with some damson and raspberry fruit.

HUNGARY: Blue Frankish or Kékfrankos from Hungary is often mistakenly believed to be the Gamay of Beaujolais, which it is not, but there is a similarity of taste, with some light peppery fruit, a little acidity, and just a touch of tannin.

AUSTRIA: A peculiarly Austrian grape making Blauer Zweigelt, a light fruity wine.

CALIFORNIA: The lighter styles of ▷Zinfandel.

AUSTRALIA: The lighter styles of ▷Shiraz.

☙ Beaujolais Nouveau

The commercial success of Beaujolais Nouveau (or Beaujolais Primeur as it is sometimes called) over the last ten years or so is such as to warrant separating it from ordinary Beaujolais. It does in fact account for something like half the production of the region. The charm of Beaujolais Nouveau is that it is a fresh, lively wine that is ready to drink within a few short weeks of the harvest, with a release date fixed for the third Thursday in November. Its appeal stems from the thrill of drinking a wine that is barely out of the fermentation vats. The reality is often far from appealing if the vintage is not so good and the grapes unripe. Then Beaujolais Nouveau is sour and acidic. However, in good years its charm is undeniable and there is a note of excitement in the first wine of the year.

● **Vintages:** In theory Beaujolais Nouveau is drunk only in the November and December of the same year. However in practice, in a good vintage it often tastes much better the following Easter.

● **Recommended producers:** Georges Duboeuf, Sarrau, Pierre Ferraud, Thorin, Chanut Frères, Mommessin, Pasquier-Desvignes.

 Taste on:

FRANCE: The success of Beaujolais Nouveau has encouraged widespread imitation, not only in France but elsewhere too. Try ▷Gaillac Nouveau, ▷Côtes du Rhône Nouveau, as well as Nouveau *vin de pays* from the south of France, which can be released even sooner, in early October. The chances are that, with a warmer climate and consequently riper grapes, they will be more palatable than Beaujolais Nouveau.

ITALY: Italy has not escaped the craze for *vini novelli* with wines such as Banfi's Santa Costanza and Antinori's San Giocondo in Tuscany, and Vinòt from Gaja in Piedmont. Also young ▷Dolcetto.

PORTUGAL: For those who take a masochistic delight in sour red wine, red ▷Vinho Verde is just the thing, with its eyewatering acidity. I will admit to enjoying it in Portugal, but it certainly does not travel well.

AUSTRALIA: But why wait until October or November when you have the new wine of the year as early as February or March from the southern hemisphere, such as Hardy's Early Bird Red.

⚘ Beerenauslese

Beerenauslese is the fourth category of German Prädikat wines, and also features in Austrian wines. It means literally a selection of berries. They will be berries affected by noble rot, so that they are dehydrated with concentrated sweet juice. Beerenauslese wines are made only in the best years. As young wines they are rich and honeyed, but always with a firm balancing backbone of acidity, so that they develop greater depth of flavour with bottle age, with a slightly roasted taste originating from the noble rot, and fruit flavours depending upon the grape variety. In Germany, ▷Riesling makes the finest, most elegant Beerenauslese wines, but always with an underlying richness.

The French equivalent, or more precisely, the equivalent terminology in Alsace is *Sélection de Grains Nobles*, again implying a choice of the best berries. *Doux*, meaning sweet, will also be an indication that a wine is quite lusciously sweet, as in ▷Vouvray Doux. Other appellations such as ▷Sauternes or Bonnezeaux also depend upon grapes affected by noble rot but do not actually say so on the label.

In the New World the literal translation is Individual Berry Selected, while the term 'botrytis affected' is also common usage, or even 'botrytis bunch selected'.

● **Vintages:** In Germany: 1990, 1989, 1988, 1985, 1983, 1976, 1975, 1971.

Taste on:
GERMANY: ▷Bernkastel, ▷Johannisberg, ▷Nierstein, ▷Nahe-Schlossböckelheim, ▷Rheinpfalz-Deidesheim.

AUSTRIA: Beerenauslese, but heavier than most German Beerenauslesen. Ausbruch, a term unique to Austria, also denotes a wine made from grapes affected by noble rot, coming between Beerenauslese and ▷Trockenbeerenauslese in degree of sweetness. The village of Rust in the Burgenland is particularly famed for its Ausbruch wines.

FRANCE: Alsace *Sélection de Grains Nobles* for ▷Riesling, ▷Pinot Gris, ▷Gewürztraminer, and very occasionally, ▷Muscat.

The sweet wines of the Loire Valley, such as Bonnezeaux, Quarts de Chaume, Chaume, ▷Vouvray, Montlouis.

The sweet wines of Bordeaux, like Ste-Croix du Mont, Loupiac and Cadillac, as well as ▷Sauternes and ▷Barsac, and also nearby ▷Monbazillac.

▷Muscat *vin doux naturel* from the south of France, such as ▷Muscat de Beaumes-de-Venise, Muscat de Rivesaltes and so on. Although the method of vinification is different, there is a similarity in the degree of sweetness.

ITALY: Muffato Nobile describes a wine made from grapes affected by noble rot.

Torcolato from Maculan in the Veneto, Recioto di ▷Soave.

USA: Botrytis Affected or Late Harvest ▷Riesling and ▷Gewürztraminer from California and Oregon.

AUSTRALIA: Wines labelled Late Harvested or Botrytis Affected, such as Noble Late Harvested Botrytis Sémillon from de Bortoli.

NEW ZEALAND: Wines made from grapes affected with noble rot will say so, such as Dry River Riesling botrytis bunch selected ▼, or Redwood Valley Late Harvest Rhine Riesling.

▼ Bergerac

Bergerac can be red, white and even pink. The vineyards adjoin those of ▷St-Emilion and so there are inevitable similarities with Bordeaux. Red Bergerac comes from the same grape varieties, ▷Cabernet Sauvignon, Cabernet Franc and Malbec, while the white wines are also made from the traditional grapes of Aquitaine, ▷Sauvignon, Sémillon and occasionally Muscadelle. An extra degree of alcohol allows red Bergerac to be called Côtes de Bergerac, while white Côtes de Bergerac is always slightly sweet or *demi sec*. However the best white Bergerac is firmly dry and often made purely from the Sauvignon grape, in which case it will say so on the label.

Red Bergerac usually has a certain lean stalkiness, with some underlying dry cedarwood fruit, laced with hints of blackcurrants. These wines will develop a little, but no more than a ▷claret from one of the peripheral appellations of Bordeaux.

Bergerac Blanc can be crisp and fresh, and deliciously pungent if it comes from Sauvignon alone. If some Sémillon and maybe a drop of Muscadelle are included in the blend, it will be fuller and grassier and maybe a little flatter and less lively.

The occasional pink Bergerac is usually fresh and dry with some attractive raspberry fruit.

• **Vintages:** Follow those of Bordeaux, so 1990, 1989, 1988, 1986, 1985, 1983, 1982.

• **Recommended producers:** Château la Jaubertie, Château Belingard, Château la Plante, Château Court-les-Mûts, Domaine de Gourgeuil.

Taste on:

RED

FRANCE: Pécharmant is an enclave within the vineyards of Bergerac, where the wines are a little tougher and longer-lived, but still similar in taste. Try Château Tiregand and Domaine du Haut-Pécharmant.

Other wines of the southwest such as ▷Buzet, Côtes de Duras.

The lighter wines of ▷St-Emilion and satellite vineyards, such as Lussac-St-Emilion and Montagne-St-Emilion.

Other ▷claret, such as wines from the peripheral appellations like Côtes de Castillon, Côtes de Francs, Lalande de Pomerol, Fronsac, Côtes de Bourg, Premières Côtes de Bordeaux and even simple Bordeaux Rouge.

WHITE:

FRANCE: ▷Bordeaux Blanc, ▷Entre-Deux-Mers, ▷Graves.

Other white wines from the southwest, made from the same grape varieties, Côtes de Duras, ▷Buzet Blanc, Côtes du Marmandais Blanc.

Bergerac Sauvignon has an affinity with Sauvignon de St-Bris, but not the ▷Sauvignon of the Loire Valley.

Côtes de Bergerac, which is neither really sweet nor dry, has affinities with ▷Anjou Blanc, or ▷Vouvray *demi sec*, with sugar masking the underlying acidity.

The little-known appellations of Saussignac and Montravel which form part of the vineyards of Bergerac, are virtually interchangeable with Côtes de Bergerac.

PINK:

FRANCE: Clairet de Bordeaux, the little-known pink wine of the Gironde or even the occasional Bordeaux Rosé; ▷Chinon Rosé.

ITALY: Vin Ruspo from Carmignano in Tuscany.

🐂 Bernkastel – Mosel

The Mosel with its two tributaries, the Saar and Ruwer, represents some of the best of German winemaking. Villages such as Bernkastel, Piesport, Graach, Trittenheim and Zeltingen in the Mittelmosel, as well as Waldrach and Eitelsbach on the Ruwer and Ayl and Wiltingen on the Saar produce delicate flowery wines for summer days. As in all the German wine regions the quality scale ranges from basic table wine or *Tafelwein* right up to ▷Trockenbeerenauslese. There is no doubt that the ▷Riesling grape produces the best wines of the Mosel, while Müller-Thurgau is popular for more basic flavours.

Good Mosel has a delicate flowery quality about it, but always with a steely backbone of acidity. There is a slatey character to the wines, that originates from the soil. As they mature, the higher-quality wines can develop an overpowering petrolly bouquet of kerosene, but always with some underlying honeyed flavours. For my tastebuds, there is nothing to better a Mosel ▷Auslese from a top producer, which one can drink in the garden on a summer's evening, with its elegant balance of delicately honeyed but slatey fruit and firm acidity. That is what German wine is all about. Forget ▷*trocken* and ▷Liebfraumilch. Give the ▷Spätlesen and Auslesen from a good vintage three or four years' bottle age, or even longer, and they will develop even more delicately complex flavours.

Bereich Bernkastel is the simplest of the wines of Bernkastel, covering a wide area of vineyards around the town, including a large part of the Mittelmosel. The grape variety is usually Müller-Thurgau. Next up the scale comes Bernkasteler Badstube and Bernkasteler Kurfürstlay, the two *Grosslage* or group of vineyards, close to the town.

The best-known *Einzellage*, or single vineyard, of Bernkastel, is the Doktor vineyard, labelled Bernkasteler Doktor, where the grape variety is Riesling. It will always be sold with a Prädikat, a quality description, such as Spätlese or Auslese. Other vineyards from the Mosel to remember include Wehlener Sonnenuhr, Piesporter Goldtröpfchen, Bernkasteler Bratenhöfchen, Urziger Würzgarten, Ayler Kupp, Scharzhofberger, Wiltinger Braune Kupp, Eitelsbacher Karthaüserhofberg. Do not be put off by the apparent complexity of these names. German wines labels have an unfailing logic. First comes the village name, then the vineyard name, next the grape variety and finally the Prädikat, which tells you how sweet the wine is.

● **Vintages:** 1990, 1989, 1988, 1985, 1983, 1976, 1971.

● **Recommended producers:** J. Lauerburg, Bert Simon, Deinhard, Dr. Thanisch, J. J. Prüm, Vereinigte Hospitien, von Hövel, Dr. Fischer, Egon Müller, Höhe Domkirche, Bischöfliches Priesterseminar, Bischöfliches Konvikt, Friedrich Wilhelm Gymnasium, Weingut Klusserath, Max Ferdinand Richter.

Taste on:

GERMANY: The elegance and balance of a Mosel Riesling is hard to beat and almost impossible to find elsewhere. Rieslings from the Rheingau village of ▷Johannisberg are riper; those of ▷Rheinpfalz-Deidesheim are heavier, and those of the ▷Nahe Bereich of Schlossböckelheim, grassier.

FRANCE: ▷Riesling d'Alsace, although they are steelier and higher in alcohol.

ENGLAND: Wines with Müller-Thurgau on the label.

Body

Full-bodied is one of those wine terms that is bandied around as something of a joke, to conjure up images of plump, even buxom wines. What it really describes is the weight and even the alcohol content of a wine. A full-bodied wine fills the mouth, with a richness of flavour that really makes an impact. By implication wines that are high in alcohol tend to be full-bodied, for the more alcohol a wine has, the weightier and heavier in the mouth it will seem. Such wines are unlikely to be described as elegant. In contrast, other wines are light and lacking in body, and also lower in alcohol. Weight is really a synonym for body, again describing the feel of the wine in the mouth, be it light, medium or heavy.

Taste on:

FULL-BODIED: ▷Châteauneuf-du-Pape, ▷Bandol, ▷Jumilla, ▷Australian Shiraz.

LIGHTWEIGHT: ▷Vinho Verde, ▷Muscadet, ▷English wines, ▷Sancerre, most German wines.

Bordeaux Blanc

Not so very long ago Bordeaux Blanc stood for all that was worst in white winemaking. It usually reeked of sulphur and had a bouquet reminiscent of wet wool. The taste was nondescript, neither sweet nor dry, but indecisively in between. Small wonder that Bordeaux Blanc and kindred appellations such as ▷Entre-Deux-Mers represented a declining market. But in the last five years things have changed dramatically for the better. In an attempt to appeal to modern tastebuds the basic white appellation of Bordeaux has become a different animal. It is no longer faintly sweet but positively dry, not acidic but firm, with some real flavour. Good white Bordeaux will have some fresh, stoney fruit, with fragrant over-tones. If it is made predominantly of Sauvignon, the flavour will be slightly pungent, but fuller and less delicate than the Sauvignon-based wines of the Loire Valley. Sometimes it contains a substantial proportion of Sémillon as well, in which case the wine will be fuller and more rounded. If it has been matured in oak – which is unlikely for a basic appellation, but nonetheless a growing trend amongst some of the more go-ahead producers, especially from appellations with a higher profile, such as ▷Graves and maybe ▷Entre-Deux-Mers – the taste may have more in common with ▷Fumé Blanc from California. In the Médoc and in the Sauternes, where the principal wines are red and sweet respectively, any dry white wines carry the appellation of Bordeaux Blanc.

• **Vintages:** 1990, 1989, 1988. Drink the youngest vintage available. Simple Bordeaux Blanc, unlike the white wines of the Graves and Pessac-Léognan will not improve with bottle age.

• **Recommended producers:** Sirius, the white Bordeaux produced by Peter Sichel, Trois Moulines, Vin Sec de Doisy Daëne, Y (pronounced 'Ygrec'), the dry white wine of Château Yquem, Pavillon Blanc de Château Margaux; J. & F. Lurton – le Blanc, R de Rieussec.

 Taste on:

FRANCE: All the white wines of Bordeaux, as well as those of the immediately adjoining appellations of ▷Bergerac and the Côtes de Duras are made predominantly from Sauvignon, with some Sémillon. Also try ▷Entre-Deux-Mers, the ▷Graves, or the new appellation of Pessac-Léognan. There is a small production of white ▷Buzet and Côtes du Marmandais, which again are very similar in taste, coming as they do, from the same grape varieties. Sauvignon de St-Bris falls between the Sauvignons of the Loire and Bordeaux in taste, although not in geography, as the little village of St-Bris-le-Vineux is the one place in Burgundy where it is permitted to grow Sauvignon. Recommended producers here include Robert Defrance, Luc Sorin, Jean-Marc Brocard. Sauvignon in ▷*vin de pays* from the Midi, such as Listel's Vin de Pays d'Oc.

CHILE: Of all the Sauvignons of the New World, those of ▷Chile most resemble the flavours of Bordeaux Blanc and Entre-Deux-Mers, for they have a fuller, more solid, flatter taste than the pithy flavours of ▷New Zealand Sauvignon. Try Viños Underraga and Los Vascos, which incidentally is half owned by the Rothschilds of Château Lafite.

🍇 Bordeaux Rouge (House Claret)

Bordeaux Rouge is the most basic of the appellations of Bordeaux. It comes from all over the department of the Gironde and is usually a fruity, slightly stalky wine, for drinking in early youth. The best-known example, but not the best, is Mouton Cadet, a popular brand created originally by Baron Philippe de Rothschild of Château Mouton-Rothschild back in the 1930s. At first it was appellation Pauillac, but since then its scope has been stretched to encompass Bordeaux Rouge.

This may be a SAFE choice. In buying a recognised brand, you are buying reassurance. Instead consider other alternatives from Bordeaux. A wine merchant's or supermarket's house claret, if you like their other wines, can be equally reassuring. A good house claret has all the basic characteristics of Bordeaux, but in a diluted form. It will have tannin and structure, backbone and balance, a fresh, youthful stalkiness, with some blackcurrant fruit. Inevitably it will not have the finesse and elegance of a classed-growth claret, nor the staying power. A house claret is designed for immediate drinking.

Any good wine merchant worth his salt will have a selection of what are commonly called in Bordeaux parlance *'petits châteaux'*, or little properties, names that are quite unknown and never aspire to any serious reputation. However in their own way, they are important for they form the backbone of a good wine merchant's claret list. The simplest of these are appellation Bordeaux, or Bordeaux Supérieur, which simply denotes an extra half-degree of alcohol.

- **Vintages:** 1990, 1989, 1988, 1986, 1985.

- **Recommended producers:** Château Méaume, Château Thieuley, Domaine de Toutigeac, de Sours, but more often sold under a brand name like Sirius, Sichel's Belair Claret, Harvey's No. 1 Claret, or a supermarket or wine merchant's own label.

 Taste on:
FRANCE: ▷Bergerac, Côtes de Duras, ▷Buzet, ▷Madiran, ▷Cahors.
▷*Vin de pays* from the Midi, made from Cabernet Sauvignon. Tursan, from the Landes.

BULGARIA: Bulgarian Cabernet Sauvignon has the recognisable qualities of the grape variety, a one-dimensional blackcurrant fruitiness and some stalky tannin, tinged with a little earthiness. Finesse it lacks, but so does Bordeaux Rouge.

CHILE: The basic Cabernet Sauvignon of most Chilean wineries has the stalky fruitiness of young claret.

ITALY: ▷Chianti. There is a leanness and an underlying astringency in both young claret and young Chianti. While sour cherries are the dominant fruit flavour of Sangiovese, the main grape variety of Chianti and blackcurrants typify Cabernet Sauvignon, the two grape varieties have distinct similarities in the structure of the wines they produce. There is tannin and a youthful stalkiness that gives the wines vigour. Neither is rich or opulent, but somewhat lean and reticent.

⚘ Brunello di Montalcino ♥♥♥

Brunello di Montalcino is one of Italy's finest red wines. It comes from the delightful hilltop town of Montalcino, in southern Tuscany, where Brunello is the local name for the Sangiovese grape that grows all over central Italy. In the last century the Biondi Santi family did much to establish the reputation of Brunello di Montalcino, including identification of the particular strain or clone of Sangiovese, that grew in their vineyards. Ferruccio Biondi Santi began to make his wine from Sangiovese alone, a revolutionary step at the time, when most Tuscan wine was a blend of different grape varieties. Brunello di Montalcino is still made only from Sangiovese and must be aged for a minimum of three and a half years in large oak vats.

From a talented producer, in a good vintage, Brunello di Montalcino is one of the most stylish wines of central Italy, if not of the whole country. Young Brunello has the sour cherry flavours of Sangiovese, which develop with age to make delicious wine, with a flavour redolent of herbs and cedarwood, with spicey, smokey fruit and a firm backbone of tannin. Good Brunello is beautifully balanced in its elegance.

● **Vintages:** 1990, 1988, 1985, 1983, 1982, 1977, 1975, 1970.

● **Recommended producers:** Caparzo, Altesino, Il Poggione, Talenti, Case Basse, Villa Banfi, Pertimale, la Chiesa Santa Restituta, Poggio Antico Fattoria dei Barbi, Col d'Orcia, Argiano, Il Paradiso, Val di Suga, Biondi Santi.

Taste on:
ITALY: If you like the taste of Brunello, but cannot afford it too often, try Rosso di Montalcino ♥, from the same grape and

vineyards, but kept for only one year in wood, so a lighter version with the same flavour.

Pure Sangiovese *vini da tavola* from numerous ▷Chianti Classico estates: Cepparello from Isole e Olena, Brunesco di San Lorenzo from Montagliari, Sangioveto from Badia a Coltibuono, Fontalloro from Felsina Berardenga, La Pergole Torte from Montevertine, Vinattieri Rosso from Maurizio Castelli, Grosso Sanese from Il Palazzino, Flaccianello della Pieve from Fontodi, Coltassala from Volpaia, to name but a few.

FRANCE: The finesse and elegance of fine Brunello di Montalcino is unrivalled elsewhere in Italy, but in France it competes with the classed growth clarets of Bordeaux, and in particular those of the ▷Médoc, rather than of a Pomerol and St-Emilion. The cedarwood quality that develops in mature Brunello di Montalcino is also to be found in St-Julien and Margaux, while a slightly more austere example may lead to St-Estèphe. In the same way Rosso di Montalcino may therefore equate with a young, lesser claret, from one of the outlying appellations of Bordeaux, such as Côtes de Bourg or Premières Côtes de Bordeaux.

PORTUGAL: ▷Bairrada, for the combination of fruit and backbone.

USA: There are a few new plantings of Sangiovese in California, notably by the Tuscan house of Antinori, but as yet no wines to taste.

☕ Bulgarian Cabernet Sauvignon

Bulgarian Cabernet Sauvignon has been one of the great success stories of the last few years. Like all the wine production of the countries of Eastern Europe, that of Bulgaria has until very recently been state controlled, but it has succeeded more than the others in adapting its wines to meet the demands of western tastebuds. Cabernet Sauvignon was identified as a key varietal, a popular flavour imitating Bordeaux and wines from the New World. State subsidies dictated by the need for foreign currency meant that Bulgarian Cabernet Sauvignon, as well as other Bulgarian wines reached our wine merchants' shelves at prices that offered irresistible value for money.

It must be said that Bulgarian Cabernet Sauvignon does not attain the quality that we normally associate with that grape variety in Bordeaux, nor does it have the intense cassis flavours of Cabernet Sauvignon from the New World. It lacks impact. However, Bulgaria does produce some perfectly acceptable Cabernet Sauvignon, with recognisable varietal characteristics, with tannin and blackcurrant fruit, depending upon the quality level, which may range from a basic Bulgarian Cabernet Sauvignon with no indication of provenance, to a wine from a specified region such as Svichtov or Oriahovitza. Sometimes it can be a little dry and stalky, a little too grassy and herbaceous, or clumsy and inky sweet, but sometimes it may be quite full and rich, with hints of cedarwood and blackcurrants. Sometimes it is blended with ▷Merlot with some success.

- **Vintages:** No significant variation in Bulgaria.

- **Recommended producers:** Not relevant.

Taste on:

EASTERN EUROPE: Bulgarian Cabernet Sauvignon is probably the best of the Eastern European Cabernets, although it is also produced in Hungary and Yugoslavia; ▷Merlot from Eastern Europe.

ITALY: Cabernet from the Trentino.

FRANCE: ▷*Vin de pays* from the Midi made from Cabernet grapes, and also ▷Merlot; ▷Bordeaux Rouge or one of the peripheral appellations of Bordeaux.

Bulgarian Chardonnay

Chardonnay is the fashionable white grape variety of the moment, so it is no surprise that the Bulgarians have planted it almost as enthusiastically as Cabernet Sauvignon. Flavour and quality vary, as do vinification methods, in that some Bulgarian Chardonnay reeks of oak and little else, while others have not touched a stave of oak and smell of grass and lemons and maybe a whiff of cheese. I have had the occasional Bulgarian

Chardonnay that has impressed me with its varietal character, its grassy fruit and firm acidity, but a recent tasting left a rather dull impression of wines that were coarse and clumsy, over-oaked and overblown, and even oxidised. The younger vintages lacked fruit and any real flavour of Chardonnay, or were overwhelmingly oaky.

- **Vintages:** No significant vintage variation.

- **Recommended producers:** Irrelevant, but look instead for specific regions, Khan Krum, Novi Pazar and Varna.

 Taste on:
EASTERN EUROPE: Hungary, Yugoslavia.

FRANCE: Basic white ▷burgundy, ▷Mâcon Blanc Villages, ▷Chablis and Petit Chablis.

ITALY: Chardonnay from the Alto Adige and Trentino, and also ▷Pinot Bianco.

SPAIN: The over-oaked Chardonnays of Bulgaria have more in common with old-style white ▷Rioja.

Bulgarian Melnik

Melnik is an indigenous Bulgarian grape variety. Its true name is a real mouthful, Shiroka Melnishka Losa, meaning 'broad vine of Melnik' but usually it is simply called by the name of the town close to the Greek border in south west Bulgaria. This is a wine with lots of tannin, fruit and body, so that it benefits from some time in an oak barrel and ages pretty well. A 1983 Damianitza Melnik Reserve, tasted when it was six years old, had some dry cedarwood fruit, with tarry overtones and hints of fruitcake on the finish.

- **Vintages:** Irrelevant.

- **Recommended producers:** Irrelevant.

Taste on:

BULGARIA: Mavrud.

ITALY: ▷Barolo, ▷Barbaresco and other Nebbiolo-based wines; Aglianico del Vulture.

PORTUGAL: ▷Dão.

FRANCE: ▷Cahors.

♈ Bulls Blood

Bulls Blood used to be a popular brand of Hungarian wine. Its name originated from a story that is probably apocryphal, relating to the Turkish invasion of Hungary. The Magyars, who were defending the town of Eger against overwhelming odds, are said to have smeared their beards with the local red wine, claiming that it was the blood of bulls, in order to frighten the invaders.

The more authentic Hungarian name for Bulls Blood is Egri Bikavér, describing a red wine from the vineyards around the town of Eger. Once upon a time there was some real flavour, with regional characteristics in the wine, but sadly these seem to have been diluted, so that it is now just another rather ordinary red wine, with some stewed, inky jammy fruit, an underlying sweetness and a curious hint of tea leaves on the finish.

● **Vintages:** Insignificant, but drink when no more than three or four years old.

● **Recommended producers:** The state cooperative monopolises the production.

Taste on:

FRANCE: Basic ▷*vin de pays* from the Aude or Hérault; ▷Coteaux du Languedoc; ▷Côtes du Rhône, for a little more spice and character.

BULGARIA: ▷Cabernet Sauvignon or Merlot.

YUGOSLAVIA: ▷Merlot, Cabernet Sauvignon and ▷Vranac.

🍇 Burgundy (Red)

The basic appellation of red burgundy is simple Bourgogne Rouge, for which the grape variety is ▷Pinot Noir, as it is for all red burgundy, excepting ▷Beaujolais, ▷Mâcon and Passe-tout-grain, which is a blend of Pinot Noir and Gamay.

Pinot Noir is one of the most difficult and temperamental grape varieties. Vinified with talent, it can attain great heights, while in the wrong hands it can be downright nasty. The producer's name on the label is all-important when choosing a red burgundy. Red burgundy is usually light in colour, depending on the vintage, but especially in contrast to claret. A young burgundy has a raspberry-flavoured, sweet fruitiness, with acidity and some tannin, but again never as much as young ▷claret. As it ages, it develops the most wonderful chocolatey flavours, with vegetal overtones, a smooth, delicate richness and intrinsic sweetness, but only when it comes from the best vineyards and growers.

Taste on:
FRANCE: ▷Irancy, ▷Mâcon, ▷Beaujolais, ▷Rully in the Côte Chalonnaise, ▷Gevrey-Chambertin in the Côte de Nuits, ▷Volnay in the Côte de Beaune.

🍇 Burgundy (White)

White burgundy is an all-embracing term that covers vineyards from ▷Chablis and St-Bris, through the Côte d'Or down to ▷Pouilly-Fuissé and ▷Mâcon. Although the grape variety is mostly ▷Chardonnay, the flavours can change enormously with vineyard and vinification method. Chardonnay can be light and grassy or rich and buttery; full and oaky or delicate and subtle.

Bottles labelled simply Bourgogne Blanc or White Burgundy are likely to follow the light, grassy style. They generally come from the inferior vineyards of the Côte d'Or, from vineyards in the Yonne that do not fall within the appellation of Chablis, or from the Côte Chalonnaise, in which case they may now be called Bourgogne Côte Chalonnaise. Otherwise Bourgogne Blanc gives little indication of provenance, apart from the producer's address on the label.

Taste on:
FRANCE: ▷Chablis,   ▷Meursault,   ▷Rully,   ▷Mâcon,
▷Pouilly-Fuissé. Also Bourgogne ▷Aligoté, a white burgundy,
but not made from Chardonnay.

Buzet ⍦

Buzet, or Côtes de Buzet as it was called until the 1988 vintage, is one of
the several wines of southwest France that bear a marked resemblance to
those of Bordeaux, by virtue of the same grape varieties and a similar
maritime climate. The vineyards lie in the heart of Gascony, between the
towns of Marmande and Agen. Buzet is predominantly a red wine,
although you can occasionally find white and pink Buzet.

The taste of Buzet Rouge is very close to that of young ▷claret, with
firm tannin, blackcurrant fruit and hints of cedarwood.

●   **Vintages:** 1990, 1989, 1988, 1987, 1986, 1985.

●   **Recommended producers:** The growers' cooperative is the
main producer and is working well for its appellation, making some
stylish oak-aged wines, such as Cuvée Napoléon as well as two individual châteaux, Château de Gueyze and Château de Bouchet. Among
the independent producers, try Domaine de Versailles and Château
Sauvagnères.

Taste on:
FRANCE: ▷Claret, from the peripheral appellations of
Bordeaux, such as Côtes de Castillon, ▷Côtes de Bourg,
Fronsac, Premières Côtes de Bordeaux, or lesser wines of the
▷Médoc.
▷Bergerac and other wines of the southwest such as ▷Cahors,
Côtes de Duras, Côtes du Brulhois, ▷Madiran.

ITALY: Rosso di Montalcino, for the similarity with claret.

PORTUGAL: ▷Bairrada.

CHILE: ▷Chilean Cabernet Sauvignon.

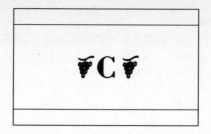

Cabernet d'Anjou

Cabernet d'Anjou is the best-known pink wine of the Loire Valley, made from Cabernet Franc and/or Cabernet Sauvignon grapes grown around the town of Angers. It may be firmly dry or slightly sweet. If the latter, sadly, it tends also to be over-sulphured and rather dull and uninspiring. Consequently, some of the better producers have abandoned it, to concentrate on making red wine instead from their Cabernet grapes. However, the dry versions can have some delicately fresh raspberry fruit, which makes them a wonderfully refreshing drink on a hot summer's day and add a note of frivolity to a picnic.

● **Vintages:** Drink the youngest available, and nothing more than two years old.

● **Recommended producers:** Mostly produced by regional merchants or *négociants*, such as Rémy-Pannier and Ackerman-Laurance, or sold under a supermarket own label.

Taste on:
FRANCE: Other pink wines from the Loire Valley, such as ▷Anjou Rosé, Rosé de la Loire, ▷Saumur Rosé, Touraine Rosé, ▷Chinon Rosé.
For dry rosé try ▷Sancerre rosé, made from Pinot Noir, which is delightfully ethereal and very delicate, as is pink Menetou-Salon.
Pink ▷Irancy, Rosé de Marsannay from the Côte d'Or; pink ▷Bergerac; Haut-Poitou rosé, made around the town of Poitiers; Bordeaux Clairet, an unusual appellation of Bordeaux.

Other pink wines from France, such as ▷Tavel and ▷Côtes de Provence, tend to be fuller and more alcoholic.

USA: Blush wines from California, made from white ▷Zinfandel or Cabernet Sauvignon. Such is the power of marketing jargon, that blush is fashionable, while pink is not.

BULGARIA too has ventured into blush wine.

PORTUGAL: ▷Mateus Rosé, apart from the bubbles.

Cabernet Sauvignon

Some of the finest wines of France and the New World are based on the Cabernet Sauvignon grape (particularly in the ▷Médoc and ▷Graves vineyards). In Bordeaux, Cabernet Sauvignon forms a substantial part of the wine, along with ▷Merlot and Cabernet Franc, while in the New World, notably in Australia and California it makes some of those countries' finest red wines, often without the addition of any other grape variety.

The flavours of Cabernet Sauvignon are typified by ripe blackcurrants or pencil shavings, with the slightly spicey smell of a cigarbox or cedarwood. The colour is always a deep red; you will never find an anaemic Cabernet Sauvignon, while mature wines develop an orange brick-coloured rim. The nose is characterised most often by blackcurrants, sometimes tempered by the vanilla of new oak. The taste will always have a substantial backbone of tannin, so that young Cabernet Sauvignon of quality can be a mouth-puckering experience, but with enough fruit to allow the tannins to mellow with age and give a long-lived wine of great subtlety. Lesser Cabernet Sauvignon can be a little stalky, but always with the underlying blackcurrant notes.

Cabernet Sauvignon as a pure varietal can be a little one-dimensional, and for that reason is sometimes blended with other grape varieties, both in France and in the New World. The traditional blend of the Médoc is Cabernet Sauvignon, Cabernet Franc and Merlot, and maybe a tiny amount of Petit Verdot, which also appears in many of the wines of southwest France. Cabernet Sauvignon is sometimes used as an improving grape variety in the south of France, lending extra flavour and weight to otherwise less inspiring wines. There are numerous ▷*vins de pays* from the Hérault and Aude and elsewhere made from Cabernet Sauvignon.

The great attraction of Cabernet Sauvignon to the winemaker is its versatility while retaining its essential style and structure. This is a grape variety that adapts easily to various conditions and usually with good results. Consequently it has spread to Italy, Spain, Bulgaria, Yugoslavia, Hungary, Greece and the Lebanon. However the closest rivals to fine claret come from ▷Australia and ▷California, with some increasingly good examples too from ▷Chile, ▷New Zealand, Spain and ▷South Africa.

Taste on:

FRANCE: The fine classed-growth ▷clarets of the Médoc represent the epitome of Cabernet Sauvignon, even though they may contain a substantial proportion of Cabernet Franc and Merlot. Other clarets and wines of the southwest like ▷Bergerac and Côtes de Duras.
▷*Vins de pays*, usually marked *cépage* Cabernet Sauvignon. The star of these, in a class of its own, is Mas de Daumas Gassac, a blend mainly of Cabernet Sauvignon and other grape varieties.

ITALY: Cabernet Sauvignon is an increasingly fashionable grape variety, not only in Tuscany, with wines like Sassicaia ❦❦❦, Solaia ❦❦❦ and Sammarco ❦❦❦, but elsewhere, with Pasqua's Morago from the Veneto, Gaja's Darmagi from Piedmont and Lungarotti's Cabernet Sauvignon di Miralduolo in Umbria, to name but three.

SPAIN: Jean Léon Cabernet Sauvignon ❦❦❦, Torres Gran Coronas Mas la Plana, Raimat Cabernet Sauvignon ❦, Marques de Griñon.

PORTUGAL: Quinta da Bacalhõa ❦, with a high proportion of Cabernet Sauvignon.

GREECE: Château Carras.

USA: The best red wines of California are made principally from Cabernet Sauvignon; Heitz Martha's Vineyard, Opus One, Dominus, Simi and others. Also wines from Oregon, Washington State, Long Island, Texas.

AUSTRALIA: Notably in Coonawarra, but with good results all over the vineyards of the continent.

NEW ZEALAND: ⊳New Zealand Cabernet Sauvignon improves with every vintage. The best wines come from Hawke's Bay, such as Te Mata's Coleraine ♥♥♥, Brookfields and Vavasour. Also Villa Maria, Kumeu River, St Nesbit.

SOUTH AFRICA: Nederburg, Rustenburg, Zevenwacht, Blaauwklippen, Groot Constantia.

CHILE: Santa Rita Medalla Real, Don Maximiano from Errazuriz Panquehue.

ARGENTINA: Etchart, Michel Torino.

EASTERN EUROPE: ⊳Bulgaria, Hungary and Yugoslavia also make wine from Cabernet Sauvignon.

♥ Cahors

Cahors is one of the larger appellations of southwest France, centred on the town of the same name in the valley of the Lot. Cahors means red wine and is unusual for that part of France in that it contains no Cabernet Sauvignon at all. Instead Malbec, locally called Auxerrois, which only plays a very small part in ⊳claret, is the dominant grape variety. This is a tough, somewhat rugged, stalky grape variety, which needs to be softened with some ⊳Merlot. There is also Tannat in the blend which, as the name implies, is a sturdy, tannic variety.

The final result is a rather tough, ungiving red wine, with an underlying austerity and a rigid backbone of tannin, sometimes tempered by some cherry fruit. Young Cahors has a youthful stalkiness about it, while older bottles can mature into more mellow wines, with a certain fruitcake quality about them. They can be very long-lived wines. Winemaking methods in Cahors vary between the rustic and unsophisticated to modern, high technology and there is a trend among more forward-looking winemakers to produce softer, more accessible wines. Nonetheless there is a rustic, sturdy quality about Cahors. Sometimes it has charm, but more often it does not.

- **Vintages:** 1990, 1989, 1988, 1986, 1985, 1983, 1982.

- **Recommended producers:** Château Haute Serre, Clos de Gamot, Château du Cayrou, Clos Triguedina, Domaine de la Pineraie,

Château de Chambert, Domaine Eugénie, Domaine des Savarines, Domaine de Gaudou, Clos de Lagarde.

 Taste on:

FRANCE: The most austere appellation of the ▷Médoc, and therefore similar to Cahors, is St. Estèphe.

The nearby VDQS of Côtes du Brulhois can be somewhat ungiving in character too.

Young ▷Madiran, with a noticeable percentage of Tannat, can have a similar austerity of flavour.

Red Côtes de St-Mont from the foothills of the Pyrenees is lighter than a Cahors, but has a similar stalky fruitiness and underlying tannin.

ITALY: ▷Barolo, as one of the most austere and tannic of all Italian wines, also develops an attractive mellow fruitcake quality in older bottles; Aglianico del Vulture from the south, which has some similar tough fruit and rugged structure; also Taurasi, made with Algianico in Campania.

PORTUGAL: ▷Dão.

ARGENTINA: The one other country where Malbec or Malbeck, as it is spelt there, is grown in any quantity. Argentinian Malbeck can vary in taste, depending on how it is vinified, but it can have a coarse, rugged flavour, such as wines from Trapiche and Etchart.

California Cabernet Sauvignon

California Cabernet Sauvignon has more immediate impact than reticent Bordeaux. It leaps out of the glass, reeking of blackcurrants, with lots of instant appeal. Only recently has it begun to aspire to subtlety too. It has rich, ripe blackcurrant fruit, with tannin and some herbaceous, minty undertones, making a mouthfilling wine, with a lingering finish. In contrast, the charms of most claret are more discreet, which is why California Cabernet Sauvignon has in the past sometimes overwhelmed classed growths from Bordeaux in those comparative blind tastings, which try to prove that one is better than the other.

California is much less concerned about the precise provenance of grapes than traditional Europe. Wineries can buy and blend grapes from all over the Golden State, if they so choose. However, the Napa Valley, north of San Fransisco, with some of the state's cooler vineyards, produces much of California's best Cabernet Sauvignon, notably those of the Rutherford Bench which includes vineyards owned by wineries such as Robert Mondavi, Freemark Abbey, Heitz, Joseph Phelps and Sterling. There are some good wines too from Sonoma and Mendocino, as well as the long Coastal Region between San Fransisco and Los Angeles. The mention of the grape variety on the label implies a minimum of 85 per cent of that variety. In the case of Cabernet Sauvignon, ▷Merlot may be included in the blend, while Cabernet Franc is a more recent and experimental innovation.

● **Vintages:** 1991, 1990, 1989, 1987, 1986, 1985, 1984, 1983, 1982, 1980, 1978.

● **Recommended producers:** Robert Mondavi, Opus One, Freemark Abbey, Clos du Val, Heitz Cellars, with Martha's Vineyard, Beaulieu Vineyards, Simi Winery, Stag's Leap Wine Cellars.

 Taste on:

USA: Washington State: Columbia Great Winery, Gordon Brothers Cellars, Hogue Cellars. However ▷Merlot does better here, as it ripens better.
Long Island: Hargrave Winery.
Texas: Pheasant Ridge, Llano Estacado.

AUSTRALIA: ▷Cabernet Sauvignon.

CHILE: ▷Cabernet Sauvignon.

FRANCE: ▷Claret, ▷Médoc, ▷St-Emilion.

SPAIN: Jean Léon Cabernet Sauvignon, Torres Gran Coronas Mas la Plana and also the wines of ▷Ribera del Duero.

ITALY: Wines from Tuscany labelled Predicato del Biturica indicate a noticeable proportion of Cabernet Sauvignon. Also Gaja's Darmagi, Castello dei Rampolla's Sammarco, Pasqua's Morago, Antinori's Solaia.
Or for something really unusual without a drop of Cabernet Sauvignon in it, but with the same ripe blackcurrant fruit, try

Sagrantino di Montefalco, from Umbria, which has a sweet, New World quality about it, as well as some firm tannin.

PORTUGAL: Quinta da Bacalhõa.

🍇 California Chardonnay

Some of the best examples of ▷Chardonnay, outside Burgundy, come from California. This fashionable and highly adaptable grape variety produces wines that are lean and understated, with a tight, nutty, dry flavour, or in contrast, wines that are riper and more opulent, with flavours of tropical fruit, pineapples and mangos. I prefer the understated wines, and that is what I look for in good California Chardonnay. The best will age, developing subtle nuances of flavour, akin to good white Burgundy, as they mature. Others that are more one-dimensional, simply fade. As with all California wines, it is producer and grape variety, rather than vineyard, that determine quality. Most bottles labelled Chardonnay from California are pure Chardonnay.

- **Vintages:** 1991, 1990, 1989, 1988, 1987, 1986, 1985, 1984.

- **Recommended producers:** Saintsbury Winery, Simi, Au Bon Climat, Schug Cellars, Edna Valley, Sonoma Cutrer, Long Vineyards, Robert Mondavi, Vita Nova, Stag's Leap Wine Cellars, Far Niente.

 Taste on:

USA: Chardonnay grows in as many as 42 other American states; Washington State with Salisham Vineyards, Kiona Vineyards, Hogue Cellars, Château Ste Michelle and Barnard Griffin, and Oregon with Sokol Blosser Winery, Ponzi Vineyards, Adelsheim Vineyard and others, are doing well. There are also some respectable Chardonnays in New York State, from Long Island, from the Hargrave Vineyard, Pindar, Bridgehampton, Palmer and Bidwell Vineyard, as well as Wagner from the Finger Lakes. Texas and Virginia are also-rans in the Chardonnay stakes.

▷AUSTRALIAN Chardonnay.

▷NEW ZEALAND Chardonnay.

▷CHILEAN Chardonnay.

FRANCE: White burgundy from the Côte d'Or like ▷Meursault and Puligny Montrachet. ▷Chablis would be too lean, apart from *Grand Cru* Chablis in a fat year, and ▷Mâcon is too light.

ITALY: Chardonnay from central Italy, rather than the northeast, such as I Sistri from the ▷Chianti Classico estate, Felsina Berardenga. Predicato del Muschio has a substantial proportion of Chardonnay.

SPAIN: Jean Léon Chardonnay, Torres Milmanda, Raimat Chardonnay.

🐂 California Pinot Noir

California Pinot Noir is getting better and better. If it is really good, it should be virtually indistinguishable from the red Burgundies of Côte d'Or, like ▷Volnay and Nuits St-Georges. And sometimes it is. Pinot Noir is a notoriously difficult and temperamental grape variety. It has none of the easy adaptability of Cabernet Sauvignon or Chardonnay. It likes a long, cool growing season, as in Burgundy and even there success is not always assured. Often it responds badly to the hotter climates of California, so maybe cooler Oregon will do better, but that is not yet proven.

Meanwhile there are indications that a determined handful of Californians, with vineyards in cooler regions of the state, such as Carneros at the southern end of the Napa Valley, are beginning to master the elusive character of Pinot Noir and produce some of the lovely ripe chocolate and vegetal fruit for which that grape variety is appreciated. Good Californian Pinot Noir does compete with the *Grands Crus* of the Côte d'Or. In its youth it has a fruity raspberry flavour, with a firm level of acidity and a touch of tannin, and the underlying hint of sweetness that is essential in Pinot Noir. The best will mellow into fine mature bottles. But at its worst, California Pinot Noir is even more unpleasant than some of the failures of the Côte d'Or. The heat can make it clumsy and jammy, or the flavour is burnt and bitter, completely dried out and devoid of any fruit.

- **Vintages:** 1991, 1990, 1989, 1988, 1987, 1986, 1985, 1984.

● **Recommended producers:** Saintsbury Winery, Carneros Creek Winery, Williams Selyem Winery, Au Bon Climat, Schug Cellars, Acacia, Chalone, Robert Mondavi, Sanfold Wines.

Taste on:

USA: Oregon Pinot Noir, from producers such as Eyrie Vineyards, Elk Cove, Ponzi.

AUSTRALIA: The producers here are still very much on a learning curve which is beginning to show results, especially in cooler areas, such as the Yarra Valley in Victoria, the Adelaide Hills in South Australia and even across the water in Tasmania. The best are Coldstream Hills, Tarrawarra, Pipers Brook, Bannockburn Vineyards.

NEW ZEALAND: Martinborough Vineyards ₹, Waipara Springs and St. Helena are achieving the best results to date and the potential is enormous.

FRANCE: Côte d'Or burgundies, such as ▷Gevrey-Chambertin, ▷Volnay.

ROMANIA: Pinot Noir.

☙ California Sauvignon Blanc/Fumé Blanc

There are two basic styles of Californian ▷Sauvignon Blanc, determined by the vinification method; with oak and without oak. The version that is kept in small oak barrels for a few months before bottling is sometimes labelled Fumé Blanc, a name originally coined by Robert Mondavi, which harks back to ▷Pouilly Fumé in the Loire Valley. However, the problem with oak and Sauvignon is that the oak tends to mask the real flavours of the grape variety. You are left with a full, rounded mouthful of buttery oak, with some lingering acidity from the grape, but none of the pithy pungency normally associated with Sauvignon. The taste is not unattractive, but it is not the true flavour of the grape. For that you need the non-oaked version, with the characteristic grassy, flinty, gooseberry flavours, or even tinned asparagus and a rich, underlying ripeness and weight that you do not find in the Sauvignons of the Loire Valley.

Sometimes there is a little Sémillon in the blend, following the practice of the ⊳Graves.

●   **Vintages:** 1991, 1990, 1989, 1988, 1987. Drink within three or four years.

●   **Recommended producers:** Fumé Blanc: Robert Mondavi, Murphy-Goode Estate Winery, Dry Creek Winery, Grgich Hills. Sauvignon Blanc: Quivira Vineyard, Ojai, Carmenet, Matanzas Creek, Clos du Bois, Château St. Jean, Simi.

 Taste on:

NON-OAKED:

USA: Sauvignon from Texas, Long Island, Washington State, notably the Snoqualmie Winery.

⊳NEW ZEALAND: Sauvignon.

SOUTH AFRICA: ⊳Sauvignon.

FRANCE: ⊳Graves and Pessac-Léognan.

ITALY: Sauvignon from Tuscany, sometimes labelled Predicato del Selvante, such as Vergena from Castelgiocondo, also Poggio alle Gazze. Sauvignon from northeast Italy.

OAKED:

The oaked Fumé Blanc style of wine has a similarity to Chardonnay, originating from the taste of the oak, rather than the taste of the grape, with a comparable buttery ripeness so:

⊳CALIFORNIA Chardonnay.

⊳AUSTRALIAN Chardonnay.

⊳AUSTRALIAN Sémillon, which is sometimes blended with Sauvignon, generally making a more successful wine than pure Sauvignon.

Cassis

Cassis is an attractive sailing port on the Mediterranean coast, close to Marseille. Frédéric Mistral said of it, 'He who has seen Paris, but has not seen Cassis, has seen nothing', which is something of an exaggeration. The reputation of the wine of Cassis rests upon the white, although the appellation also includes red and pink. The grape varieties are a blend of Ugni Blanc, Clairette and Marsanne, with the occasional drop of Sauvignon. There is an old-fashioned feel about white Cassis, with its rather solid, dry nutty flavours. It lacks the zingy, fruity acidity of modern winemaking, but the best have a mouthfilling dry, but not acid, tang, but of no very great character.

- **Vintages:** Drink within three or four years.

- **Recommended producers:** Domaine Clos Ste-Magdelaine, Domaine du Paternel, Domaine de la Ferme Blanche.

Taste on:
FRANCE: The white versions of ▷Côtes de Provence, such as Clos Mireille, and nearby Coteaux d'Aix-en-Provence, as well as Palette, a tiny appellation close to the town of Aix; ▷Bandol; ▷Côtes du Rhône; ▷Châteauneuf-du-Pape; ▷Graves; Pessac-Léognan.

ITALY: Fiano di Avellino and Greco di Tufo from Campania.

SPAIN: ▷Penedés, with wines like Torres Viña Sol.

Cava

Cava is the Spanish term used to define sparkling wine made by the champagne method. It is a *Denominación de Origen* in its own right, covering sparkling wines from several parts of northeast Spain, mainly in the province of Catalonia. Most of those are produced in Penedés, in the singularly unprepossessing town of San Sadurni de Noya, which is home to as many as eighty-five different Cava companies.

Cava is traditionally made from three grape varieties, Parellada, Xarello and Viura, which is known as Macabeo in Penedés. Parellada gives a little aroma and Xarello some body, but none are very positive in character, so that there has been a move towards planting more flavoursome Chardonnay, as in ▷Champagne, to boost the sometimes bland taste of Cava.

Cava generally has a lemony, dusty bouquet, with some full, biscuity, yeasty fruit. It is not as acid as champagne, nor is it as elegant. However, from a good producer it has much more to offer than champagne from an indifferent source. So far there are a couple of pure Chardonnay Cavas, notably Raimat, with some delicate buttery fruit on nose and palate.

Most Cava is sold as *brut* which means that it is dry, but not as firmly dry as *brut* champagne. There is little to be gained from giving Cava any bottle age, as the lack of acidity makes it fade relatively quickly.

- **Vintages:** Mostly non-vintage, like champagne.

- **Recommended producers:** Codorníu, Raimat, Juve y Camps, Cavas Hill, Mont-Marçal, Segura Viudas.

Taste on:

FRANCE: All sparkling-wine producers aspire to emulate ▷champagne, and if any one Cava comes close to champagne it is Raimat, with its pronounced flavours of Chardonnay, that could equate it with a Blanc de Blancs. However, champagne it is not.

The sparkling wines of the Loire Valley, such as Crémant de la Loire, sparkling ▷Saumur, although the acidity level in these is significantly higher.

ITALY: Traditional Cava is more akin to Italian sparkling wines, which are labelled *metodo classico*, to indicate the champagne method, such as Prosecco di Conegliano, or Prosecco di Valdobbiadene. Like the Cava grapes, Prosecco is not particularly rich in flavour, so that the taste is similar; dry, but not acid, with some slightly dusty fruit.

NEW WORLD: Australia and California produce sparkling wines, which tend to be more buttery and lemony in the case of Australia, while California bubbles are heavier and more yeasty.

Chablis

Chablis is the northernmost vineyard of ▷Burgundy. Here the combination of ▷Chardonnay grown on chalky soil in a cool climate makes for lean, grassy, dry wines, with a touch of what the French call *pierre à fusil*, or gunflint. There is a firm, stoney quality about good Chablis, which develops more complex flavours with bottle age, and there is no doubt that good Chablis does age. Apart from the basic appellation and some unimportant *Petit* Chablis, there are, as in other Burgundy villages, recognised *Premier Cru* and *Grand Cru* vineyards. The *Grand Crus* ♥♥♥, such as Les Clos, Valmur, and Grenouilles, will have greater depth and concentration, with richer, more substantial flavours. There should also be a marked difference in the weight and feel in the mouth between a simple Chablis and a *Premier Cru*. Sometimes the *Premiers* and *Grands Crus* wines, and very occasionally the simple Chablis are aged in oak barrels, depending on the producer's personal preference.

● **Vintages:** 1990, 1989, 1988, 1986, 1985, 1983, 1982, 1981, 1975, 1971.

● **Recommended producers:** François Raveneau, René Dauvissat, Louis Pinson, Domaine Laroche, William Fèvre, Louis Michel, Jean Durup, A. Régnard, Domaine des Malandes, Domaine des Maronniers, Jean-Pierre Grossot.

Taste on:

FRANCE: For Chablis, comparable Chardonnays include ▷Mâcon and Mâcon Villages, ▷Bourgogne Blanc, St-Véran, lighter wines of the Côte d'Or, such as Hautes Côtes de Beaune and Hautes Côtes de Nuits, St-Aubin ♥, St-Romain ♥; Chardonnay du Bugey ♥, Chardonnay de l'Ardèche, Chardonnay du Franche-Comté, Chardonnay du Haut Poitou.
For *Grand Cru* Chablis see ▷Meursault entry for greater details. Chardonnay apart, ▷Pinot Blanc d'Alsace.

ITALY: ▷Soave, ▷Gavi dei Gavi, Bianco di Custoza (Le Vigne di San Pietro), Lugana (Ca'del Frati) can all have a delicate grassy flavour with some firm acidity; as can some white wine from Sicily, notably a newcomer, Terre di Ginestra ♥♥, as well as Regaleali Bianco, and Feudo dei Fiori from Settisoli.
Montecarlo ♥♥, from Tuscany, which has a slight leafy, nutty bite, made from ▷Trebbiano and other more unusual grape varieties, like Roussanne and ▷Sémillon. Chardonnay also grows successfully in Tuscany, but is sometimes over-oaked.

Wines that do not touch a stave of wood, like Terre di Cortona from Avignonesi and Tenuta di Capezzana's Chardonnay best resemble Chablis.

Chardonnay also grows in the Alto Adige, as one of the permitted grape varieties of the DOC. You find it too in Trentino and Friuli, in DOCs like Grave del Friuli, Colli Orientali, Collio (Jermann) and all-embracing Trentino (Pojer e Sandri).

The distinction between ▷Pinot Bianco and Chardonnay has been somewhat blurred in the past in northeast Italy, so Pinot Bianco from the Alto Adige, Trentino and Friuli has some of the delicate, buttery flavours associated with Chardonnay.

▷Pinot Grigio from the same DOCs has a little more spice. Franciacorta Bianco from vineyards near Brescia in Lombardy is a stylish blend of Chardonnay and Pinot Bianco.

SPAIN: ▷Rueda made by Marqués de Riscal.

PORTUGAL: Planalto from the ▷Douro.

NEW ZEALAND: At a recent wine tasting I was not alone in mistaking a Pinot Blanc ▼ from the St. Helena Winery for Chablis.

USA: Pinot Blanc from the Cameron Winery in Oregon's Willamette Valley. Any bottles labelled Chablis have nothing at all to do with the real thing. The name has been borrowed to describe a vaguely dry white wine of indeterminate origins, and certainly without a single drop of Chardonnay.

▼ Champagne

Champagne is quite simply the best sparkling wine that there is. The process of production, entailing a second fermentation in the bottle and then the removal of the sediment arising from that fermentation by the techniques of *remuage* and *dégorgement* was developed in the Champagne area of Reims and Epernay by Dom Pérignon and Madame Veuve Clicquot and has been copied the world over. Hitherto the label for these other sparkling wines has said 'champagne method' on it, or words to that effect in French, Italian or whatever, but now the Champenois are trying to protect their interests and restrict the use of the term, so phrases like *metodo classico* or *méthode traditionnelle* are appearing. What is worse, however, is that in less scrupulous parts of the world, notably the United States, the name champagne has been borrowed and applied to the local production of sparkling wine, even if the method is not that of champagne.

There is no doubt that champagne is unique. What makes it so is the soil of the vineyards in northern France. The chalky soil, called *belimnita quadrata*, gives the ▷Chardonnay, ▷Pinot Noir and Pinot Meunier grapes a particular, distinctive flavour. It has an indefinable, yeasty, nutty taste, that other sparkling wines aspire to emulate, but never quite manage to imitate.

Champagne comes in various degrees of sweetness, according to the dosage or amount of sugar added at the time of *dégorgement*. It can also be pink. There is extra *brut*, or very dry indeed, which does not include any dosage, brut which is dry, *extra sec* (medium dry), *sec* (medium sweet), *demi sec* (sweet) or *doux* which is very sweet. Most champagne is *brut*. The term Blanc de Blancs means that it comes only from Chardonnay, while Blanc de Noirs means that there is no Chardonnay in the blend.

Basic champagne is sold without a vintage, as the producers' aim is to make a wine with a consistent house style, year-in year-out. For this, reserves of older wines are kept to blend with the new wine, so that the average champagne blend may contain as many as 70 different wines. However in the better years, which these days seem to be most years, a vintage wine is produced as well, (which must, by law, spend a minimum of three years (as opposed to one year for non-vintage champagne) on the lees of the second fermentation.

While there is nothing to beat the real thing, there is also no doubt that champagne is too expensive to drink every time you are in the mood for bubbles. It must also be said that bad cheap champagne is one of the nastier drinks around; it is coarse and sour, and worst of all, completely dampens any note of celebration. Broadly speaking, there are two styles of champagne, the lighter lemony ones and the richer, fuller wines, but that is an enormous generalisation, with many blurred distictions in between.

• **Vintages:** 1990, 1989 and 1988 are all good enough to produce vintage, but not yet. 1986, 1985, 1983, 1982, 1981, 1979, 1975.

• **Recommended producers:** Or rather, favourite champagne houses. Mine include Veuve Clicquot, Ruinart, Roederer, Alfred

Gratien, Billecart-Salmon, Bollinger, Henri Abelé, Krug, Laurent Perrier, Joseph Perrier, Perrier Jouët, Pol Roger.

Taste on:

FRANCE: For the lighter style, the closest parallel is Crémant de Bourgogne, which comes from the same grape varieties. Crémant de la Loire and the other sparkling wines of the Loire Valley such as sparkling ▷Saumur and sparkling ▷Vouvray, can also have some affinity with Champagne, although they come from a completely different grape variety, ▷Chenin Blanc.

Other French alternatives include Crémant d'Alsace mainly from Pinot Blanc; Blanquette de Limoux ❦ from the south of France, sparkling Gaillac ❦❦, Seyssel from Savoie, as well as sparkling wine from the Jura ❦❦, which is usually made from Chardonnay.

Ayze, the other sparkling wine of Savoie, has a firm acidity, with more in common with a Brut Nature champagne, a champagne which has not had sugar added to it.

ITALY: The dry sparkling wines of Italy are coming into their own, labelled *metodo classico* to describe the champagne method. Some of the best are the sparkling wines from Franciacorta, from producers like Ca'del Bosco, Bellavista, Berlucchi and Cavalleri. The Prosecco grape makes some successful sparkling wine too, in the Veneto, but perhaps the somewhat dusty, appley flavours have more in common with ▷Cava than champagne. There are other reputable producers of sparkling wine, scattered over the northern half of Italy, such as Ferrari, Lungarotti, Antinori, and Carpineto.
Sparkling Recioto di ▷Soave for rich champagne.

NEW ZEALAND: One of the very best New World imitations of champagne comes from New Zealand, where the champagne house Deutz has joined up with Montana to produce a deliciously elegant, creamy sparkling wine, Cuvée Deutz ❦. Also Lindauer.

INDIA: Omar Khayyam ❦❦, produced in cool, high altitude vineyards, with Champenois expertise.

USA: The richer, fuller champagnes have more in common with the sparkling wines of the New World. Indeed, several champagne houses are now producing sparkling wine across the Atlantic and in the southern hemisphere, but normally for the domestic American market. Champagne houses with interests in California include Moët & Chandon, Roederer, Mumm, Deutz and Piper Heidsieck. The warmer climate of California means that acidity, or rather lack of it, can be a problem. Try as they may, they never quite emulate the elegance of champagne. The flavours are rich, yeasty, broad and mouthfilling. Schramsberg has established a reputation as the first truly Californian champagne-method wine. Also Iron Horse, Cuvée Napa from Mumm, Schaffenberger.

AUSTRALIA: The warmer climate of Australia encourages comparison with richer styles of champagne, with wines like Yellowglen, Angas Brut, Killawarra, Great Western, Seaview, Croser.

SPAIN: ▷Cava, notably Chardonnay-based Raimat.

• **Pink champagne** Pink champagne is pretty, with its delicate colour and light, raspberry fruit. It is made in the same way as other champagne, except that the juice is left on the skins of the red grapes for a very short time so that it absorbs just the desired amount of colour, or more commonly, a tiny amount of red wine is added to the final blend to give some colour. Apart from that the vinification process is identical.

• **Recommended producers:** Billecart-Salmon, Bollinger, Perrier Jouët, Taittinger, Veuve Clicquot, Laurent Perrier.

 Taste on:

FRANCE: Pink wines from the Loire valley, such as Crémant de la Loire and sparkling ▷Saumur; Crémant de Bourgogne rosé; Crémant d'Alsace rosé; sparkling Côtes de Toul, a crisp, raspberry-flavoured wine, from vineyards around the town of Toul and not so far from Champagne. Mas de Daumas Gassac Rosé Frissante, a lightly sparkling, refreshing, fruity wine from the south.

SPAIN: Cava rosado.

ITALY: Pink spumante, from the DOC of Franciacorta; Bellavista, Berlucchi and Ca'del Bosco are all good; Also Equipe 5 from Trentino and Monsupello from Oltrepò Pavese.

USA: Pink sparkling wines from California, such as Schramsberg Cuvée de Pinot.

AUSTRALIA: Yalumba Angas Brut Rosé.

Chardonnay

Chardonnay is the fashion leader in white wine. If there's Chardonnay on the label, then it sells. It seems as though you can't go wrong with Chardonnay. It looks good; it tastes good.

Above all it is the grape variety of all fine white ▷Burgundy. It is grown from ▷Chablis down to ▷Mâcon, via the Côte d'Or, as in ▷Meursault, and Côte Chalonnaise, as in ▷Rully. Like its fashionable red counterpart, ▷Cabernet Sauvignon, it travels well. You find it in other vineyards in eastern France, the Jura, the Bugey, as well as in ▷Champagne, and it has spread south to improve the white wines of the Midi, and even across the sea to ▷Corsica. Nor is the Loire Valley without Chardonnay, in Vin de Pays du Jardin de la France, as well as Chardonnay du Haut Poitou. It seems as though Bordeaux is the one wine region of France where Chardonnay is absolutely forbidden in any form, shape or size.

Chardonnay is one of the grape varieties allowed in the vineyards of north eastern Italy, in the DOCs of the Alto Adige, Friuli and Trentino. It has been introduced into Tuscany as a more flavoursome alternative to the ubiquitious ▷Trebbiano and Malvasia. A wine labelled Predicato del Muschio implies a substantial proportion of Chardonnay in the blend. It has spread as far as Apulia too.

As for Spain, it has been planted in vineyards in ▷Penedés, with some success, and in Portugal it is planted in one isolated vineyard.

It features in the eastern European vineyards of Bulgaria, Yugoslavia and Hungary, with their quest for western European flavours.

And naturally Chardonnay has adapted well to the vineyards of the New World. Some of the classiest Chardonnay outside Burgundy is to be found in California, while other States, such as Oregon and Long Island are working on it.

Australia is producing some successful Chardonnay, as is cooler New Zealand. Chardonnay is now well established in Chile, while in Argentina it is still relatively insignificant, though of growing importance. There is even Chardonnay to be found in China.

The taste of Chardonnay varies very much with climate and vinification methods. Take two extremes. Compare an unoaked ▷Chablis with an ▷Australian Chardonnay from the Hunter Valley. The differences are considerable. Chardonnay grown in a cool climate like Chablis will have a gentle grassy, lightly buttery taste with some firm, stoney acidity. With the hotter climate of Australia, or even Tuscany or northern Spain, its flavours become richer and fuller, with less acidity, reminiscent of what the French call exotic fruits, by which they mean pineapples, mangoes and lychees, but always with the underlying buttery nuttiness. Chardonnay matured, or even fermented in oak barrels, changes again. Oak fills out the wine, giving it more substance and weight, as well as some toasted flavours, as epitomised by a fine ▷Meursault or Puligny.

A young Chardonnay can be amazingly easy to drink, with instant appeal, while a mature wine demands food for full appreciation. Young Chardonnay can have an almost austere, steely acidity, while Chardonnay from a hotter climate will be ripe and opulent. The flavours can vary enormously, making it one of the most versatile of grape varieties, but always with that underlying flavour of buttery Chardonnay.

Taste on:

FRANCE: Blanc de Blancs ▷champagne for the taste of Chardonnay with bubbles, such as Ruinart Blancs de Blancs, or Le Mesnil; ▷Chablis; the white wines of the Côte de Beaune, such as Puligny Montrachet, ▷Meursault, Corton Charlemagne and so on; the white wines of the Côte Chalonnaise, ▷Rully, Montagny, ▷Pouilly-Fuissé and adjoining St-Véran; ▷Mâcon Blanc, Beaujolais Blanc; Vin du Bugey ▼▼, with Chardonnay on the label. ▷*Vins de pays* from the south of France, and elsewhere, with the mention of Chardonnay on the label; Chardonnay du Haut Poitou; ▷Côtes du Jura, made from Chardonnay.

ITALY: Chardonnay from DOCs of the Alto Adige, Trentino, Friuli; *vini da tavola* from Tuscany, Piedmont, Umbria, the

Veneto and Puglia, often with fantasy names like I Sistri from Tuscany and Preludio No. 1 from Puglia.

SPAIN: Jean Léon Chardonnay, Torres Milmanda and Raimat Chardonnay, all from ▷Penedés.

PORTUGAL: Quinta da Valprado, a Chardonnay from the Douro produced by Caves da Raposeira, which at the moment still allows plenty of room for improvement.

USA: ▷California, as well Oregon, Washington State, Texas, Long Island.

CANADA: Of which the best example comes from Inniskillen Winery.

SOUTH AMERICA: ▷Chile: Villa Montes, Santa Rita, Errazuriz Panquehue, Los Vascos.
Argentina: Finca Flichman, Trapiche.

AUSTRALIA: Yarra Yering, Coldstream Hills, Tarrawarra.

NEW ZEALAND: Babich, Te Mata, Kumeu River, Cloudy Bay, Morton Estate, Neudorf Vineyards.

CHINA: Sold under the name of Tsingtão, with some stewed (as in apples) leafy, oaky fruit.

EASTERN EUROPE: Try also Chardonnay from Bulgaria, Hungrary and Yugoslavia.

🍇 Château Musar ♥♥

The Lebanon is not the obvious home of a fine wine, but despite the difficulties caused by the civil war – what do you do if there are armoured tanks blocking the road between your vineyards and your winery at harvest time? – Château Musar continues to produce some wonderfully distinctive wines. ▷Cabernet Sauvignon is the main grape variety, blended with some Cinsaut and Syrah to make an unusual blend, which is vinified like a ▷claret, with ageing in small barrels, for Serge Hochar, the owner of Château Musar, trained at Bordeaux university.

Although Cabernet Sauvignon is the main grape variety, the wines of Château Musar have a warm spiciness not normally associated with that variety. They have more in common with wines from the south of France, from the Rhône Valley or Provence, for any blackcurrants from the Cabernet Sauvignon are drowned by warm, meaty flavours, with leather and liquorice, pepper and spices. Château Musar makes full-bodied wines with enough body and tannin to ensure a measure of longevity.

- **Vintages:** 1989, 1983, 1982, 1981, 1980, 1978, 1975, 1972, 1970.

Taste on:

LEBANON: Coteaux de Kefraya.

FRANCE: ▷Châteauneuf-du-Pape, Gigondas, ▷Côtes de Provence, Coteaux d'Aix-en-Provence, notably Domaine de Trévallon, ▷Bandol.

AUSTRALIA: ▷Shiraz.

CALIFORNIA: ▷Zinfandel.

Châteauneuf-du-Pape

Châteauneuf-du-Pape is the most famous wine of the southern Rhône valley, coming from vineyards around the ruined château of the Avignon popes. The red version is heady and alcoholic, rich and warming, and from a mixture of grape varieties, including Grenache, Syrah and Mourvèdre. Thirteen are allowed altogether, but not all are used and the minimum alcohol level is a potentially heady 12.5°. In practice it is often much higher. The vineyards are covered with large, flat stones that reflect heat onto the ripening grapes. Originally the area was delimited according to where the herbs thyme, lavender and rosemary grew, and those to some extent determine the flavours of Châteauneuf-du-Pape. It is a rich, scented wine, redolent of the warm south. Sadly, some of the heady flavours have been diluted in the hands of less conscientious producers, who have been content with more anaemic Châteauneuf-du-

Pape. However, in the right hands it is still a powerful, full-flavoured wine, firmly tannic in its youth and deserving several years of bottle age.

White Châteauneuf-du-Pape does rather take second place to the red, but with a little bottle age, it can be distinctively leafy, with herbal and nutty overtones; unfortunately there are flat, flavourless versions too, which are best avoided.

- **Vintages:** 1990, 1989, 1988, 1986, 1985, 1983, 1981, 1979, 1978.

- **Recommended producers:** Château Fortia, Château Rayas, Domaine de Beaucastel, Domaine du Vieux Télégraphe, Clos des Papes, Clos du Mont Olivet.

Taste on:

RED:

FRANCE: Palette ▼▼, a tiny appellation outside Aix-en-Provence; lighter versions of blends of similar grape varieties such as ▷Côtes du Rhône and Côtes du Rhône Villages, Vacqueyras and Gigondas; ▷Côtes du Roussillon; ▷Fitou.
One particular estate in the ▷Coteaux du Languedoc near Pézenas, called Prieuré de St-Jean-de-Bébian, prides itself on growing all thirteen grape varieties of Châteauneuf-du-Pape, a decision inspired by the similarity of the soil.

ITALY: Cannonau di Sardegna, because Cannonau is a synonym for Grenache, the dominant grape variety of Châteauneuf-du-Pape, and there is a warm, alcoholic earthiness about the wine.
Red wines from Sicily have a similar warm headiness, with some fruit and tannin, such as those from the estate of Donnafugata, or the best red of the Corvo range, Duca Enrico.
Cerasuolo di Vittorio, a DOC from Sicily, is deep in colour, with some heady, herbal fruit and tannin; Copertino from Apulia has some rich, warming fruit, akin to Châteauneuf-du-Pape; Cirò from Calabria, full-bodied, meaty wine with good chewy fruit. Librandi is the best producer; Salice Salentino from Puglia; Recioto della Valpolicella Amarone.

SPAIN: Some of the lesser-known DOs of central Spain have a warm, heady flavour, not unlike a Châteauneuf-du-Pape. They are high in alcohol, with some spicey flavours, and sometimes warm, earthy overtones, like Almansa and Priorato, which are made from the Cencibel grape.

SOUTH AFRICA: Rustenberg Red for some warm, chewy fruit.

USA: California has taken some interest in the grape varieties of the southern Rhône, notably Mourvèdre, and is producing some distinctively spicey, full-bodied warming wines, such as Joseph Phelps' Vin du Mistral, Domaine de la Terre Rouge (Yes, it is in California), Bonny Doon's Le Cigar Volant, and Jade Mountain Mourvèdre.

WHITE:
FRANCE: White ⟡Hermitage, and other white wines from the Rhône valley, such as ⟡Côtes du Rhône and Lirac; Palette.

PORTUGAL: ⟡Dão, ⟡Douro.

🐂 Chenin Blanc

Chenin Blanc is the most characteristic grape variety of the central part of the Loire Valley, of the vineyards around the towns of Angers and Tours. It demonstrates an amazing versatility, producing not only still and sparkling wines, but a whole range of taste from the severely dry to the opulently sweet, but always retaining a firm backbone of acidity. In Savennières it is dry and grassy; in ⟡Vouvray it may be *sec, demi sec, moelleux* or *doux*, while in the appellations of Bonnezeaux, ⟡Coteaux du Layon and Quarts de Chaume it is sweetly honeyed and at its best with some years of bottle age. However, like most sweet wines these can be remarkably appealing in their youth, with flavours of peaches and apricots. In contrast dry young Chenin Blanc can sometimes be rather dull. I can decent overtones of wet dogs or damp hay, spoilt even more by a sweet and sour finish. There is no doubt that Chenin Blanc is at its most delicious in a mature Bonnezeaux or Quarts de Chaume.

Chenin Blanc has travelled to California where it is used for everyday dry or off-dry table wines, labelled simply with the grape variety. In South Africa it makes some easy-to-drink dry white wine, but without the sometimes seering acidity of the Loire Valley. These are often called ⟡Steen, rather than Chenin Blanc, while Edelkeur is a lusciously rich sweet wine. Some Chenin Blanc is also produced in Argentina, Australia and New Zealand, more often for bag-in-box wines than for bottles, but it has not captured the imagination of the wine world in the same way as varieties like Chardonnay or even Syrah or Pinot Noir and has been largely ignored in Europe, outside France.

 Taste on:

FRANCE: ▷Anjou Blanc, ▷Saumur Blanc, Savennières, Jasnières, ▷Vouvray, both still and sparkling, Montlouis, Bonnezeaux, Quarts de Chaume, ▷Coteaux du Layon, sparkling ▷Saumur, Crémant de la Loire.

SOUTH AFRICA: ▷Steen, Edelkeur.

USA: California, with Dry Creek and Kenwood; Washington State, with Kiona, the Hogue Cellars and Snoqualmie, and also Texas.

NEW ZEALAND: A particularly good example of Chenin Blanc comes from Collards ▼▼.

Chianti

Chianti is the red wine of Tuscany. The vineyards cover a large area, from Pisa to Arezzo, with several sub-zones, namely Chianti Classico, Rufina, Colline Pisane, Colli Aretini, Montalbano, Colli Fiorentini and Colli Senesi. Chianti Classico is the heart, lying between Florence and Siena, and in terms of taste it may be grouped with Rufina and distinguished from the other, lighter Chianti, which are often sold without any reference to their sub-zone. A distinction must also be made between young *normale* and wood-aged *riservas*. *Riserva* denotes a wine of three years' ageing before sale, while *normale* is the description for a young Chianti, usually of the previous year's vintage.

In Chianti Classico and Rufina the wines have body and structure, and good vintages develop into fine bottles with age, while the other areas tend to produce light, cheerful, fruity wines that are best drunk while they are young.

Chianti is made from a mixture of grape varieties, mainly Sangiovese, but also Canaiolo, a little white Trebbiano and Malvasia and maybe even a drop of ▷Cabernet Sauvignon. Sour cherries is the keynote of Sangiovese, with an underlying astringency which complements the olive oil of Tuscany. In Chianti from the Colline Pisane or Colli Senesi the sour cherries have a fresh, fruity flavour, with a lively acidity. In contrast Chianti Classico and Rufina, especially when they are of *riserva* quality, have much more body and backbone. These are wines that develop with bottle age all kinds of subtle flavours, even to the extent of resembling old burgundy or old claret.

● **Vintages:** 1990, 1988, 1985, 1983, 1982, 1977, 1974, 1971, 1970.

● **Recommended producers:** Chianti Classico: Badia a Coltibuono, Castello dei Rampolla, Castello di Ama, Castello di Cacchiano, Castello di Querceto, Castello di San Polo in Rosso, Felsina Berardenga, Isole e Olena, Monsanto, Montagliari, Montevertine (labelled Vino da Tavola di Radda, but to all intents and purposes a Chianti), Capannelle (likewise called Vino da Tavola di Gaiole), Vecchie Terre de Montefili, Riecine, Villa Antinori, Le Masse di San Leolino, Fonterutoli, Vignamaggio, Fontodi.
Rufina: Selvapiana, Villa di Vetrice, Castello di Nipozzano.
Colline Pisane: Bruno Moos.
Colline Aretini: Villa Cilnia.
Colli Fiorentini: Pasolini dall'Onda Borghese, Fattoria di Lilliano, San Vito in Fior di Selva, Fattoria di Sammontana.
Colli Senesi: Poliziano, Avignonesi.

 Taste on:
YOUNG CHIANTI:
ITALY: Other Sangiovese-based wines, from central Italy, such as Sangiovese di Romagna; Rosso delle Colline Lucchesi; Rosso Cònero; Montecarlo Rosso; Barco Reale from Carmignano; ▷Dolcetto; ▷Barbera.

FRANCE: ▷Beaujolais.

CHIANTI CLASSICO AND RUFINA:
Carmignano ▼; some of the Sangiovese Super-Tuscan wines, such as Cepparello, Flaccianello and ▷Tignanello; Morellino di Scansano ▼, from southern Tuscany; ▷Vino Nobile di Monte-pulciano; Rosso di Montepulciano; ▷Brunello di Montalcino;

Rosso di Montalcino; Pomino Rosso; Rubesco di Torgiano from Umbria.

FRANCE: Patrimonio from ▷Corsica, as the principal grape variety, Nielluccio is said to be related to Sangiovese.
▷Claret: Young claret has a stalky astringency, like young Chianti Classico *riserva*, with hints of cedarwood as the wines mature. They may not actually taste the same but there is a similarity in the structure and feel of the wine. Comparisons may be taken further in that both come from a blend of grape varieties and from a large area that is further divided into smaller zones.

PORTUGAL: Tinta da Anfora from J. M. da Fonseca in Setúbal, with some sweet fruit, balanced by some Italian astringency and tannin.

ᵺ Chilean Cabernet Sauvignon ᵥ

Chile has a fabulous climate for grape-growing and is often described as a viticultural paradise, with its warm summers, mild winters and limited rainfall, supplemented by irrigation from the melted snows of the Andes, and the additional bonus of phylloxera-free soil. European grape varieties like Cabernet Sauvignon were brought across the Atlantic in the mid-1850s, happily before the vine-killing pest phylloxera had arrived in Europe from North America.

It is Cabernet Sauvignon that offers some of Chile's most individual flavours. There is ripe blackcurrant fruit, with a backbone of tannin and hints of herbs and eucalyptus. Sometimes it may be a little coarse, leathery and earthy, but sometimes it makes a wine with considerable depth of flavour, and increasingly so, as winemaking techniques in Chile improve apace. Sometimes Cabernet Sauvignon may be blended with ▷Merlot or Malbec.

• **Vintages:** No significant vintage variation.

• **Recommended producers:** Santa Rita, Torres, Cousiño Macul with their Antiguas Reservas, Viña Carmen, Concha y Toro,

Errazuriz Panquehue, Caliterra, Los Vascos, Villa Montes, Santa Helena, San Pedro, Villa Montes.

 Taste on:

FRANCE: ▷Bordeaux provides the obvious comparisons. Wines such as Santa Rita's Medalla Real and Errazuriz Panquehue Don Maximiano could equate to a good *cru bourgeois* of the Médoc, with some ripe blackcurrant fruit. However they may tend to be a little softer and less tannic, and therefore with less ageing potential than their Bordeaux counterparts. In contrast, a supermarket own-label Chilean Cabernet Sauvignon would have more in common with basic Bordeaux Rouge. ▷Bergerac, Côtes de Duras, ▷Buzet, ▷Cahors, ▷Madiran. ▷*Vin de pays* from the Midi, marked *cépage* Cabernet Sauvignon.

NEW WORLD: Cabernet Sauvignon from other parts of the New World, notably Argentina, with the Andean Vineyard label, ▷Australia, ▷California.

♈ Chilean Sauvignon

Sauvignon seems more established in Chile and, at first taste, more successful than Chardonnay. From that one grape variety it is possible to detect three distinct styles. Two come from Miguel Torres of ▷Penedés fame, who has achieved so much for Chilean viticulture by introducing techniques such as temperature-controlled fermentations and judicious ageing in small, new oak barrels.

His standard Sauvignon from Curicó has some deliciously pithy gooseberry fruit, with some fresh acidity. It does not quite have the elegance of a Sauvignon from ▷Sancerre, but more the fruit and impact of a ▷New Zealand Sauvignon. In contrast, his second Sauvignon, called Bellaterra after the vineyard, is partially matured in wood. To my tastebuds this masks the true flavour of the grape, though if you like the taste of oak, you will undoubtedly enjoy this. It is full-flavoured with a dry, oaky, biscuity taste and quite a soft finish.

The third string to Chilean Sauvignon is a cross between the two, wines without the oak of the Torres Bellaterra but also lacking the pithy, fruity acidity of the unoaked wines from Torres or Canepa. A Sauvignon from a winery like Underraga has a soft, grassy flavour, with some body and acidity, not unlike an old-fashioned white ▷Bordeaux, but without the definition of character associated with modern Sauvignon. One reason for this may be that not all the Sauvignon planted in Chile is true Sauvignon, but an inferior relative of it. Sometimes they can be just a touch dull, but they are showing a marked improvement in flavour as winemaking in Chile develops.

● **Vintages:** Drink the youngest possible.

● **Recommended producers:** Torres and Canepa produce the pithiest, liveliest Sauvignons of Chile; also Los Vascos, Underraga and Santa Rita.

 Taste on:

FOR FRESH PITHY SAUVIGNON:
FRANCE: The Sauvignons of the Loire Valley such as ▷Sancerre, ▷Pouilly Fumé, ▷Sauvignon de Touraine.

ITALY: Sauvignon from the Alto Adige, Friuli and Trentino regions.

▷NEW ZEALAND: Sauvignon.

▷CALIFORNIA: Sauvignon.

FOR SOFTER SAUVIGNON:
FRANCE: White ▷Bordeaux and ▷Entre-Deux-Mers, and also ▷Graves.

FOR OAKY SAUVIGNON:
FRANCE: Oak-aged white ▷Bordeaux, ▷Entre-Deux-Mers, and ▷Graves.

SPAIN: Old-style white ▷Rioja, such as Marques de Murrieta or Bodegas Riojanas' Monopole, which tastes of oak rather than of the grape.

CALIFORNIA: Fumé Blanc style of Sauvignon.

AUSTRALIA: Oak-aged Fumé Blanc.

☙ Chinon

Chinon is the most characteristic red wine of the Loire Valley. It comes from vineyards around the town of the same name, with its ruined castle that played a part in English history.

Cabernet Franc is the dominant grape variety here, very occasionally blended with some Cabernet Sauvignon. Whereas in ▷Bordeaux it is usually the lesser part of the blend, in Chinon and neighbouring Bourgueil, it dominates the wine. Cabernet Franc is easily identifiable. In these northern vineyards it has a somewhat rustic, earthy flavour, reminiscent of potato peelings, with some herbaceous flavours and lots of raspberry and cherry fruit as well. There is a little tannin, but not usually much staying power. However, in the hottest years like 1990, 1989 or 1976, the red wines of the Loire Valley really come into their own, for then they have more tannin and concentration, so that they do age very successfully. Normally, however, a Chinon is destined for relatively early drinking.

- **Vintages:** 1990, 1989, 1988, 1986, 1985, 1983, 1982, 1976.

- **Recommended producers:** Charles Joguet, Domaine de la Perrière, Bernard Baudry, Olga Raffault, Domaine du Colombier, Couly-Dutheuil, Jean-Maurice Raffault.

Taste on:

FRANCE: The nearby appellations of Bourgueil and the much smaller St-Nicolas-de-Bourgueil are made mainly from Cabernet Franc, as is ▷Anjou Rouge. ▷Saumur Champigny is another Cabernet Franc-based wine, with more structure and flavour than plain Saumur Rouge. However, Domaine Langlois-Château Vieilles Vignes, although a basic Saumur has more flavour than most as it comes from old vines.

▷Beaujolais Villages, or one of the Beaujolais *crus* like ▷Moulin-à-Vent, have a similar degree of immediate fruity appeal but without so much tannin.

Marcillac ☙☙, from the upper reaches of the Lot Valley, is a combination of blackcurrant fruit, with hints of green peppers and spice.

ITALY: Cabernet is grown extensively in northern Italy. Often the label does not specify Sauvignon or Franc and many of the wines from Friuli, the Trentino and Alto Adige are a blend of the two. The flavours are a little riper and softer than those from the Loire, but with a comparable fruity, herbaceous taste, and the distinctive note of potato peelings.

Franciacorta Rosso ▼▼ in Lombardy comes mainly from Cabernet Franc, with some Cabernet Sauvignon and Merlot, giving a soft, ripe berry fruit flavour.

Teroldego Rotaliano from Trentino; the grape is the Teroldego which produces some ripe cherry fruit, with a slightly earthy finish.

NEW ZEALAND: The cool climate vineyards of the Antipodes produce some herbaceous Cabernet flavours. Sauvignon is planted more than Franc, but the wines often have a grassy taste, with acidity as well as tannin, like those of the Loire Valley.

▼ Claret

Claret is the traditional name that the English-speaking world gives to the red wines of Bordeaux. It covers a wide range, not so much of taste but of quality. The difference between simple unpretentious ▷Bordeaux Rouge and a prestigious classed growth of the ▷Médoc can be considerable. The grape varieties for each are similar, but the proportions may vary, to include greater or lesser amounts of ▷Cabernet Sauvignon, Cabernet Franc and ▷Merlot, and there may be a sprinkling of Malbec and Petit Verdot as well. However, the fine variations in soil and microclimate make the difference between a first growth and, say, a *cru bourgeois*, even though they may be separated by as little as a road.

Vinification methods matter too. They may be more or less sophisticated, with finely tuned temperature control for fermentation, a considerable annual expenditure in new oak barrels or, in contrast, the wine may see no oak at all and just spend a few months in concrete vats or stainless-steel tanks before bottling in time to leave the vats empty for the next vintage. Flavour, therefore, can range from fruity, young, stalky wines with a underlying taste of blackcurrants, to rich opulent, mature, complex flavours of cigar boxes, cedarwood and more subtle blackcurrant. It is impossible to consider claret as a whole, so for simplicity's sake I have divided it into various taste categories.

The first difference is between the two broad regions of Bordeaux, the right and left banks of the Gironde, the ▷Médoc or ▷St-Emilion and Pomerol. There is also ▷Graves and Pessac-Léognan between the two. Secondly there is the quality difference between basic ▷Bordeaux Rouge or house claret and a classed growth. Finally there are the peripheral appellations of Bordeaux, the wines from the outlying areas like ▷Côtes de Bourg, Côtes de Francs, Fronsac, Côtes de Castillon and so on.

 Taste on:
FRANCE: ▷Medoc, ▷St-Emilion, ▷Bordeaux Rouge, ▷Côtes de Bourg, ▷Graves.

🍇 Commandaria

Commandaria is the traditional dessert wine of Cyprus, made from weird and wonderful-sounding grape varieties, both black and white, like Xynisteri, Mavro and Ophthalmo. The name Commandaria originates from associations with the Knights Templar of the 12th century, who played an important part in the chequered history of Cyprus. The ripe grapes are dried in the sun so that they become rich and raisin-like and ferment very slowly. No fortification with brandy is necessary and yet the taste of Commandaria is not unlike a sweet sherry, with rich raisiny fruit, reminiscent of Moscatel grapes, with a walnut and marmalade aftertaste. However, it lacks the alcohol of sherry, so that it is softer and less intense in flavour. The colour is a deep brown.

- **Vintages:** Irrelevant.

- **Recommended producers:** Made by the large cooperative producers of Cyprus and usually sold under a brand name, like Alasia, Grand Commandaria, St Barnabas, Commandaria St John.

 Taste on:
SPAIN: Cream ▷sherry, ▷Màlaga, Montilla.

PORTUGAL: Moscatel de ▷Setúbal.

AUSTRALIA: ▷Liqueur Muscat.

🍇 Condrieu ♀♀♀

Condrieu is one of the most distinctive wines of France, let alone the Rhône Valley. The grape variety is Viognier, a rather fragile, sensitive vine that is rarely found outside the appellation of Condrieu and adjoining Château Grillet. However the flavour is quite individual, reminiscent of dried apricots with somewhat oily undertones. You either love it or hate it. I love it.

● **Vintages:** Some say that Condrieu should be drunk as young as possible and that there is no virtue in keeping it. I disagree and find that a wine that is about five years old, will develop more nuances of flavour. The good recent vintages of the northern Rhône are 1990, 1989, 1988, 1986, 1985.

● **Recommended producers:** Domaine Pinchon, Georges Vernay, Château du Rozay, Dumazet, Guigal.

 Taste on:

FRANCE: Château Grillet, a single property and an appellation in its own right, adjoins the appellation of Condrieu. It too comes from the Viognier grape, so that the flavour is very similar, with any difference stemming from slight variations in terrain, microclimate and vinification techniques.

Viognier is one of the several grape varieties allowed in ▷Côtes du Rhône Blanc, but you rarely find it as a pure variety. However, when you do, and it will say so on the label, it is a good alternative to expensive Condrieu, such as Domaine Ste-Apolinaire, and Château du Rozay, which makes a Côtes du Rhône from young Condrieu vines.

Over in southwest France, close to the foothills of the Pyrenees there is a little-known wine, called Pacherenc du Vic Bilh ♥♥, that is currently enjoying something of a revival. You pronounce it 'pash er rank du vick beel', or words to that effect. Although the grape varieties are peculiar to this part of France, with Gros Manseng, Petit Manseng and Arrufiat, the flavour has a similarity with Condrieu. It is not as heavy, but there are the same hints of apricots with an underlying unctuousness. Domaine Crampilh is the best producer.

ITALY: Arneis ♥♥ is one of the more obscure grape varieties of Piedmont in northwest Italy, making a wine of the same name. The best is Arneis San Michele made by Carlo Deltetto, a delicate white wine, again with the distinctive apricot fruit. His

Favorita, another obscure Piedmontese grape variety, also has a light taste of apricots, with some grassy fruit.

SPAIN: ▷Rias Baixas.

PORTUGAL: Apricots are the theme-tune of Condrieu, but I have also found them in good ▷Vinho Verde, by which I mean a wine from a single estate, not one of the popular, gently swee-tened commercial blends; for example, Palacio de Brejoeira, where the wine is made just from the best grape variety of the area, Alvarinho. It is delicious, elegant, with acidity balancing the delicate flavour of apricots.

CALIFORNIA: Viognier ♥♥ presents a challenge to some of the pioneering winemakers of the west coast. To date, Calera is the only winery to produce a Viognier which successfully holds its own alongside Condrieu.

♥ Corbières ∨

Corbières is a warm, sturdy, southern French wine, forming a pair with ▷Minervois. It comes from the foothills of the Pyrenees, with Minervois facing it on the opposite side of the valley of the Aude. It can be pink and white, but the better wines are firmly red, made from Carignan, Cinsaut, Grenache and some improving Syrah and Mourvèdre. These last two give extra spice and character to the solid flavours of the more traditional Midi varieties.

The taste is very similar to Minervois, perhaps a little tougher and more rugged, but the underlying flavours are comparable. There is an attractive fruity spiciness, with a firm backbone of tannin, making for full-flavoured wines with plenty of character.

- **Vintages:** 1990, 1989, 1988, 1986, 1985.

- **Recommended producers:** Domaine la Voulte-Gasparets, Domaine de Villemajou, Château la Baronne, Château St-Auréol, Domaine de Fontsainte, Château des Ollieux.

 Taste on:
FRANCE: ▷Minervois, ▷Fitou, ▷Coteaux du Languedoc.

PORTUGAL: ▷Bairrada.

SPAIN: There are Spanish wines with the some of the firm spiciness of Corbières, such as Torres Gran Sangre de Toro, with some peppery flavours reminiscent of the south of France. The red wines of La Mancha in central Spain.

Priorato, a small DO in northeast Spain, where the grape varieties are Garnacha and Cariñena, the Spanish equivalents of Grenache and Carignan.

🍇 Cornas

Cornas, a robust red wine, from the northern Rhône Valley, is very similar to nearby ▷Hermitage. The grape variety is identical, namely Syrah, and the vineyards conparable, with steep granite hillsides. In other words, it is difficult to distinguish good Cornas from good Hermitage. Both are puckeringly tannic in their youth, with the characteristic blackcurrant gum flavours of the Syrah, which develops more complex tastes as it ages, with spice, tobacco and a rich, opulent warmth that comes from such sunny climes. Forget about Cornas until it is at least ten years old.

- **Vintages:** 1990, 1989, 1988, 1985, 1983, 1980, 1978.

- **Recommended producers:** Auguste Clape, Guy de Barjac, Marcel Juge, Alain Voge, Jean-Luc Colombo, Robert Michel, Sylvain Bernard.

Taste on:

FRANCE: ▷Hermitage, ▷Côte Rôtie, ▷Crozes Hermitage, St-Joseph and lighter Syrah wines, like Coteaux de Tricastin and ▷vin de pays from the Midi made from Syrah.

ITALY: One lone Chianti producer is experimenting with Syrah, with some success. Look out for a Syrah under the Collezione de Marchi label.

CALIFORNIA: Syrah from the wineries of Joseph Phelps, Qupe, Ojai, Bonny Doon, Kendall-Jackson and Zaca Mesa, but do not confuse the popular California grape, Petite Sirah, with Syrah.

▷AUSTRALIA: Shiraz is the name for ▷Syrah here. The star example is Grange Hermitage, now called simply Grange, to avoid confusion with the wine from the Rhône valley.

☙ Corsica ♥♥

Corsica is a ruggedly individual island with particular flavours of its own. There are grape varieties that you find nowhere else, such as Sciacarello; others like Vermentino, or Nielluccio (otherwise known as Sangiovese), that are grown in Italy, while less interesting Carignan, Grenache and Cinsaut are common throughout the south of France. A small amount of Muscat is grown too, as well as recently introduced varieties like Cabernet Sauvignon, Chardonnay and Chenin Blanc for the exotic-sounding Vin de Pays de l'Ile de Beauté.

The principal appellation of the island is quite simply Vin de Corse, with various *crus*, namely Calvi, Figari, Sartène, Porto Vecchio and Coteaux de Cap Corse. Patrimonio and Ajaccio are the other two appellations of the island.

The red wines of Corsica made from Corsican grape varieties have a perfumed individuality, reminiscent of the scents and herbs of the *maquis* or scrubland with which the island is covered. There is thyme and rosemary, laurel and lavender. The wines are rounded and soft, with a chewy fruitiness and not much tannin, making them eminently easy to drink. Patrimonio tends to be more solid and substantial, but with an underlying southern warmth. White wines from Vermentino have a firm, dry, slightly bitter almond flavour and are sometimes a touch dusty on the finish.

● **Vintages:** Corsican wines do not have any great ageing potential, nor is there any significant quality difference from year to year. For whites drink the youngest available, and for reds nothing older than about five years.

● **Recommended producers:** In Patrimonio, Dominique Gentile, Yves Leccia and Antoine Arena; Clos Nicrosi ♥♥ in Coteaux de Cap Corse makes the best white wine of the island; Domaine de Torraccia for Porto Vecchio; Domaine Peraldi in Ajaccio; Clos Reginu in Calvi; Domaine du Petit Fournil; Vin de Pays de l'Ile de Beauté under the Pieve label.

Taste on:

RED:

FRANCE: Patrimonio has similarities with the ▷Côtes du Rhône, for although Nielluccio may be Italian in origin, the island flavours are more in keeping with France.

Other red wines of Corsica lead to ▷Côtes de Provence, Costières de Nîmes (until 1988 called Costières du Gard), ▷Corbières, ▷Minervois, ▷*vin de pays* from the Midi, such as the Collines de la Moure or Vallée du Paradis.

For something a little more structured, but with some comparable spicey fruit, try Côtes du Fronton and Côtes du Marmandais from the southwest.

ITALY: ▷Chianti for a fruitier version of Sangiovese.

WHITE:

FRANCE: *Vin de pays* from the Midi made from Grenache Blanc and Terret Blanc, which have a touch more character than usual.

ITALY: The white wines of Sardinia are also made from Vermentino, and are virtually indistinguishable from those of Corsica. Also try Torbato di Sardinia. You also find a little Vermentino of the Tuscan mainland.

Still Prosecco di Conegliano from the Veneto has a similar dusty flavour, not unlike Vermentino.

The one exception is Clos Nicrosi, which has an individual, leafy, buttery flavour which any ▷Chardonnay or ▷Chablis fan would appreciate. The same estate makes some delicious ▷Muscat which has more in common with a good ▷Muscat de Beaumes-de-Venise.

Corvo

Corvo is Sicily's best-known wine, both red and white, thanks to successful marketing by the producer, the Casa Vinicola Duca di Salaparuta, whose brand name it is. It is a plain *vino da tavola*, with no more precise a definition than Sicily, which means that grapes can be bought from all over the island to achieve a consistent blend, year in year out.

The white, when it is last year's vintage, is dry and fresh, with a touch of almonds and a neutral finish, while the red has a rustic flavour with a bit of astringency and tannin, but not too much, with some raspberry and damson fruit. When in doubt it is a pretty safe choice in an Italian trattoria. Then there are two better qualities of white, Colomba Platina which is a little fuller, with some buttery fruit, not unlike a light ▷Mâcon, and Bianca di Valguarnera, which is nothing but an infusion of oak chippings in a fancy bottle. The better quality of red, called Duca Enrico, is also pretty oaky, but less obviously so, with a little more fruit.

● **Vintages:** There is little vintage variation in the southernmost part of Italy. Drink the latest vintage of the white and red that is no more than three or four years old. Duca Enrico needs more bottle age; give it six or seven years.

 Taste on:
WHITE:
ITALY: Other Sicilian *vini da tavola*, also often sold under a brand name, usually related to the name of the cooperative that makes them, such as Cellaro and Settesoli. Regaleali Bianco from an aristocratic estate in the centre of Sicily; the Sicilian DOC, Bianco di Alcamo from Rapitalà.

FRANCE: ▷Muscadet.

RED:
ITALY: Other Sicilian reds, such as Cellaro, Donnafugato.

FRANCE: ▷Coteaux du Languedoc.

☙ Coteaux du Languedoc

The Coteaux du Languedoc is one of those all-embracing appellations that covers a multitude of little villages in the south of France, stretching from just south to Narbonne, round the Mediterranean to the east of

Montpellier, with numerous different *crus*, some of which, such as Faugères, St-Chinian and La Clape, are much better-known in their own right than the overall appellation. The grape varieties are those of the Midi, Carignan, Cinsaut and Grenache, with some improving Syrah and Mourvèdre for red wine and Ugni blanc, Macabeo and Bourboulenc for white.

Winemaking techniques are improving apace in this part of France, making it one of the most exciting regions of viticultural development. However, most of that experimentation is more likely to be demonstrated in wines labelled ▷*vin de pays* than in a wine that has to conform to the regulations of its appellation. That is not to say that there are not some good things in the Coteaux du Languedoc, especially from Faugères, St-Chinian and la Clape. There is an underlying similarity between the various *crus*, with individual differences, originating from vineyard and producer.

At their best, the flavours of red Coteaux du Languedoc are warm and southern, spicey with tannin and backbone. With too much Carignan in the blend, they can be just a bit dull, dry and lacking in charm and fruit. They are not as full-bodied as ▷Côtes du Roussillon, nor as sturdy as ▷Minervois or ▷Corbières. The further east you go through the Coteaux du Languedoc, the lighter the wines become, so while La Clape is not dissimilar to nearby ▷Fitou, the wines of Lunel have more in common with the adjoining Costières de Nîmes.

White Coteaux du Languedoc is less exciting, rather dry and flat, with one or two exceptions. Picpoul de Pinet is white rather than red, with some dry, nutty fruit. La Clape too can have more complex flavours, with hints of nuts and herbs.

- **Vintages:** There is little significant vintage variation in this part of France.

- **Recommended producers:** Henri Arnal in the village of Langlade, Prieuré de St-Jean-de-Bébian.
Cave Cooperative de St-Georges d'Orques.
La Clape: Domaine la Rivière-Haute, Château la Rouquette-sur-Mer, Château Moujan, Domaine la Pech-Céleyran.
St-Chinian: Cave Cooperative de Berlou, with its brand name, Schisteil, Château Coujan, Domaine Guiraud Boyer.
Faugères: Château de Haut Fabrègues, Gerard Alquier.

Taste on:

RED:

FRANCE: ▷Corbières, ▷Minervois, ▷Fitou, Costières de Nîmes, ▷*vins de pays* from the Midi, ▷Côtes du Rhône.

PORTUGAL: ▷Bairrada, as well as southern reds like Reguengos de Monsarez from the Alentejo.

GREECE: Naoussa and red wines made from the Xynomavro grape, which has a sweet and sour fruity flavour, not unlike some Coteaux du Languedoc.

WHITE:

FRANCE: ▷Corbières, ▷Minervois, Costières de Nîmes, ▷Côtes de Provence, ▷Bandol, ▷*vin de pays* from the Midi.

PORTUGAL: ▷Dão, ▷Bairrada.

GREECE: Robola of Cephalonia, an old-fashioned, dry, nutty white wine.

Coteaux du Layon

Coteaux du Layon is a sweet white wine from the Loire Valley coming, as the name implies, from vineyards in the valley of the river Layon, a tributary of the Loire. ▷Chenin Blanc is the grape variety here and the growers hope for noble rot, to which it is particularly susceptible, but only in the right climatic conditions. A combination of damp autumnal mornings, followed by brilliantly warm afternoon sunshine to dry the grapes, results in the development of *botrytis cinera*, or noble rot, which forms on the skins of the ripe grapes, making them dehydrated and raisin-like.

The juice becomes concentrated and sweet, resulting in some deli-ciously honeyed wines. Chenin Blanc always gives wines with a high degree of acidity to balance the ▷sweetness, so they are never cloying, but delicately rich, with honey, apricots, peaches and cream, with a slightly roasted tang coming from the botrytis. The degree of sweetness depends on the vintage. Years with a higher proportion of grapes affected with noble rot will make richer and more concentrated wines, while in less successful vintages, Coteaux du Layon is light and lemony and much less honeyed.

The appellation of the Coteaux du Layon comprises six villages, the names of which may also appear on the wine label. Chaume is regarded as the best, and within the village of Chaume there is a small vineyard called Quarts de Chaume, which produces some particularly luscious wine.

Also in the valley of the Layon is the small appellation of Bonnezeaux which, along with Quarts de Chaume, makes the finest sweet wines of the Loire Valley. Production is limited, with very low yields, resulting in wines that have an intensity that is sometimes lacking in Coteaux du Layon. However the sweetness is always balanced by the acidity of the Chenin grape.

- **Vintages:** 1990, 1989, 1988, 1986, 1985, 1982, 1979, 1976.

- **Recommended producers:** Domaine du Petit Val, Château de la Roulerie, Domaine de la Soucherie, Clos Ste-Catherine, Château du Breuil.

Taste on:

FRANCE: Bonnezeaux, with Château de Fesles, Renou; Quarts de Chaume, with A. Laffourcade; Chaume with Jacques Lalanne; ▷Vouvray *moelleux* ❦ and Montlouis; Moulin Touchais, an exceptional sweet ▷Anjou Blanc; lighter sweet Bordeaux, from ▷Barsac, rather than ▷Sauternes; ▷Jurançon *moelleux* ❦.

ITALY: Piccolit, which is one of the few Italian wines made from grapes affected with noble rot. Sadly, more often than not it fails to meet expectations; ▷Orvieto *abboccato*; Recioto di ▷Soave.

GERMANY: ▷Auslese and ▷Beerenauslese wines.

AUSTRIA: Auslese wines.

❦ Côtes de Bourg

For Côtes de Bourg, also read Premières Côtes de Blaye, Côtes de Castillon, Premières Côtes de Bordeaux, Fronsac, Côtes de Franc and the other peripheral appellations of Bordeaux. These areas are made up of numerous little-known estates. Again they swell the ranks of the *petits châteaux* that make up a good wine merchant's claret list. They are generally more substantial wines, richer, with a little more subtlety and staying power than basic ▷Bordeaux Rouge.

- **Vintages:** 1990, 1989, 1988, 1986, 1985, 1983, 1982.

- **Recommended estates:** Côtes de Bourg: de Barbe, du Bousquet, la Croix-Millorit, Rousset.
Fronsac: la Rivière, la Vieille Cure, la Dauphine, Richotey.
Côtes de Francs: Puygueraud de Francs.
Côtes de Castillon: Pitray.
Premières Côtes de Blaye: Haut-Sociondo.
Premières Côtes de Bordeaux: du Juge, Reynon, Cayla, Tanesse.
Canon-Fronsac: Canon, Canon-de-Brem, Haut-Mazeris, Canon-Moueix; du Gaby, Moulin-Pey-Lebrie.

 Taste on:
FRANCE: The adjoining appellations, separated from Bordeaux by the departmental boundary, such as ▷Bergerac, Côtes de Duras and ▷Buzet, where the grape varieties and methods of vinification are virtually identical.
▷Madiran.
▷Cahors.
Côtes de la Malepère ▼▼ and Cabardès ▼▼. This pair of wines to the north and south of the city of Carcassonne are where Languedoc meets Aquitaine, or in wine terms where the grape varieties of the south west, namely Cabernet and Merlot, meet the grape varieties of the Midi, such as Syrah, Grenache and Carignan. Producers here are allowed an enormous flexibility in what they put into their wines and some are made almost entirely from Bordeaux grape varieties, resulting in a definite similarity. There is a leanness about these wines that you do not find in the Midi. Look for estates like Château Malviès, Château de Routier.
▷*Vin de pays* from the Midi, made from Cabernet Sauvignon.

ITALY: ▷Chianti.

PORTUGAL: ▷Bairrada.

94

🍇 Côte Rôtie ▼▼▼

Côte Rôtie translates literally as the 'roasted slope', a description which gives some idea of the taste and concentration of flavour in the wine. this is the most northern appellation of the Rhône Valley, coming from steeply terraced vineyards on the hills behind the town of Vienne. As with other red wines from the northern end of the Rhône Valley, the grape variety is Syrah and in the Côte Rôtie it is sometimes softened with a drop of Viognier. Côte Rôtie is a long-lived wine, with rich, concentrated flavours, meriting several years of bottle age. In its youth it is thickly tannic, with the firm peppery flavours of blackcurrant gums, and as it ages it becomes more mellow, but always with a solid, meaty mouthful of flavour, with plenty of pepper and spice, and a ripe, long finish.

- **Vintages:** 1990, 1989, 1988, 1985, 1983, 1980, 1978.

- **Recommended producers:** Guigal, with la Mouline, la Turque and la Landonne labels, Jasmin, Champet, Dervieux-Thaize, Jaboulet, Vidal-Fleury.

 Taste on:
FRANCE: The other red wines of the northern Rhône: ▷Hermitage, ▷Crozes Hermitage, ▷Cornas, St-Joseph, as well as the Coteaux du Tricastin, Vin de Pays de l'Ardèche, made from Syrah, and other ▷*vin de pays* from the south made from Syrah. ▷Bandol.

USA: Examples of Syrah from California, notably from Joseph Phelps, Ojai, Qupe, Bonny Doon, Kendall-Jackson and Zaca Mesa. Do not confuse with Petite Sirah, which is no relation.

AUSTRALIA: ▷Shiraz.

🍇 Côtes de Gascogne ▼

The Vin de Pays des Côtes de Gascogne is one of the rising stars of southwest France. For the moment it is still classified as a mere ▷*vin de pays* but its aspirations, which are generally substantiated in the glass, are much higher. It was born of the decline in sales of Armagnac. The vinification of white wine destined for distillation could be a rather hit-and-miss affair, as any defects would disappear in the still. As sales of Armagnac have declined, the grape growers have begun to pay attention to their vinification methods, with the result that the wine has changed out of all recognition. It is today a dry white wine distinguished by an attractive, smokey, stoney-flavoured fruitiness. There is a firm acidity, and sometimes a delicate perfumed fragrance.

- **Vintages:** Drink the youngest available.

- **Recommended producers:** Domaine de San Guilhem, Domaine de Tariquet and other estates belonging to the Grassa family, Domaine de Cassignoles, Domaine de Mestre Duran, Cave Cooperative de Plaimont.

 Taste on:

FRANCE: There are similarities with other dry white wines of southwest France, such as the nearby but little-known Côtes de St-Mont; ▷Entre-Deux-Mers; ▷Bordeaux Blanc; ▷Bergerac Sec; ▷Gaillac Blanc; ▷Muscadet; Vin de Pays de l'Hérault, made from Terret Blanc, with some smokey, pithy fruit.

AUSTRIA: ▷Grüner Veltliner, with a smokey, stoney flavour and firm acidity.

▷English wine.

☙ Côtes du Jura ▾▾

There is an originality about the wines of Jura. It must be the isolation of this mountainous region that breeds a determined nonconformity amongst its winemakers. I remember my first taste of white Côtes de Jura. Frankly I thought it was oxidised, in that it had been exposed to air for much too long. I was prepared to accuse it of all kinds of heinous faults, while the assembled company of Jurassien winemakers were voluble in their enthusiasm. So I stopped and listened and tasted again and realised how wrong my initial impressions had been. This wine was not oxidised. It had been exposed to oxygen, yes, but it had a distinctive firm nuttiness, not unlike a light ▷Vin Jaune. In more familiar terms, it was a lighter, less alcoholic version of fino ▷sherry or, tongue in cheek perhaps, I could find a resemblance with rather flat, rather old champagne or even very mature ▷Meursault! It is the kind of wine you love or hate. Friends in London have rejected it out of hand. I have come to love it.

Red Côtes du Jura is almost identical with ▷Arbois.

- **Vintages:** 1990, 1989, 1988, 1986, 1985, 1983, 1982.

- **Recommended producers:** Beware; there is a confusion with white Côtes du Jura. There are producers who follow more conventional winemaking practices, so that their white wines have the fruit and buttery flavours that you might normally expect from the ▷Chardonnay grape. For these try Rollet Frères, but for traditional white Jura go to Claude Bernard, Michel Rameaux, Pierre de Boiseau at the Château de Gréa, Christian Bourdy or the wines of Jean Cros from L'Etoile ▼▼, another tiny appellation of the Jura.

Taste on:
FRANCE: Very old white burgundy, such as ▷Meursault; very old ▷champagne.

SPAIN: Fino ▷sherry.

 ## Côtes de Provence

Côtes de Provence can be red, white or pink. Pink is most common, but red is more interesting, while white is made only in small quantities. The vineyards cover a large part of the department of the Var, behind the towns of St-Tropez and Toulon.

Pink Côtes de Provence comes into its own for a seaside picnic. At its best it is a refreshing summer wine, tasting of herbs and raspberries. It is quite solid and full-flavoured, dry but not acid, substantial rather than ethereal. However, drink only the youngest vintage available as it quickly looses its freshness and charm to turn tired, flabby and a little stewed.

As a result of some of the disenchantment with pink Côtes de Provence, the red wine of the appellation has been the subject of some enormous improvements in vinification techniques in recent years. The old-fashioned method was to leave the wine sitting in large oak barrels for several months, if not years, and you do still find some wines like this, that are rather heavily flavoured, solid and meaty. The new style is lighter, softer and fruitier, with the warm herbal flavours of thyme and rosemary, so reminiscent of the scents of Provence. They have enough tannin to give them some backbone, but not so much as to need more than a couple of years ageing.

White Côtes de Provence is generally fresh and dry, with some nutty fruit and hints of almonds and herbs, well made, but sometimes rather neutral in flavour. The better wines have a fresh, leafy flavour.

●   **Vintages:** 1990, 1989, 1988.

●   **Recommended producers:** Domaines Ott with Clos Mireille and Château de Selle; Domaine de la Bernarde, Château Minuty, Maîtres Vignerons du Presqu'île de St-Tropez, Château Pamplonne, Château Ste-Rosaline, Commanderie de la Peyrassol, Château de Barbeyrolles, Château St-André de Figière.

 Taste on:

RED:

FRANCE: ▷Côtes du Rhône and Côtes du Rhône Villages; Coteaux d'Aix-en-Provence ▼, Coteaux Varois, Côtes du Lubéron, Côtes du Ventoux, Costières de Nîmes, Lirac; ▷Bandol; wines from the Midi, such as ▷Corbières, ▷Minervois and ▷Coteaux du Languedoc, which have a little more structure, but similar warm, spicey fruit.

▷Beaujolais, for there is a similarity in vinification methods, making for wines with a similar weight and feel to them, even if with a difference in fruit flavour.

PINK:

FRANCE: ▷Tavel, Lirac, ▷Corsica and the pink versions of other appellations and *vins de pays* from the south of France, such as Bellet, Palette, Coteaux d'Aix-en-Provence; ▷Corsica; Rosé de Béarn, from the Pyrenees.

ITALY: Vin Ruspo from Carmignano.

SPAIN: ▷Rioja Rosada and pink wines from Navarre and ▷Penedés.

CHILE: Torres Rosado, quite the best pink wine from the southern hemisphere.

WHITE:

FRANCE: Other white wines of the south of France, such as white ▷Bandol, ▷Cassis, Bellet ▼▼, the tiny appellation outside the town of Nice, Côtes du Lubéron, ▷Côtes du Rhône, white wine from Corsica, ▷Minervois, ▷Corbières, ▷Côtes du Roussillon.
▷Graves for wines with a little more character and flavour.

GREECE: Robola of Cephalonia, for the old-fashioned, nutty style of white wine.

▼ Côtes du Rhône

Côtes du Rhône is the basic appellation of the whole of the Rhône valley, but with a greater concentration of vineyards in the south around Avignon. It can be red, white or pink. The best is red, while Côtes du Rhône Villages, often with the village name on the label, like Chusclan, Rasteau and so on, has stricter production regulations to lend greater individuality.

Good red Côtes du Rhône should taste of the south, with an aura of warmth, laced with the herbs of the Midi, notably thyme and lavender, as well as a touch of spice and liquorice. It comes from a mixture of grape varieties, Grenache, Syrah, Mourvèdre, Cinsaut and Carignan. Grenache usually dominates, making a wine that is quite high in alcohol, full-bodied and mouth-filling and just the thing to take away the winter chill. Modern trends have lightened Côtes du Rhône, so that feeble versions do not have much more body than a Beaujolais.

White Côtes du Rhone has a dry, rather flat, nutty flavour, while a well-made pink is quite full and fruity.

● **Vintages:** 1990, 1989, 1988, 1986, 1985.

● **Recommended producers:** Pascal, Jaboulet, especially Parallèle 45, Château du Grand Moulas, Cru du Coudoulet, Guigal.

Taste on:

RED:

FRANCE: Adjoining appellations, made from similar grape varieties, such as Gigondas, Vacqueyras, Côtes du Ventoux, Côtes du Lubéron; Vin de Pays des Bouches du Rhône, Vin de Pays de l'Ardèche, Coteaux de Tricastin.

▷Châteauneuf-du-Pape for something even heavier and more full-bodied.

Patrimonio from ▷Corsica.

▷Corbières, ▷Minervois, ▷Côtes du Roussillon.

PORTUGAL: Quinta de Santa Amaro from the Setúbal Peninsular, with some warm peppery fruit, as well as Periquita ▼, which is a little fuller and spicier, from the same producer, J. M. da Fonseca.

SPAIN: ▷Penedés, with Torres Gran Sangredetoro, with its chewy, spicey fruit; ▷Valdepeñas, notably Viña Albali with some warm spice.

ITALY: Red wines of Sicily, such as ▷Corvo, Donnafugata, Cellaro and so on. Salice Salentino from Puglia.

CYPRUS: Afames, made by one of the large cooperatives, Sodap, has some of the earthy, peppery fruit of more rugged, old-fashioned Côtes du Rhône, as do other Cyprus reds.

HUNGARY: Blue Frankish or Kékfrankos, with some dry, peppery fruit, is not unlike a lightweight Côtes du Rhône.

WHITE:

FRANCE: Côtes du Lubéron, ▷Côtes de Provence, Coteaux d'Aix-en-Provence, Vin de Pays des Bouches du Rhône, white wine from ▷Corsica, ▷Minervois, ▷Corbières, ▷Côtes du Roussillon.

PINK:

FRANCE: ▷Tavel, Lirac, ▷Côtes de Provence, Coteaux d'Aix-en-Provence, Côtes du Lubéron, Bellet, ▷Bandol, Gigondas, Côtes du Ventoux, ▷Minervois, ▷Corbières.

SPAIN: Rosado from ▷Rioja, Navarra and ▷Penedés.

☙ Côtes du Roussillon ▾

Côtes du Roussillon can be red, white or pink, of which the red version is by far the most interesting. The vineyards are in the foothills of the Pyrenees behind the town of Perpignan, where the landscape is wild and dramatic, with arid slopes where little else but vines and olive trees will grow. The wines are rugged to match, full-flavoured, warm spicey wines, with the flavours and scents of the south of France. Carignan, Cinsaut and Grenache are the main grape varieties, with increasing amounts of Syrah and Mourvèdre for added flavour.

Red Côtes du Roussillon has a solid backbone of tannin, with the herbal overtones to make a mouthfilling wine, with some rich, spicey fruit. It is also tends to be quite high in alcohol, coming as it does from sunsoaked vineyards. It is neither elegant nor subtle, nor is it a wine to age for more than three or four years.

● **Vintages:** Vintage variations are not significant.

● **Recommended producers:** Château de Jau, Château de Corneilla, Vignerons Catalans, Arnaud de Villeneuve.

Taste on:
RED:
FRANCE: Côtes du Roussillon Villages, which is only ever red, comes from a smaller area and tends to be more concentrated in flavour. Two villages can add their names to the label, Caramany and Latour de France.

Collioure, from precipital vineyards around the fishing village of the same name. The wines are even sturdier, more full-bodied and longer lasting.

▷Fitou, ▷Côtes du Rhône, ▷Châteauneuf-du-Pape.

ITALY: Montepulciano d'Abruzzo, with some warm spicey fruit.

101

PORTUGAL: Wines from the Alentejo, such as Reguengos de Monsarrez.

CYPRUS: Typical Cypriot reds like ▷Othello and Afames.

WHITE: Apart from the whites of the south such as ▷Côtes de Provence and ▷Côtes du Rhône, try Torbato di Sardegna, with a dry, green, peppery flavour.

Crépy

The vineyards on the southern shores of Lake Geneva have more in common with those of Switzerland on the opposite side of the lake than with the other wines of Savoie. Crépy, which comes from the Chasselas grape, is the best-known wine here, although it must be said that its reputation has not travelled that far. It is a rather soft, easy-to-drink, innocuous white wine, with a gentle, leafy flavour. It makes a pleasant enough drink, but is far from memorable.

● **Vintages:** Drink the youngest available, as these are not wines with any great staying power.

● **Recommended producers:** Métral, Fichard.

Taste on:
FRANCE: The adjoining *crus* of Vin de Savoie, namely Marignan and Ripaille, produced entirely by the medieval Château de Ripaille, are very similar, as is the aspiring *cru* of Marin, for they too are all made from Chasselas.
▷Gaillac Blanc, with a similar rather neutral flavour.

SWITZERLAND: On the other side of Lake Geneva, in the Vaud, the Swiss call the Chasselas grape Dorin, and Fendant in the Valais, and anything white from these two cantons is likely to taste very similar to Crépy. However, Swiss wines tend to travel even less than those of Savoie.

❦ Crozes Hermitage

Crozes Hermitage is a lesser, more accessible version of ▷Hermitage, coming from vineyards that encircle the more prestigious appellation. As always in the northern Rhône, Syrah is the grape variety for the red wine, while Marsanne and Roussanne make the white.

Both are very similar to Hermitage, but without the same intensity or longevity. The red is softer and less robust, but always with the characteristic, spicey, peppery, blackcurrant-gum fruit that makes Syrah so appealing. From a good producer, the whites have a fragrant, leafy flavour, with hints of honey and are quite mouthfilling and rich. They are dry, but not acid. In less talented hands they can be just a bit dull and boring, with little to distinguish them from an indifferent ▷Côtes du Rhône.

- **Vintages:** 1990, 1989, 1988, 1986, 1985.

- **Recommended producers:** Jaboulet, notably with Domaine Thalabert, Château Curson, Fayolle, Alain Graillot, Domaine des Clairmonts, Desmeure.

 Taste on:
RED:
FRANCE: ▷Hermitage, ▷Côte Rôtie, ▷Cornas, St-Joseph, Vin de Pays de l'Ardèche, Coteaux de Tricastin.

USA: Syrah from California.

AUSTRALIA: ▷Shiraz.

WHITE:
FRANCE: Vin de Pays de Vaucluse, ▷Côtes du Rhône, ▷Hermitage.
Bellet from outside Nice, with similar dry, leafy flavours.
▷Cassis, ▷Châteauneuf-du-Pape, ▷Graves.

ARGENTINA: Shiraz from Finca Flichman.

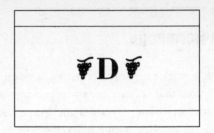

D

 Dão

Dão comes from northern Portugal, from the hillsides around the town of Viseu to the south of the ▷port vineyards of the Douro river. Pronounced something like 'downg', with a nasal twang, it can be either red or white, although its reputation is based on red. No one grape variety determines the flavour, for either red or white, but a motley hotchpotch of instantly forgettable names.

White Dão is quite full-flavoured, with lemon and honey and high acidity in its youth. As it matures, it becomes fatter and richer, with a nutty, piney quality. Good white Dão has an old-fashioned feel about it, in the best possible way. It must be aged for at least six months before bottling, while *garrafeira* indicates a year's ageing, half in vat and half in bottle.

Red Dão requires a minimum of eighteen months' ageing while the *garrafeira* wines, which are those that the producer deems to be his very best, must spend at least two years in vat and one in bottle. Often it is longer, indeed too long. Sadly there has been a tendency to keep Dão in wood for so long that it looses any fruit. Dão is firmly tannic in its youth and certainly needs some ageing, but not an excessive amount. Mature Dão has a firm, spicy character, with some peppery fruit and a rugged quality about it. It never quite loses the rough, puckering edge of tannin and retains quite an austere, dry finish.

- **Vintages:** 1991, 1990, 1989, 1987, 1985, 1983, 1980, 1975, 1974,

- **Recommended producers:** Caves Aliança, Caves São João, Sogrape under the Grão Vasco label, J. M. da Fonseca under the Terras Altas label, Conde de Santar.

Taste on:

WHITE:

PORTUGAL: ▷Bairrada and Bucelas, a dry white from just north of Lisbon.

FRANCE: ▷Châteauneuf-du-Pape; ▷Hermitage, ▷Crozes Hermitage and nearby St-Péray, which comes from the same grape varieties; La Clape in the ▷Coteaux du Languedoc; Château Simone in Palette, the tiny appellation outside the town of Aix-en-Provence; old-fashioned white ▷Graves.

GREECE: Robola of Cephalonia and white Patras, which have an old-fashioned nutty fruitiness.

SPAIN: Dry white wines of La Mancha in central Spain; Terra Alta from northeast Spain.

RED:

PORTUGAL: ▷Bairrada and ▷Douro.

SPAIN: ▷Jumilla.

FRANCE: ▷Cahors, and St-Estèphe in the ▷Médoc, for the austerity and the tannin. ▷Crozes Hermitage in the northern Rhône for the peppery spiciness, and maybe other adjacent appellations like St-Joseph, ▷Cornas and even ▷Hermitage. ▷Fitou.

ITALY: ▷Barolo.

Taurasi from near Naples has an earthy, rugged flavour.

GREECE: Naoussa and other red wines made from the Xynomavro grape.

Dealcoholised wine/low alcohol wine

Dealcoholised wine is not really wine at all, but a concocted, manufactured drink, which may have its origins in grapes, but from which the alcohol that is the natural product of the fermentation process has been removed, thereby completely distorting the taste. The technology for doing this is improving apace, with distillation, filtration or centrifuging, whereby the alcohol is literally spun out of the wine, leaving no more than 0.05° alcohol. In contrast, an ordinary table wine has anything between 9° to 16° alcohol.

Low alcohol wines may contain as much as 4.5° alcohol. Often the fermentation is stopped, leaving some sugar. Sparkling water can also be an ingredient in low alcohol wine, used quite simply to reduce the alcohol level.

The low alcohol wines tend to be slightly sweet and grapey. There are some very acceptable ▷Muscat-based ones, which only have a degree or two less alcohol than the average ▷Asti Spumante. In these the lack of alcohol is successfully compensated for by sweetness. In contrast, the dealcoholised wines are usually lacking not only alcohol, but sugar too, so the taste seems very hollow and artificial.

- **Vintages:** drink youngest available.

Taste on:
It is now obligatory to mention the alcohol level of a wine on the label, so careful reading of wine labels saves a degree or more. Look for wines like ▷Vinho Verde, ▷Bernkastel in the Mosel and ▷Asti Spumante, which are significantly lower in alcohol than, say, ▷California Chardonnay or ▷Australian Shiraz. Alternatively take a light white wine and make a spritzer, by diluting it with sparkling water. The effect is much the same as a low alcohol wine, and probably more palatable.

Deidesheim *see* Rheinpfalz – Deidesheim

Demestica

Demestica, both red and white, is a popular brand of Greek wine, marketed by one of the country's largest wine producers, Achaia-Clauss. The label gives no more details of origin than Greece. The white is dry and pretty nondescript, lacking the fruit of a cooler climate, while the red is warm, with a touch of spice and herbs, but surprisingly light for a hot-climate wine.

Demestica is useful in providing an introduction to Greek wines, but there are others of more interest and flavour. Greece is moving towards the concept of appellations, with names like Patras and Nemea in the Peloponnese and Naoussa to the west of Thessalonica in the north. White Patras has some dry, rather dusty fruit and is quite full and rounded, with little acidity and a rather old-fashioned feel to it. Red Nemea has a soft, peppery flavour, with a bit of spice and warm fruit, while Naoussa is a little richer and fuller.

● **Vintages:** Insignificant; drink whites as young as possible and reds within five or six years.

● **Recommended producers:** Achaia-Clauss for Demestica. Other good Greek producers include Boutari, Calliga, Château Carras, Château Semeli, Château Pegasus.

 Taste on:

WHITE:
GREECE: Patras, Robola of Cephalonia.

CYPRUS: ▷Aphrodite.

ITALY: Fiano di Avellino and Greco di Tufo from Campania.

FRANCE: ▷Minervois, ▷Corbières and ▷Coteaux du Languedoc.

PORTUGAL: ▷Bairrada and ▷Dão.

RED:
GREECE: Patras, Nemea and Naoussa.

CYPRUS: Afames and ▷Othello.

FRANCE: Soft, spicey, peppery flavours from the Midi like ▷Corbières, ▷Minervois, ▷Coteaux du Languedoc and ▷Côtes du Rhône.

🍇 Dolcetto

Do not be misled. Although *dolce* means sweet in Italian, this is not a sweet wine. The name is indeed a diminutive of *dolce* but the sweetness refers to the grape juice and not the wine. Dolcetto does indeed have some ripe berry fruit, which is always balanced with firm, lively acidity, making a deliciously refreshing bittersweet drink. It is never heavy or tannic. There are seven DOCs altogether from Dolcetto, all in Piedmont, some of which are rarely found outside the production zone. Most characteristic is Dolcetto d'Alba, closely followed by Dolcetto d'Asti.

• **Vintages:** Drink the youngest available, even as a *novello* wine. These are not wines to age.

• **Recommended producers:** Often prominent ▷Barolo and ▷Barbaresco producers such as Gaja, Giacomo Conterno, Giuseppe Mascarello, Prunotto, Ratti, Vietti, Bruno Giacosa, Cavallotto, Pio Cesare.

Taste on:

ITALY: ▷Barbera, young ▷Chianti and ▷Valpolicella. Although the grape varieties of these are quite different, there is a similarity in the feel and weight of the wine.

FRANCE: ▷Beaujolais and other Gamay-based wines for the liveliness of the fruit, combined with refreshing acidity.

GREECE: The sweet and sour flavours of the Xynomavro grape as in the Château Pegasus from Naoussa.

☙ Douro

Not all the grapes grown in the Douro valley are turned into ▷port, so that there is a significant production of red and white table wine from the area, usually from the same varieties as port.

The most characteristic white is Planalto, from the producers of ▷Mateus Rosé, who have applied their expertise to produce a soft grassy, dry white wine, with fresh acidity and fragrance.

Reds are usually more interesting. Some have the liquorice taste that reminds you instantly of ruby port, but without the spirity finish. They can be pretty tough and tannic, with a dry, stalky quality. At their worst you can quite see why a hefty dollop of brandy improved them beyond recognition. However, at its best, a red wine from the Douro will taste of liquorice and plums, with plenty of fruit, to fill the mouth, and a firm backbone of tannin.

- **Vintages:** 1991, 1990, 1989, 1988, 1987, 1985, 1984, 1982, 1981, 1980.
- **Recommended producers:** Ferreira with a young, peppery, stalky Esteva, and much better Barca Velha ♥♥♥, which is in a class of its own, with lovely spicey fruit and ▷Syrah-like pepperiness and a long finish Quinta do Cotto, with Grande Escolha Tinto; Sogrape with Planalto; Quinta da Pachera.

The one Portuguese ▷Chardonnay comes from the Douro, made by Caves do Raposeira at Quinta da Valparado. There are hints of varietal character, but to date it lacks definition. Older vines may well help.

 Taste on:
WHITE:
PORTUGAL: ▷Bairrada, ▷Dão.

FRANCE: with Planalto in mind, ▷Chablis, ▷Mâcon.

RED:
PORTUGAL: ▷Dão, ▷Bairrada.

FRANCE: The spicy, liquorice flavours of the Douro have something in common with the south of France, ▷Corbières, ▷Minervois, and maybe ▷Côtes du Roussillon and ▷Fitou.
Also from the northern Rhône, ▷Crozes Hermitage, ▷Cornas and ▷*vin de pays* made from Syrah.

Eiswein/Ice Wine

Eiswein means quite literally 'ice wine', a wine that is made from grapes that have been picked and then pressed while still frozen. It is something of a commercial gimmick in Germany. Ripe, healthy grapes are left on the vines until December or January in the hope that the appropriate climatic conditions will prevail to enable ice wine to be made, which does not happen every year. The water content of the grapes is thus removed in the form of ice, so that all the flavours in the grapes, sugar as well as acidity, become very concentrated. The sugar level must be at least the equivalent of a ▷Beerenauslese. However, the wine does not always have the balance of more conventional sweet German wines. While the alcohol level is low, only about 5°, the sugar is very intense, with quite searing acidity and very concentrated, honeyed, apricot and marmalade fruit. The best are made from Riesling, but other grapes like Scheurebe and Optima can also be used. With such a high level of acidity, they can be very long-lived wines, as long as a hundred years, I was told by one producer.

• **Vintages:** 1990, 1989, 1988, 1985, 1983.

• **Recommended producers:** The good German estates of the Rhine and Mosel, namely ▷Bernkastel, ▷Johannisberg, ▷Rheinpfalz-Deidesheim, ▷Nahe-Schlossböckelheim, ▷Nierstein.

Taste on:

GERMANY: ▷Trockenbeerenauslese, ▷Beerenauslese.

AUSTRIA: Eiswein from the Burgenland, and also Trock-beerenauslese and Beerenauslese.

CANADA: Climatic conditions here are even more favourable than in Germany for making ice wine. Inniskillin is one of the most sucessful producers.

USA: Washington State: Riesling ice wine, from Kiona and Covey Run.
California: December Harvest Arroyo Seco Riesling from Wente Bros, and other Late Harvest Rieslings from California.

NEW ZEALAND: Late Harvest Wines have an intensity of flavour not unlike an Eiswein, such as Matua Valley Late Harvest Muscat and Dry River Riesling Botrytis Bunch Selection.

ITALY: Recioto di ▷Soave.

English Wine

With two brilliant summers in 1989 and 1990, English, and Welsh, wine is coming into its own and gathering momentum and stature. Vineyards are more established; winemakers are more experienced. Many favour a Germanic style with grape varieties like Müller-Thurgau, Reichensteiner, Huxelrebe, Bacchus, as well as Seyve Villard and Madeleine Angevine. Most of the English vineyards are in the southwest, East Anglia and the Home Counties. As yet there are few discernable regional differences, but an overall style of light, fragrant, flowery, slightly spicey, ethereal wines, that are generally low in alcohol and fairly light in body, as well as being quite high in acidity and sometimes slightly sweet, like some German wines. There is the occasional pink wine, and not so successful red wine, but usually English wine is white.

British wine on the other hand has nothing at all to do with English wine and is a manufactured product, originating from reconstituted, dehydrated grape juice, and to be avoided at all costs.

● **Vintages:** 1990, 1989. Most English wines are best drunk within a couple of years.

● **Recommended producers:** Westbury, Loddiswell, Breaky Bottom, Carr Taylor, Three Choirs, Barton Manor, Adgestone, Staple St James, Biddenden, Penshurst, Chiltern Valley, Elmham Park,

Tenterden, Wootton, Pilton Manor, Nutbourne, Barkham Manor, Mumfords and a wine called simply English Vineyard, made at High Weald Winery.

 Taste on:

GERMANY: The slightly sweet, floweriness of English wines resemble a Mosel, so try wines from the village of ▷Bernkastel. Try also ▷*Trocken* and ▷*Halbtrocken* wines.

AUSTRIA: Wines made from ▷Grüner Veltliner.

FRANCE: ▷Jurançon, ▷Muscadet, ▷Côtes de Gascogne, ▷Pinot Blanc d'Alsace, ▷Aligoté, ▷Anjou Blanc.

PORTUGAL: ▷Vinho Verde.

Entre-Deux-Mers

The wines of the Entre–Deux–Mers, a white appellation from some of the prettiest vineyards of Bordeaux, are very similar to simple ▷Bordeaux Blanc. They have undergone the same improvements in vinification methods, resulting in the same drastic transformation of flavour. Entre–Deux–Mers no longer epitomises the worst of winemaking, as it once did, but produces a shining example of just what can be achieved with a change of attitude and some investment in new equipment. The flavours are fairly neutral, crisp, dry and stoney, with the grassy pungency of the ▷Sauvignon grape, which is sometimes filled out by some Sémillon. The judicious use of oak barrels can add an extra dimension of flavour too.

● **Vintages:** Drink the youngest available.

● **Recommended producers:** The cooperative of Rauzan in the heart of the Entre–Deux–Mers is working well for its appellation. Château Ducla, Moulin–de–Launay, Thieuley.

Taste on:

FRANCE: Côtes de Duras on the other side of the departmental boundary and made from the same grape varieties, as are nearby Côtes du Marmandais and ▷Buzet; ▷Bergerac Sec; ▷Côtes de

112

Gascogne and other ▷*vins de pays* of the southwest, such as Vin de Pays Charentais from Cognac country, and Vin de Pays des Terroirs Landais, from vineyards in the pine forests of the Landes.

On the edge of the Landes is the little-known appellation of Tursan. Here again vinification methods have improved significantly and white Tursan is an unusual alternative to Entre-Deux-Mers, with a similar dry fruitiness; ▷Gaillac, for wines with a little more body; ▷Graves.

SPAIN: Torres Green Label Vina Sol from ▷Penedés.

F

 Finish

The finish of a wine is the taste left in your mouth after you have swallowed a wine, or spat it out, if you happen to be at a formal tasting! A top quality wine should have a long finish, in that its flavour will linger quite noticeably for several seconds after the wine is no longer in your mouth. In contrast, inferior wine will have a short finish, in that the taste ends very abruptly. This is a defect in a wine that aspires to some quality.

A wine with high acidity may have a crisp finish, but with too much acidity, a sour finish, or a wine with too much sugar and not enough acidity may be cloying on the finish. Essentially the finish should be clean and enticing, making you want another taste of this delicious liquid!

Taste on:

FOR A LONG FINISH:

Good quality ▷claret and Cabernet Sauvignon from ▷Australia and ▷California.

Good quality burgundy, both red and white, namely ▷Gevrey-Chambertin, ▷Meursault; ▷Australian Shiraz.

▷Hermitage and other good Rhône wines; ▷Ribera del Duero; ▷Brunello di Montalcino.

In fact just about anything really classy!

 Fitou

Fitou comes from the hills behind the towns of Perpignan and Narbonne. The grape varieties are those of the south of France, Carignan, Cinsaut and Grenache, with some improving Mourvèdre and Syrah. All Fitou, and it is only red, has a rugged sturdiness about it that somehow goes with the countryside. It always has a solid backbone of tannin, with warm, rustic fruit, tasting of liquorice, prunes and spice, with a dry, earthy finish. Elegant it is not, but warming and mouthfilling, and quite high in alcohol.

• **Vintages:** There is little significant vintage difference in this part of France.

• **Recommended producers:** Château de Nouvelles, Château d'Aguilar, Domaine de Roudène.

Taste on:
FRANCE: ▷Côtes du Roussillon and Côtes du Roussillon Villages, as well as the smaller, adjoining appellation of Collioure.
▷Corbières, ▷Minervois.

PORTUGAL: ▷Dão.

ITALY: Cannonau di Sardegna, a warm, spicey red wine from the island of Sardinia; ▷Barolo.

SPAIN: ▷Jumilla, and nearby Almansa.

 Fortified Wines

Fortified wine is the term used to describe a wine with an alcoholic strength that is higher than that of ordinary table wine, as it has been fortified by the addition of some grape brandy at some stage during its production process. These are wines like port and sherry, which are usually drunk before or after a meal, rather than during it. The range in taste is quite considerable, from very dry to very sweet, with various other permutations in the vinification process.

Taste on:
▷Sherry; ▷Port; ▷Madeira; ▷Marsala; ▷Málaga; ▷Setúbal; ▷Muscat de Beaumes-de-Venise; ▷Liqueur Muscat.

🍇 Franconia

Franconia is best known for the distinctive shape of its bottles rather than for the taste of its wine, which is rarely exported and little known outside the vineyards in northern Bavaria around the town of Würzburg. However, traditionally all the wines of Franconia are sold in dumpy, fat flagons called *bocksbeutel*. Steinwein is another name for the wine of Franconia, after the most famous vineyard, Würzburger Stein. Müller-Thurgau and Silvaner, rather than Riesling, are the main grape varieties here. The tastes are stoney and flinty, stemming maybe from the association with Steinwein, with a mouthful of spice and apricots. The wines are never as sweet as those of the Rhine and Mosel, but always quite soft and dry, but not acidic.

- **Vintages:** 1990, 1989, 1988, 1985, 1983.

- **Recommended producers:** Burgerspital, Juliusspital, Furstlich Castell'sches Domänenamt, Weingut Hans Wirsching, Staatlicher Hofkeller.

 Taste on:

GERMANY: ▷Baden; ▷*trocken* and ▷*halbtrocken* wines from elsewhere in Germany.

FRANCE: Alsace, especially ▷Pinot Blanc, Sylvaner (spelt with a y in France), and for something a little richer, ▷Pinot Gris.

AUSTRIA: ▷Grüner Veltliner, with its pithy, stoney, grassy fruit.

ITALY: Smokey Silvaner, and also Müller-Thurgau from the Valle Isarco, Italy's most northern DOC area, in the foothills of the Dolomite mountains.

🍇 Frascati

Frascati is the wine the Romans drink. It waters the numerous *trattorie* of the capital where it tastes cheerfully quaffable. The grape varieties are a mixture of various types of Trebbiano and Malvasia, which are not guaranteed to provide much flavour or interest. On the contrary, away from its homeland Frascati can taste dull and insipid, or even worse, can epitomise some of the prime defects in Italian winemaking. But things are looking better and it is possible to find Frascati with a bit of character. The most obvious fruit flavour is bananas. Good mouthfilling Frascati reminds me of mushy, ripe bananas, with a touch of cream, and takes me back to my childhood. All that is missing is the brown sugar. Occasionally you come across an *amabile* version of Frascati, which is medium dry, while *superiore* on the label indicates a touch more alcohol than usual.

● **Vintages:** Drink the youngest available.

● **Recommended producers:** Colli di Catone, with the single vineyard, Colle Gaio; Villa Simone, Fontana Candida, with the Santa Teresa vineyard and also their *vino da tavola* Villa Fontana.

Taste on:
ITALY: If you like the taste of Frascati, the chances are that you will enjoy most of the white wines of central Italy. The grape varieties are all similar; some of the wines have a touch more flavour than others. The adjoining DOC is Marino, where Paola di Mauro is the best, under the Colle Picchioni label, and also nearby Colli Albani.
▷Orvieto.
There's Est! Est!! Est!!! di Montefiascone in northern Lazio near the Lago di Bolsena. Since acquiring its reputation and the exclamation marks back in the 12th century (if you have not heard the story before, it is said that Archbishop Fugger who was on his way to Rome, sent his servant on ahead to seek out the inns serving the best wine, to be indicated with an exclamation mark. The wine was supposed to be so good at Montefiascone, that the archbishop went no further), Montefiascone seems to have rested on its laurels. Mazzioti is the best producer and makes some palatable, dry, rather neutral white wine.
The white wines of Sicily, especially ▷Corvo.

FRANCE: White wines from the south of France, ▷Corbières, ▷Minervois, ▷Côtes du Roussillon, ▷Côtes de Provence, ▷Coteaux du Languedoc.

☿ Fruit

Wines are often described as fruity, as indeed you may have noticed in this book! It is hard to escape from the term. What it means is the appealing flavour that comes from ripe grapes. It does not describe the smell of the grapes themselves, but the intrinsic taste that may remind you of raspberries, cherries, strawberries, plums, blackcurrants, or whatever. The fruit is the flavour that fills the mouth, giving the wine its essential character. Some wines are more obviously fruity than others, while characteristics such as ▷tannin or ▷acidity may dominate in others.

 Taste on:

For wines with an immediately fruity impact: young ▷Beaujolais, ▷Australian Shiraz, ▷California Cabernet Sauvignon, ▷Dolcetto.

Muscat-based wines, tasting vividly of grapes: ▷Muscat d'Alsace, ▷Asti Spumante.

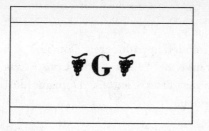

𝔾 Gaillac

The name Gaillac on a label can mean a lot of different things, for Gaillac may be red or white, dry or sweet, still or sparkling, and even *perlé*, which is hardly sparkling at all. Of all the appellations of southwest France, this is the one with the most varied range of flavours.

Take red Gaillac first. Several different grape varieties are grown, including Duras, which has no relation with the Côtes de Duras, Fer Servadou, Syrah, Gamay and Négrette, as well as the Bordeaux varieties, Cabernet Franc, ▷Cabernet Sauvignon and ▷Merlot. In fact a pattern emerges from these. Duras is the grape that gives Gaillac its individuality. Usually it is either blended with Fer Servadou and Syrah, in which case the wine has some distinctive spicey flavours, or it is put with Cabernet and Merlot to bring out any affinities with Bordeaux. The problem is that the label does not tell you which is which and there is really no way around that. Gamay is used purely for the recently developed Gaillac *nouveau*.

As for white Gaillac, it may come from Mauzac, Loin de l'Oeil, Sauvignon, Muscadelle or Sémillon. Gaillac Perlé is a dry white wine, made from any combination of the above, but usually Mauzac and Loin de l'Oeil, in which a little carbon dioxide is retained from the malolactic fermentation. The bubbles in the glass should look like tiny pearls, hence its name, and the wine will taste soft and dry, with hints of apples and almonds, but with no really distinctive flavour. Gaillac with a substantial proportion of Sauvignon may have a little more character, but again there is no way of telling from the label. Fortunately, sweet Gaillac will say so, with the words *moelleux* or *doux*. It is delicately sweet and quite full in flavour.

119

- **Vintages:** 1990, 1989, 1988, 1987, 1986, 1985.

- **Recommended producers:** Domaine Jean Cros, Château Larroze, Cooperative de Labastide dé Levis, Cave Cooperative de Técou, Domaine des Trois Cantous, Domaine de Labarthe, Château Lastours, Mas Pignou.

 Taste on:

NOUVEAU: ▷Beaujolais Nouveau, Italian *vino novello*.

RED: May resemble young ▷claret.
Other wines from the southwest like the lesser-known red ▷Côtes de Gascogne, red Côtes de St-Mont, nearby Côtes du Brulhois and Côtes du Marmandais.
There can also be a pepperiness about Gaillac, which is not unlike a young Rhône wine, say a light ▷Côtes du Rhône.

WHITE AND *PERLÉ*: a soft white wine from Savoie such as ▷Crépy; Côtes de St-Mont; ▷Bordeaux Blanc; a pure Mauzac *vin de pays* from the Aude.

SPARKLING: Blanquette de Limoux.

MOELLEUX: FRANCE: *Moelleux* wines from the Loire valley such as ▷Vouvray, Montlouis; ▷Coteaux du Layon; ▷Jurançon.

ITALY:▷Orvieto.

DOUX: A lesser sweet Bordeaux, like a Premières Côtes de Bordeaux or a Ste-Croix-du-Mont, rather than ▷Sauternes, ▷Monbazillac.

☙ Galestro

Galestro was born of the glut of white grapes in central Tuscany, after the percentage of Trebbiano and Malvasia allowed in Chianti was drastically reduced. This pair are not the most flavoursome of grape varieties and so other, slightly more aromatic ones can be used for Galestro, such as Vernaccia, ▷Pinot Grigio, ▷Pinot Bianco and so on. Galestro has also benefitted from modern technology, particularly from carefully controlled fermentations in pristine stainless steel vats. However, the end result is still a neutral, dry white wine, with remarkably little flavour, that has been a marketing success in Italy, but has made much less impact abroad. Despite the addition of supplementary grape varieties, Galestro still seems bland. Somehow, its most distinguishing characteristic is its lack of flavour, making it ideal for those who want a dry (but not acidic) white wine, with relatively low alcohol, to drink well chilled, without having to think about the taste. You might say, a safe but unadventurous choice in an Italian trattoria.

- **Vintages:** Drink the youngest available.

- **Recommended producers:** Antinori, Frescobaldi, Ricasoli.

Taste on:

ITALY: Other pretty neutral whites from central Italy include Bianco Val d'Arbia, Bianco Pisano di San Torpè, Bianco della Lega, Bianco Vergine Valdichiana; ▷Trebbiano di Romagna; ▷Verdicchio.

For a little more flavour, ▷Orvieto and ▷Frascati; ▷Pinot Grigio and ▷Pinot Bianco from north eastern Italy.

FRANCE: Neutral white wines from the south of France, such as ▷Minervois, ▷Corbières, ▷Côtes du Rhône; ▷Muscadet.

SPAIN: ▷Penedés, notably Torres Viña Sol.

PORTUGAL: ▷Vinho Verde, for lightness and dryness, but with more flavour.

Gavi

Gavi is a white wine, made from the Cortese grape. However, if the label says Gavi dei Gavi, this means that the wine comes from the village of Gavi itself, rather than any of the other surrounding villages in this DOC of Piedmont. Gavi di Cortese on the label is what it says it is, but is not considered to be as good as plain Gavi, nor more emphatically, Gavi dei Gavi. I have never understood why Gavi has such a reputation, not to mention the price to match. It is a pleasant enough wine, with a firm, grassy flavour, a streak of steeliness, some dry, leafy fruit and hints of almonds, but lacks any real depth or complexity.

- **Vintages:** Drink the youngest available.

- **Recommended producers:** La Scolca, la Giustiniana.

 Taste on:
ITALY: Other white wines from northern Italy, such as ▷Soave, Bianco di Custoza, Lugana.

FRANCE: ▷Chablis, ▷Jurançon.

SPAIN: ▷Rueda.

Gevrey-Chambertin ▼▼▼

Gevrey-Chambertin is taken as an example of the red wines of the Côte de Nuits, the northern half of the Côte d'Or. These tend to be just a little fuller and richer than the lighter, more elegant wines of the Côte de Beaune. However, that said, much does depend upon a producer's individual style of winemaking.

As with all the red wines of the Côte d'Or, the grape variety of Gevrey-Chambertin is ▷Pinot Noir. In a young wine, raspberries are the key fruit, with some acidity and tannin, and maybe a some hint of vanilla from oak barrels. As it matures it will develop rich, vegetal overtones, reminiscent of farmyards and rotting leaves, and sometimes a rich, opulent, almost velvety chocolate flavour. The great wines of the Côte de Nuits have evocative names like Le Chambertin, Clos de Tart, Romanée Conti and so on. Fine burgundy is sublime, but it is rare and elusive. Sadly, even what promises well on a wine list can disappoint, but when burgundy is great, it is great indeed.

If you like good Gevrey-Chambertin, you will appreciate the other wines of the Côte de Nuits, from the villages of Morey St-Denis, Chambolle-Musigny, Clos Vougeot, Vosne-Romanée and Nuits St-Georges. The wines of the Côte de Beaune will appeal too, from

▷Volnay, Aloxe-Corton, Savigny-lès-Beaune, Beaune itself, Pommard, Auxey-Duresses and Santenay, amongst others.

- **Vintages:** 1990, 1989, 1988, 1985, 1983, 1978.

- **Recommended producers:** Not just of Gevrey-Chambertin but from all over the Côte de Nuits: Armand Rousseau, Drouhin, Faiveley, Bachelet, Magnien, Alain Michelot, Gouges, Jayer, Méo-Camuzet, Emmanuel Rouget, Boillot, Lignier, Rion, Hudelot-Noëllat, Domaine de la Romanée Conti, Dujac, Mugnier, Rossignol-Trapet, Roty, de Montille.

Taste on:

Attempts have been made to imitate the elusive qualities of Pinot Noir outside Burgundy, and not just in France. There is Pinot Noir in ▷California, Oregon, Australia, ▷New Zealand, Tuscany, Yugoslavia and Romania. To avoid repetition, ▷Volnay and ▷Pinot Noir.

FRANCE: One of the clichés of the blind tasting is the ability, or otherwise, to tell the difference between burgundy and ▷claret. This may seem obvious when you can see the label, and they do say that one glance at the label is worth twenty years in the wine trade, but on occasions it can be all too misleading. The style of the claret in question is the richer wines of ▷St-Emilion and Pomerol, which can have a sweetness about them that suggests a fine burgundy.

SPAIN: Consider too *gran reserva* ▷Rioja and some of the other red wines of northern Spain, such as ▷Ribera del Duero, that are aged for several months in American oak. This gives them a soft, ripe vanilla nose, not unlike the chocolatey aroma of mature Pinot Noir, with some of the smooth, velvet elegance of burgundy on the palate.

ITALY: Mature Chianti Classico, or Chianti Rufina, that is at least twenty years old, can take on some of the vegetal, farmyard flavours of burgundy. Grattamacco Rosso from an individual estate in the Maremma near Bolgheri also has some Burgundian vegetal and herbal flavours, with a soft sweetness in the mouth, even though the grape varieties are Cabernet Sauvignon and Malvasia Nera. Also mature ▷Barbaresco.

🐂 Gewürztraminer d'Alsace

Gewürztraminer is the most individual and distinctive of all the grape varieties of Alsace. Alsace is alone amongst the wine regions of France for giving greater emphasis on wine labels to the grape variety than the precise provenance of a wine, except in the case of the *grands crus*. *Gewürz* means spice in German and the flavours of Gewürztraminer are indeed that, sometimes elegantly so, with a firm, structured backbone, but sometimes blowsily so, with a vulgar, overpowering perfume. The question is, which spice? More often it is an opulent perfume, reminiscent of tropical fruit (lychees are often mentioned in this context), or roses, or even Nivea cold cream. You either love it or hate it. I love the more subtle Gewürztraminer, if they can ever be described as subtle. Traminer implies that this grape variety may have once originated from the town of Tramin in the Alto Adige of north west Italy.

In contrast to the wines of the Rhine and Mosel, most Alsace wines (do not describe them as Alsatian, for that indicates canine associations) are fermented completely dry, leaving no residual sugar. Although Alsace is one of the most northern vineyard areas of France, it is also one of the sunniest and driest, protected from inclement weather by the Vosges mountains. This produces wines with a fairly high degree of alcohol, which is especially noticeable in full-bodied Gewürztraminers that make for a flavour-packed mouthful, with an obviously opulent, spicey richness. Often there is an underlying characteristic oiliness. The taste can vary with individual producers' own house styles; some make more obvious blowsy Gewürztraminer, while others favour the understated, leaner style.

As well as various *grand cru* vineyard names, the terms Vendange Tardive, meaning late harvest, and Sélection de Grains Nobles, implying a special selection of individual grapes, may also feature on a Gewürztraminer label. While a *Vendange Tardive* may not have any residual sugar, but may just taste very concentrated and rich, *Sélection de Grains Nobles* will have been made from grapes affected by noble rot and will not be fermented completely dry. The result is something not unlike a good ▷Sauternes. The flavour of the grape may be different, but the body, weight and structure of the two wines is remarkably similar.

● **Vintages:** 1990, 1989, 1988, 1985, 1983, 1981, 1976.

● **Recommended producers:** Hugel, Trimbach, Léon Beyer, Domaine Weinbach, Jos Meyer, Marc Kreydenweiss, Ostertag, Blanck, Willm, Turckheim cooperative, Zind-Humbrecht.

Taste on:
Gewürztraminer is grown in other parts of the world, but nowhere quite as successfully and distinctively as Alsace. However, try:

GERMANY: Gewürztraminer from Germany, notably from the Rheinpfalz, such as Dürkheimer Feuerberg Spätlese Trocken from Weingut Fitz-Ritter.

AUSTRIA: South and east Styria, on the Yugoslav border, is the main area for Gewürztraminer, often reaching ▷Beerenauslese quality.

USA: California, Oregon, Washington State, Texas and Long Island. Dry California Gewürztraminer is sometimes spoilt by a bitter finish, so that the off-dry wines are more successful, or even better are the Late Harvest wines, notably from Mark West Vineyards in Sonoma.

NEW ZEALAND: Good producers include Villa Maria, Vidal, Hunters.

ITALY: Südtirol or Alto Adige, where it is called Traminer Aromatico, but is underplayed, more subtle and less overwhelming. Also features in the DOCs of Friuli, Grave del Friuli, Collio and so on.
Trebianco, a *vino da tavola* from Castello dei Rampolla in Tuscany, contains a substantial proportion of Gewürztraminer and is distinctively spicey.

YUGOSLAVIA: Not a lot of varietal character; an even more gentle version of Italian Gewürztraminer.

FRANCE: I certainly have on occasions confused ▷Muscat from Alsace with Gewurztraminer, so the chances are, that it you like one, you will like the other.

▷Sauternes, for similarities with *Sélection de Grains Nobles*.

SPAIN: Torres Viña Esmeralda from Penedés.

☙ Graves (Red)

Red Graves, or rather Pessac-Léognan, which since 1987 has the appellation of the better part of the original area, comes between the ▷Médoc and ▷St-Emilion in taste. The main characteristic is a certain *goût de terroir*, an underlying earthiness, that is peculiar to the Graves. The name has something to do with the soil, or rather the gravelly pebbles that make up the vineyards. The wines do not quite have the finesse of those of the Médoc, nor are they quite as rich as those of St-Emilion and Pomerol. Sometimes there is a smokey quality, reminiscent of the smell of tobacco. Château Haut-Brion is the one estate to feature in the classification of *grands crus* of the Médoc and the region also has its own more recent classification. Like the better wines of the Médoc and St-Emilion, those of the Graves will age superbly well.

• **Vintages:** 1990, 1989, 1988, 1987, 1986, 1985, 1983, 1982, 1981, 1978, 1970.

• **Recommended estates:** Domaine de Chevalier, Haut-Bailly, Haut-Brion, La Mission Haut-Brion, Smith-Haut-Lafitte, La Louvière, de Fieuzal, Rahoul, Magence, La Grave, Larrivet-Haut-Brion.

Taste on:
FRANCE: Other ▷claret, namely ▷Médoc, ▷St-Emilion.

ITALY: ▷Brunello di Montalcino; ▷Chianti Classico, maintaining the similarity between Sangiovese and Cabernet Sauvignon.

☙ Graves (White)

The appellation of the Graves, or Pessac-Léognan, as the better part of the Graves vineyards is now called, can be either red or white. It is unusual in Bordeaux to have the same appellation for both colours: usually it is one or the other. The white wines of the Graves can cover a whole range of flavours, depending on how they are made, with or without oak and whether their producers have adopted the more advanced techniques of modern winemaking or not. At their simplest the white wines of the Graves are fuller, more solid versions of ▷Bordeaux Blanc, with the lemony flavours or fruity acidity of wines intended for early drinking. Sometimes there is the merest hint of oak, sometimes none at all.

At the other end of the scale, amongst the more prestigious classed growths of the Graves, the flavours become more substantial and the use of new oak barrels widespread. These are wines that require bottle age and the flavours are more confusing and complex, as I know to my cost. With the arrogance of a three-hour old Master of Wine – I had received the exam results that morning – I told the directors of my company, whose habit it was to play guessing games with the wine over lunch, that they were all wrong, that the wine that they thought came from somewhere close to the village of ▷Meursault, was the finest of white Graves, Laville Haut-Brion. In fact it was the finest of white burgundies, Corton-Charlemagne! I had been confused by the oaky overtones, which can be found equally well in good Graves as in fine white good burgundy. However there is a difference. Some of the white wines of the Graves have what I call an old-fashioned feel about them. Not all the producers have espoused modern winemaking techniques and some remain firmly traditional, with varying results. Domaine de Chevalier and Château Laville Haut-Brion make stylish wines, which sometimes seem misleadingly dull in early youth. They demand patience which is rewarded by the development of rich, full, nutty flavours.

● **Vintages:** 1990, 1989, 1988, 1986, 1985, 1983, 1982.

● **Recommended estates:** Domaine de Chevalier, de Fieuzal, Laville Haut-Brion, La Louvière, Smith-Haut-Lafitte, Rahoul, Bouscaut, Carbonnieux, Larrivet-Haut-Brion, La Tour Martillac.

 Taste on:

FRANCE: The simplest wines of the Graves are not unlike ▷Entre-Deux-Mers, Côtes de Duras or ▷Bergerac Blanc.

In Provence there is a Sauvignon/Sémillon blend that has a flavour of the Graves about it, namely Clos Mireille ▼▼ from

Domaines Ott. There is an underlying richness, a leafy flavour, with a merest hint of spritz, the weight of the full, honeyed, mature flavours of fine white Graves. The appellation of Clos Mireille is ▷Côtes de Provence, but it is quite unlike any other white wine of that appellation. The white wine of Château Simone, the only estate of any significance in the tiny appellation of Palette outside Aix-en-Provence, also has a richness that is more akin to white Graves than the other white wines of the adjoining Coteaux d'Aix-en-Provence.
▷Meursault; ▷Hermitage Blanc.

USA: The oak-aged wines of the Graves have more in common with a ▷Sauvignon Blanc from the New World than with their neighbours in southwest France. A ▷California Sauvignon labelled ▷Fumé Blanc, rather than plain Sauvignon, immediately implies some ageing in oak. These are wines with a marked resemblance to the Graves. The link is the effects of oak ageing. There is sometimes a little Sémillon in the blend too, as there is in the Graves, as with Robert Mondavi's Fumé Blanc. Other good California Sauvignons with a similarity to the Graves include Murphy-Goode Estate Winery, Dry Creek, and Grgich Hills.

AUSTRALIA: Mature Sémillon from the Hunter Valley: Lindemans is best of all but also Rosemount and Rothbury. Oaky Sauvignon, sometimes also called Fumé Blanc, as made by Tim Knappstein, Hill-Smith etc. Blends of Sauvignon/Sémillon as from Cape Mentelle, Chittering Estate, Kies Estate.

NEW ZEALAND: Oak-aged Sauvignon from Cloudy Bay, Kumeu River, Brookfields and others.

❦ Grüner Veltliner ❧

Grüner Veltliner is *the* grape variety of Austria and, apart from crossing the border into Hungary and Czechoslovakia, grows nowhere else. In Austria however, it features in most of the country's wine regions, giving dry white wines, with smokey, slightly spicey, slightly grassy fruit and fresh stoney acidity. Grüner Veltiner is easy to drink, neither heavy nor cloying, but usually at its best within a year or two of the harvest, especially in the *heurigen* of the wine villages surrounding Vienna, where the Viennese go to sample the new wine.

Occasionally you can find Grüner Veltliner of ▷Spätlese quality, when it takes on a honeyed note, with full-bodied, ripe apricot fruit, but always with a dry finish. Nor is it unknown for Grüner Veltliner to age, taking on an attractive toasted, leafy character.

● **Vintages:** 1990, 1989, 1988, 1987, 1986, 1985.

● **Recommended producers:** Lenz Moser, Fritz Salomon, Freie Weingärtner in Wachau, Sepp Hold, Wilhelm Bründelmayer.

Taste on:

FRANCE: Grüner Veltliner has something in common with several wines: ▷Chablis for the grassy fruit; ▷Jurançon for the pithy flavour; ▷Pinot Gris or ▷Pinot Blanc from Alsace for some spice; ▷Muscadet for acidity; ▷Apremont for the stoney flavours.

ITALY: ▷Pinot Bianco and ▷Pinot Grigio from Friuli and the Alto Adige.

GERMANY: ▷Baden; ▷Franconia.

🍇 Halbtrocken

Halbtrocken (or half dry) wines represent part of the current fashion in Germany for making dry wines, along with ▷*trocken* wines. They are not as searingly dry as *trocken* wines, retaining a little sweetness to take away the sharp edges of acidity. Usually they are quite soft and fruity, with underlying acidity, and hints of honey, and quite light in alcohol and body. The depth of flavour depends upon the grape variety; Riesling gives the most stylish flavours in the Rhine, while Silvaner is best in ▷Franconia.

● **Vintages:** 1990, 1989, 1988, 1985.

● **Recommended producers:** Lingenfelder, Bürklin Wolf, Bassermann-Jordan and Fitz-Ritter in the Rheinpfalz; Werner'sches Weingut, Schloss Reinhartshausen and Balthasar Ress in the Rheingau; Heyl zu Herrensheim and Strub in Nierstein; Hans Wirsching in Franconia.

Taste on:
GERMANY: Wines from ▷Baden and ▷Franconia; only ▷Kabinett quality wine.

FRANCE: Most Alsace wines, from Edelszwicker and Sylvaner, to ▷Pinot Gris and ▷Riesling; ▷Vouvray *demi-sec*, for the combination of honey and acidity.

AUSTRIA: Qualitätswein made from Müller-Thurgau and Riesling.

Hermitage

The red wine of this northern Rhône appellation from the hills around Tournon is made from Syrah. It is here and in the ▷Côte Rôtie, a little further north, that you find the best examples of this distinctive variety. The key to its recognition is blackcurrant gums, as produced by Rowntree, not the ripe, fruity cassis of Cabernet Sauvignon, but the rubbery gum flavour of the sweets, with some pepper and tannin. Young Hermitage is a solid, mouth-puckering tannic wine, that needs years to age and develop softer, spicey flavours. Patience is well rewarded for mature bottles can be outstandingly good, magnificently rich and spicey, with complex flavours of fruit, liquorice, herbs and spice.

There is also a tiny amount of white Hermitage made from two grape varieties, Roussanne and Marsanne, which in the right hands make wine that age as well as their red counterparts. It seems a little dull and flat in its youth, but develops all sorts of wonderful nuances of honey, herbs, peaches and toasted nuts.

● **Vintages:** 1990, 1989, 1988, 1985, 1983, 1978, 1976, 1971, 1970, 1969.

● **Recommended producers:** Chave, Jaboulet, notably Hermitage la Chapelle, Desmeure, Fayolle, Guigal, Grippat, Sorel, Vidal-Fleury.

 Taste on:

RED:

FRANCE: Similar wines from the northern Rhône, also from Syrah, namely ▷Crozes Hermitage, ▷Cornas, St-Joseph, ▷Côte Rotie.

Vins de pays which mention Syrah on the label, notably Coteaux de l'Ardèche and Coteaux des Baronnies; Coteaux de Tricastin. Other wines from the Midi, such as ▷Corbières and ▷Minervois with a high percentage of improving Syrah.

ITALY: The only example of Syrah in Italy comes from Tuscany, from the Chianti Classico estate of Isole e Olena. If you like the taste of Syrah, this is not to be missed.

AUSTRALIA: The most distinctive examples of Syrah in the New World come from Australia, where it is called ▷Shiraz.

The flavours are ripe and spicey, sometimes sweeter than their French counterparts, and redolent of mint and blackcurrant gums. In the Hunter Valley Shiraz could also be called Hermitage, as in Penfold's Grange Hermitage, although that name has now been shortened to Grange to avoid any confusion with the French appellation. It is fatter and fuller than many of the leaner Hermitages of the Rhône valley, with wonderfully ripe, opulent blackcurrant-gums fruit and warm, spicey flavours and ages beautifully.

CALIFORNIA: Syrah, as opposed to the more common and much less distinguished Petite Sirah, is grown successfully by a handful of wineries in California, namely Zaca Mesa, Qupe, Phelps, Bonny Doon and Ojai.
▷Zinfandel.

SOUTH AFRICA: Shiraz made by Zandvliet and Zonnebloem.

WHITE:
FRANCE: ▷Meursault, ▷Graves, ▷Châteauneuf-du-Pape.

CALIFORNIA: Le Sophiste from Bonny Doon, a Marsanne/ Roussanne blend.

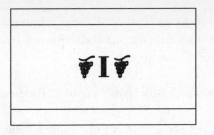

Irancy ♥♥

Irancy is one of the most northern vineyards of ▷Burgundy, lying close to ▷Chablis. Like all good red Burgundy it is made from ▷Pinor Noir, but very occasionally laced with a little César and Tressot. Here the climate is slightly cooler than in the Côte d'Or so that the young wines have an appealing fruity, raspberry acidity and develop smoother, richer flavours, as they mature. However, it is only in the ripest years that Irancy completely looses its fresh acidity. Something remains that denotes a northern vineyard, a liveliness and lightness that distinguishes Irancy from the wines of ▷Volnay and ▷Gevrey-Chambertin.

• **Vintages:** 1990, 1989, 1988, 1986, 1985, 1978, 1976.

• **Recommended producers:** Léon Bienvenu, Delaloge, Cantin.

Taste on:
FRANCE: ▷Pinot Noir from other marginal vineyards, where the grapes do not always ripen fully, as ▷Sancerre, Reuilly and Menetou-Salon.
▷Pinot Noir d'Alsace, which sometimes looks like a deep pink wine, rather than a pale red one. Refreshing acidity and raspberry fruit is the key to taste, with some sweet fruit. These are wines to drink in relatively early youth.
Hautes Côtes de Beaune and Hautes Côtes de Nuits from the cooler vineyards behind the Côte d'Or; nearby Coulanges-la-Vineuse ♥♥, as well as Epineuil.

133

Vin de Pays de Franche-Comté, another cool-climate Pinot Noir; red ▷Côtes du Jura and ▷Arbois; Bouzy Rouge, the still red wine of champagne.

GERMANY: Spätburgunder from ▷Baden and the Ahr.

SWITZERLAND: Where Pinot Noir is called Blauburgunder in the German cantons and makes very light red wine; Dôle, which is either pure Pinot Noir or pure Gamay, or a mixture of both.

AUSTRIA: Pinot Noir from Georg Stiegelmar, considered to be the best producer and also the most expensive.

ENGLAND: Pinot Noir is produced by Bernard Theobald at Westbury and by the Thames Valley Vineyard.

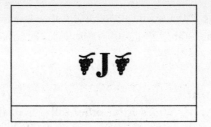

🍇 Johannisberg – Rheingau 🍇

The wines of the Rheingau are often considered to be the very best of German wine, with the village of Johannisberg representing the epitome of the Rheingau. The heart of the region runs from Rüdesheim to Rauenthal, a small stretch of vineyards on the northern banks of the Rhine. The village of Hochheim, to the east of the cities of Wiesbaden and Mainz, is also included in the Rheingau, forming a separate pocket of vineyards. Hock, an idiosyncratic English term to describe the wines of Rhine, is derived from Hochheim.

As elsewhere in the Rhine and Mosel, the best wines of the Rheingau come from the ▷Riesling grape. They are a delicious combination of honey, apricots, peaches and cream, combining elegance and balance. A firm backbone of acidity prevents them from ever being cloying, nor are they heavy, but always delicately subtle. The level of sweetness, or richness depends of course upon the Prädikat (or category); ▷Kabinett wines will be quite firm and almost steely compared with an ▷Auslese or ▷Beerenauslese. These are wines that deserve bottle age in the best vintages, developing the even more complex slatey, mineral flavours of mature Riesling.

Bereich Johannisberg is the wine district which covers the whole of the Rheingau, and the village has just one *Grosslage*, that of Johannisberger Erntebringer. The best single vineyards, or *Einzellagen*, of Johannisberg include Johannisberger Klaus, Johannisberger Hölle as well as Schloss Johannisberg.

- **Vintages:** 1990, 1989, 1988, 1985, 1983, 1976, 1975, 1971.

- **Recommended producers:** Schloss Vollrads for the drier style of wines, Schloss Johannisberg, Schloss Schönborn, Deinhard, Schloss Groenesteyn, the State Domaine at Eltville, Schloss Rheinhartshausen, Balthasar Ress.

 Taste on:

GERMANY: Wines from other villages of the Rheingau, such as Geisenheimer Schlossgarten, Rüdesheimer Schlossberg, Winkeler Hasensprung, Eltviller Sonnenberg, Erbacher Marcobrunnen, Steinberg in the village of Hattenheim, Kiedricher Wasseros, Rauenthaler Steinmächer and Hochheimer Königin Victoriaberg, which commemorates a visit by Queen Victoria.

Wines from ▷Bernkastel in the Mosel, Schlossböckelheim in the ▷Nahe, ▷Nierstein in the Rheinhessen, Deidesheim in the ▷Rheinpfalz.

Wines of ▷Kabinett, ▷Spätlese, ▷Auslese, ▷Beerenauslese and ▷Trockenbeerenauslese quality from other villages of the Rheingau.

USA: California produces some fine Rieslings, often called Johannisberg Riesling or White Riesling, but they tend to be heavier, high in alcohol and less subtle than those of the Rheingau. Cooler Oregon may be more successful.

NEW ZEALAND: Dry Riesling.

AUSTRALIA: Riesling, notably from the Barossa Valley.

❦ Jumilla ▼

Jumilla is a full-bodied, alcoholic red wine from vineyards in the arid hills behind the town of Alicante in southeast Spain. The main grape variety is Monastrell. Old-style Jumilla was kept in large oak vats for several months, if not years, with the result that the fruit flavours evaporated and you were left with a rather dry, tarry and probably oxidising red wine. High alcohol was certainly a dominant feature from these sunsoaked vineyards. However, there have been gradual improvements in the winemaking in southeast Spain, and Jumilla is becoming just a little lighter in body, with a little more fruit.

There is a warmth about good Jumilla that is reminiscent of the southern Rhône Valley and there is a dry, tarry flavour with fruitcake and walnuts that is more akin to ▷Barolo or ▷Fitou. However, modern Jumilla tends to be spicey and peppery, with some dry, stalky fruit and tannin.

- **Vintages:** No change from year to year.

- **Recommended producers:** Bodegas Juvinsa, Cooperative San Isdro, Bodegas Bleda, Bodegas Ascensio Carcelen.

 Taste on:

SPAIN: Adjoining DOs like Yecla, Valencia, Almansa, Utiel Requena, ▷Valdepeñas.

FRANCE: ▷Châteauneuf-du-Pape, or Gigondas from the southern Rhône; ▷Fitou.

ITALY: Cannonau di Sardegna, a full-bodied, rather alcoholic red from what is otherwise known as the Grenache, or Garnacha grape; ▷Barolo.

PORTUGAL: ▷Dão, Torres Vedras, ▷Arruda.

 # Jurançon

Jurançon can be either dry or sweet or rather, as one producer described it, a dry wine that is not really dry, or a sweet wine that is not very sweet. Usually the label clarifies, with the words *sec* or *moelleux*. Winemaking in this appellation in the foothills of the Pyrenees around the town of Pau, has improved beyond recognition. Jurançon, sweet or dry, used to stink of sulphur dioxide rather than any enticing flavours of fruit. In contrast dry Jurançon today is packed with pithy grapefruit flavours, with a distinctive pungency, that fills the mouth, while the sweet wines are honeyed and fresh.

There is a lightness and delicacy about Jurançon *moelleux* which has more in common with the Loire Valley than with ▷Sauternes. There is no noble rot here. Instead the grapes are dried on the vines, in order to concentrate their juice, until well into November. The taste is elegantly honeyed with an underlying lemony acidity.

- **Vintages:** 1990, 1989, 1988, 1986, 1985.

- **Recommended producers:** Domaine Cauhapé, Clos Uroulat, Château Jolys.

 Taste on:

DRY:

FRANCE: Nearby Côtes de St-Mont is made from the same obscure grape varieties, Gros Manseng and Petit Manseng; ▷Côtes de Gascogne.

ITALY: ▷Gavi dei Gavi.

AUSTRALIA: Marsanne, from Yeringberg in the Yarra Valley, has some pithy vibrant fruit, not unlike Jurançon.

SWEET:

FRANCE: ▷Coteaux du Layon, Bonnezeaux.

ITALY: ▷Orvieto *abboccato*; late-harvested Erbaluce di Caluso ♥♥, notably a delicately honeyed wine called Solativo del Canavese, made by Ferrando; Piccolit from Trentino, one of the few Italian wines affected by noble rot.

Kabinett

Kabinett on a German wine label indicates the lowest category and the driest of the quality Prädikat wines. This is the clue that the wine is not sweet, although it may have gentle hints of honey, and in some instances can be quite firmly dry. Kabinett, or Cabinet, also features on Austrian wine labels, again for the drier styles of wine.

Examples from the cooler vineyards of the Mosel will be quite crisp and flowery, maybe with a hint of underlying honey, depending on the ripeness of the vintage. In the vineyards of the Rhine they become a little fuller and richer, although a Rheingau Kabinett will always be more elegant than one from the Rheinpfalz, while Kabinetts from warmer Austria are riper and richer still.

The best Kabinett wines come from the ▷Riesling grape, which indisputably makes the finest German wines.

• **Vintages:** In Germany: 1990, 1989, 1988, 1986, 1983, 1976, 1975, 1971

Taste on:

GERMANY: ▷Bernkastel, ▷Johannisberg, ▷Nahe-Schlossböckelheim, ▷Nierstein, ▷Rheinpfalz-Deidesheim. Any Kabinett ▷*trocken* and ▷*halbtrocken* wines.

AUSTRIA: Kabinett wines from Riesling.

FRANCE: ▷Riesling d'Alsace.

ITALY: Riesling Renano from the Alto Adige.

NEW ZEALAND: Riesling.

USA: California Johannisberg or White Riesling; also Riesling from Oregon and Washington State.

AUSTRALIA: Riesling from the Barossa Valley.

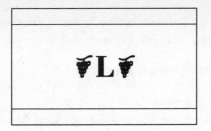

Lambrusco

Lambrusco can be red, white or pink. It can be fully fizzy or lightly sparkling, pretty sweet or firmly dry. Wine snobs may call it alcoholic Coca Cola. However, bottles of Lambrusco have provided lots of gluggable drinking pleasure and may even have sent the odd person off down the slippery path of serious wine appreciation.

Lambrusco is the name of the grape, grown around the town of Modena, in the province of Emilia Romagna in central Italy. This is where real Lambrusco is made, a positively red and firmly dry, frothy wine. It has a distinctive sour-cherry flavour with a bitter finish, and is just the thing to cut the rich cooking of the region. Look for Lambrusco di Sorbara on the label, because it is the best. Lambrusco Grasparosa di Castelvetro and Lambrusco Salamino di Santa Croce are the other two defined areas of Lambrusco. Otherwise it tends to be pretty anonymous.

Pink and white Lambrusco both tend to be slightly sweet, appealing to those who want pleasant flavours with no particular regional characteristics and the frivolity of cheerful bubbles.

- **Vintages:** Never sold with a vintage.

- **Recommended producers:** Cavacchioli, Chiarli, Giacobazzi.

Taste on:
REAL RED LAMBRUSCO:
FRANCE: Red Crémant de Bourgogne, red Crémant de Loire, red ▷Saumur Mousseux.

PINK OR BLUSH LAMBRUSCO:
PORTUGAL: ▷Mateus Rosé, Lancers.

141

FRANCE: For something a little drier, pink Crémant de Bourgogne and pink Crémant de Loire; pink ▷champagne.

AUSTRALIA: Angas Brut.

WHITE LAMBRUSCO:
FRANCE: Anonymous white sparklers like Veuve du Vernay, Kriter, Cavalier, but then trade up and try something drier with regional characteristics, like Blanquette de Limoux, Crémant de Loire, ▷Vouvray, *moelleux* rather than *sec*, Crémant d'Alsace, or even ▷champagne, *demi sec* rather than *brut*.

SPAIN: ▷Cava, a sweeter version rather than *brut*.

ITALY: For positively sweet sparkling wine, ▷Asti Spumante; Moscadello di Montalcino, from Tuscany.

☙ Laskirizling (Lutomer)

Believe it or not, Lutomer Laski Riesling (or Laskirizling) is Britain's biggest selling single wine. More bottles of this slightly sweet, soft, easy to drink white wine from Yugoslavia move off our wine shelves than any other single wine.

Laskirizling is quite a different grape from the ▷Riesling grown in Germany or the Johannisberg or White Riesling of the New World. It does not have the same depth of flavour, elegance and complexity, but can produce some fresh, fruity, grapey wines. There are various synonyms; Welsh or Wälschriesling in Austria, Olaszrizling in Hungary and Riesling Italico in Italy. It is very much a grape variety of Eastern Europe. Northeast Italy is the furthest west it comes.

Lutomer Laskirizling is Yugoslavia's answer to ▷Liebfraumilch. It has some of the same qualities, in that it is soft and grassy and slightly sweet and honeyed, with just enough acidity to stop it from being cloying. Bland is another possible description, for there is nothing in it to dislike, except its lack of positive character.

● **Vintages:** Drink the youngest available.

Taste on:
HUNGARY: Olaszrizling, which a few years ago, was almost as common as Laskirizling, but has since declined in popularity.

AUSTRIA: Wälschriesling. It is rarely exported, but in Austria provides a pleasant, undemanding glass of wine, with more fruit and flavour and a better balance of acidity than its Yugoslav counterpart.

ITALY: Riesling Italico is grown chiefly in Friuli and is to be found in the DOC of Collio. Riesling Renano from the same region tends to have more flavour.

BULGARIA: Riesling and Misket blends.

GERMANY: ▷Liebfraumilch, but also be more adventurous with village names such as ▷Nierstein or Deidesheim, wines from the Rhine rather than the Mosel.

CYPRUS: Thisbe, a soft white wine from Keo.

 # Liebfraumilch

It is somewhat ironic and a sad reflection on the state of the German wine industry that Liebfraumilch is top of the popularity stakes of German wine abroad, while Germans themselves completely ignore it at home. Liebfraumilch translates literally as the 'milk of Our Lady' and the name originates from the vineyard of the Liebfrauenkirche in the city of Wörms. While Liebfraumilch may be a blend of several grape varieties and vineyards from a region, it must not come from more than one wine region and these are the Rheinpfalz, Rheinhessen or occasionally the ▷Nahe and the Rheingau. It must also conform to the basic quality standards of German wine law.

Unfortunately the enormous quantitiy of cheap Liebfraumilch that has flooded the export market has brought the reputation not only of Liebfraumilch, but finer German wines as well into disrepute. However, Liebfraumilch from a reputable source is a perfectly agreeable and enjoyable wine. Not only that, meticulous care and attention is devoted to maintaining the standard of quality and consistency of taste of popular brands like Blue Nun, Crown of Crowns, Black Tower and so on.

A Liebfraumilch like Blue Nun, which originates from the Rheinhessen, will consist of six or more different wines and grape varieties. Müller-Thurgau forms the basis of Blue Nun, making a light, flowery framework, which is complemented by some Sylvaner, which provides body; ▷Riesling which adds some ripeness and depth of flavour, plus a little Kerner which contributes some pithy grapefruit character, a drop of Faber for some fruity acidity and a drop of Gewürztraminer for a hint of spiciness. The final result is a wine that is soft and fruity, but without any distinctive regional characteristics. This sounds rather boring, and on occasions it is. The chief virtue of Liebfraumilch is that it is a safe choice, usually devoid of any unpleasant surprises and provides reassurance in the minefield of a complicated wine list.

● **Vintages:** Drink the youngest available.

Taste on:

GERMANY: Be more adventurous, try some of the village wines of Germany, especially from the Rheinhessen and ▷Rheinpfalz, namely ▷Nierstein, Deidesheim and also Schlossböckelheim from the ▷Nahe. ▷Spätlese is the most appropriate category of sweetness, for it is neither too dry nor too sweet, but soft and gentle.

FRANCE: Edelszwicker, from Alsace.

AUSTRIA: Spätlese wines.

SPAIN: ▷Penedés, Torres Viña Esmeralda, a distinctive blend of Riesling and Gewürztraminer.

PORTUGAL: João Pires Muscat.

YUGOSLAVIA: ▷Laskirizling (Lutomer).

HUNGARY: Olaszrizling.

BULGARIA: Riesling and Misket blend, a sweet, grapey, dusty white wine.

CYPRUS: Thisbe, a medium dry wine made by Keo.

▷Riesling
▷Muscat
▷Gewürztraminer

Liqueur Muscat ♥♥

Liqueur Muscat is one of Australia's most original wines; a superbly rich dessert wine, made in the northeast corner of the state of Victoria around the town of Rutherglen. The ▷Muscat grapes are not picked until they are overripe and turning into raisins; the fermentation is stopped by the addition of brandy and then the wine is matured in oak barrels, often for several years, and sometimes in a solera system, like ▷sherry.

The resulting wine is rich and luscious, the essence of liquid walnuts and orange marmalade, with a ripe, full-flavoured nuttiness. Older wines lose the pronounced orange flavours of the Muscat grape, to become softer and more toffee-like. They can range in colour from deep amber to mahogany brown.

- **Vintages:** Not relevant.

- **Recommended producers:** Chambers, Campbells, Stanton & Kileen, All Saints, Seppelts, Bailey's.

 Taste on:

SPAIN: ▷Málaga, Moscatel de Navarra, sweet *oloroso* and cream ▷sherry.

GREECE: Muscat of Samos, which tastes of toffee apples; Mavrodaphne ♥♥, an unusual dessert wine, with some muscat fruit, as well as flavours of toffee and black treacle.

PORTUGAL: Moscatel de ▷Setúbal, Malmsey ▷Madeira.

ITALY: Muscat di Pantelleria Passito ♥♥, with flavours of orange marmalade.

CYPRUS: ▷Commandaria.

FRANCE: Vin de Paille ♥♥ from the Jura where they preserve a tradition for this wine, drying the grapes on straw for several weeks before pressing them to make a sweet dessert wine; Rivesaltes ♥♥, a fortified wine, made near Perpignan in the south.

Low alcohol wine *see* Dealcoholised wine

M

 Mâcon

Mâcon can be red, white or pink. The red version comes from Gamay and is not unlike nearby ▷Beaujolais, while the white is normally made from ▷Chardonnay and sometimes ▷Pinot Blanc. Pink Mâcon, again from Gamay, is rather rare.

Good red Mâcon has a cheerful, fruity, raspberry flavour, which is very similar to Beaujolais, though sadly often rather duller and flatter, without the same fresh, vibrant fruit.

White Mâcon, or Mâcon-Villages if it comes from one of the better villages (which may be named on the label, such as Lugny or Viré) rarely has any contact with oak, so that it is light and grassy and could be confused with a basic ▷Chablis. The Chablis however should, but does not always, have a firmer edge of acidity, while Mâcon is a little fuller in the mouth.

● **Vintages:** 1990, 1989, 1988, 1986, 1985. There is no great merit in ageing Mâcon; drink the youngest available.

● **Recommended producers:** Jean Thévenet, Domaine de la Bon Gran. Mâcon-Village cooperatives are particularly important; those at Clessé, Chardonnay, Lugny, Prissé, Viré and St Gengoux de Scissé are best.

Taste on:
RED:
FRANCE: ▷Beaujolais and other Gamay-based wines like Côte Roannaise, Côtes du Forez, Coteaux Lyonnais; Passe-Tout-Grain, a blend of Pinot Noir and Gamay from Burgundy.

WHITE:

FRANCE: Adjoining appellations such as St-Véran, Pouilly-Vinzelles and Beaujolais Blanc. ▷Pouilly-Fuissé tends to be a little heavier and fuller.

▷Chablis; Chardonnay du Haut Poitou; Chardonnay de l'Ardèche; Vin du Bugey Chardonnay; Chardonnay from the Midi, such as Vin de Pays de l'Aude from around Limoux, and also Vin de Pays de l'Ile de Beauté from Corsica; ▷Pinot Blanc d'Alsace.

ITALY: ▷Pinot Bianco and Chardonnay from northeast Italy, from the DOCs of the Trentino, Alto Adige and Friuli; ▷Vernaccia di San Gimignano.

NEW ZEALAND: ▷Chardonnay and also Pinot Blanc.

SPAIN: ▷Rueda.

Madeira

The small island of Madeira in the Atlantic Ocean lies closer to the coast of north Africa than to Portugal. Its island isolation has given it a very distinctive style of wine. As well as being fortified with grape brandy, Madeira is heated for a minimum of three months and maybe for as long as six months in an *estufa*, a special hothouse. The island was the last port of call for ships sailing to India before they crossed the equator and often they took on ballast in the form of wine, the flavour of which was found to have improved dramatically on arrival in India, after a long voyage which included two crossings of the equator. The modern *estufa* system imitates the conditions in the hold of the ship, subjecting the wine to the same constant heat.

There are four distinct styles of Madeira, from dry to sweet, Sercial, Verdelho, Bual and Malmsey, named after the principal grape variety of each wine. However all Madeira, be it sweet or dry, is characterised by a distinctive cooked flavour, combined with a high level of acidity, which contributes to its longevity. Madeira is the longest-lived of all wines and it is not uncommon to find vintages that are over a hundred years old. Within the four basic styles there are several different qualities, including five- and ten-year-old reserve wines, as well as the occasional vintage wines and even rarer wines aged in a *solera* system.

Sercial is light golden in colour and often has a rather cheesey, cooked nose. It is dry on the palate, with high acidity and a firm flavour. Verdelho is a little deeper in colour, a little sweeter on the palate and a little richer on the nose, with the characteristic cooked, caramel taste.

Bual is even richer, a mixture of caramel and cheese, developing more nutty flavours as it matures. There is a definite quality leap between Cossart Gordon's Good Company Bual, which is positively cheesey on the palate, while the five-year-old reserve is sweeter and nuttier, and the Duo Centenary Celebration Bual which is smooth and rich, with a dry caramel nose and a good underlying bite of acidity, but still leaving a full, rich mouthful of flavour.

Malmsey is richer still, especially if it is a ten-year-old reserve. It is deep brown in colour, with the distinctive yellow-green rim of sweet Madeira. It has a wonderful toasted caramel nose, with a very distinctive burnt caramel taste, with plenty of walnuts and fruit, finishing with a firm bite of acidity, to counterbalance the sweetness.

• **Vintages:** Rare and old; 1956 is one of the youngest available, also, 1950, 1934, 1927. They indicate a commercial decision, rather than a particularly outstanding year.

• **Recommended producers:** The Madeira Wine Company is a conglomeration of most of the old British firms, such as Cossart Gordon, Rutherford & Miles, Blandys and Leacocks, whose names are still preserved. Also Barbeito and Henriques & Henriques.

 Taste on:
SERCIAL:
PORTUGAL: White ▷port.

SPAIN: *Fino* and drier *amontillado* ▷sherry and ▷Málaga.

FRANCE: ▷Vin Jaune.

VERDELHO:
SPAIN: *Amontillado* ▷sherry, ▷Málaga, medium dry ▷Montilla.

ITALY: ▷Marsala, Vin Santo.

AUSTRALIA: Bleasdale in South Australia makes a comparable fortified Verdelho, a six-year-old and an even better sixteen-year-old.

BUAL:
SPAIN: *Oloroso* ▷sherry, ▷Málaga.

MALMSEY:
PORTUGAL: ▷Setúbal.

SPAIN: *Oloroso* ▷sherry, ▷Málaga, cream ▷Montilla.

ITALY: ▷Marsala.

AUSTRALIA: ▷Liqueur Muscat.

Madiran ▼

Madiran is a red wine from the foothills of the Pyrenees. The principal grape variety is Tannat, which is softened with some ▷Cabernet Sauvignon and Cabernet Franc. Madiran usually spends a few months in oak, which has a mellowing effect on this rather sturdy, solid red wine. It should have rich blackcurrant flavours, with a firm backbone of tannin, but is sometimes spoilt by puckering dryness indicating an excess of tannin. Madiran ages well and can be considered one of the most exciting and individual wines of southwest France.

● **Vintages:** 1990, 1989, 1988, 1986, 1985.

● **Recommended producers:** Château Montus, Château Boucassé, Château d'Aydie, Domaine de Teston, Château Arricau-Bordes.

Taste on:
FRANCE: Rouge de Béarn, the nearest red wine appellation to Madiran.
   Young ▷Cahors has a similar firm, rugged streak of tannin, but as Madiran matures, it becomes richer and less austere.
   ▷Claret, which is usually more elegant than Madiran.
   Other red wines from the southwest, namely ▷Bergerac, ▷Buzet.

ITALY: Cabernet Sauvignon/Sangiovese blends from Tuscany, such as Balifico, Bruno di Rocca and Alte d'Altesi, with some solid levels of tannin, balanced with rich, chewy fruit.

☙ Málaga

Málaga today is associated with package-holiday destinations whereas in the last century it was a very fashionable fortified wine, which was sometimes known as Mountain, a name you occasionally see on old decanter labels. The grape varieties are Pedro Ximénez and Moscatel, grown around the town of Málaga in southern Spain, and make a versatile range of wines. Málaga is always a fortified wine and is usually labelled according to its flavour, ranging from *seco* to *dulce*, and sometimes according to colour, *blanco*, *dorado*, *rojo-dorado*, *oscuro* or *negro*, (white, golden, tawny, dark and black). The grape variety may be mentioned, as in the case of Moscatel de Málaga, which is not so unlike ▷Muscat de Beaumes-de-Venise. The fermentation has been stopped by the addition of brandy and you are left with the ripe, pithy orange flavour of Muscatel grapes. Unlike other Málagas it is not aged in oak barrels, and so still retains the fresh flavour of the grapes.

Another possibility is Lágrima, which describes wine made only from the free-run juice pressed by the weight of the grapes, and then matured in wood for several years. It is an intense dark chocolate colour, with hints of Bovril on the nose, and the taste is rich and concentrated, so unctuously thick that you could almost stand a teaspoon up in it. It is sweet, but with a dry, firm finish, so that it does not cloy, but soothes the throat.

Finally, Málaga may be aged in a *solera* like ▷sherry and takes on some of the characteristics of sherry. Take Solera Scholts 1885 – the date here describes the starting date of the *solera* – which is quite deep brown in colour with rich moscatel flavours as well as walnuts, not unlike an old sherry or a ▷Liqueur Muscat from Australia. It is deliciously smooth and rich, with a firm finish. Málaga is undoubtedly one of the world's underrated wines, just waiting to be rediscovered.

- **Vintages:** Irrelevant.

- **Recommended producers:** Scholtz Hermanos.

Taste on:

SPAIN: ▷Sherry: equate *seco* to *fino*; *dulce* and *moscatel* to *oloroso* and cream; Solera Scholtz 1885 is reminiscent of a wonderful old *amontillado* sherry, while the Lágrima is like a very rich *oloroso*.

▷Montilla – again *seco* to dry, *dulce* to cream.

ITALY: ▷Marsala.

PORTUGAL: Moscatel de ▷Setúbal; *seco* equals a Sercial ▷Madeira and the Solera 1885 a Bual.

AUSTRALIA: ▷Liqueur Muscat.

FRANCE: ▷Muscat de Beaumes-de-Venise for Moscatel de Málaga, as well as other Muscat-based wines from the south of France.

 # Marsala

Marsala from the island of Sicily is Italy's answer to ▷sherry, with just as wide a range of flavours, depending on how long the wine is kept in wood; from one year for Fine and two for Superiore, five years for Vergine, up to as many as ten or more. There are colour variations too; *oro* (gold), *ambra* (amber) or *rubino* (ruby), and then it can be *secco* (dry) *semi-secco* or *dolce* (sweet). As with sherry, the vinification process involves the addition of brandy, as well as the ageing and blending of different wines. That is for the real thing. Unfortunately some horrible, confected wines, with flavourings like egg and coffee, have been masquerading as Marsala. A change in the regulations has reduced them to the status of *vino aromatizzato*.

Dry Marsala makes an original pre-dinner drink, as an alternative to sherry, while the sweeter Marsalas are best drunk afterwards. There is something distinctive about Marsala, a particular flavour that reminds me of Bovril. Star of all the Marsala producers is Marco de Bartoli who has upset the establishment with the quality and originality of his wines. Three are exported: Josephine Doré is firmly dry, with the distinctive Bovril nose, making it a cross between a *fino* and a dry *oloroso* sherry. Vigna La Miccia is a young Marsala, again slightly meaty on the nose with a sweetness akin to good *amontillado* sherry. Finally there is Vecchio

Samperi, aged for 20 years, which is rich and concentrated, just like a good *oloroso* sherry.

- **Vintages:** Marsala is always a blend of several years, and sold without a vintage date.

- **Recommended producers:** Marco de Bartoli is the star; also Rallo, Pellegrino, Florio.

Taste on:

SPAIN: ▷Sherry, with a comparable variety of flavours. *Dolce* would be cream sherry and *secco* would be fino, *vergine* probably *oloroso*, the permutations are infinite; ▷Málaga.

PORTUGAL: ▷Madeira for a similarity in the weight and feel of the wine.

Mateus Rosé

Mateus Rosé was one of the wine trade's great success stories. Not so long ago total sales stood at one million bottles a week, which represents no small drop in the world's wine consumption. It was the brainchild of the Guedes family in the 1930s, but sales really took off during the 1950s. It is easily recognisable by its distinctive dumpy bottle, with the picture of the Mateus Palace on the label. The owners of the palace made the wrong choice and opted for a safe option when the Guedes family offered them either a lump sum for the use of the picture of their palace or a royalty per bottle.

Mateus Rosé varies in taste on either side of the Atlantic. In North America it is a still wine and noticeably sweet, while in Britain it is lightly sparkling and only slightly sweet, light in alcohol at 11°, soft and fruity. Its appeal is that it is very undemandingly innocuous and easy to drink.

- **Vintage:** Drink as young as possible.

Taste on:

PORTUGAL: The principal Portuguese competitor is Lancers, a brand owned by another large wine company, J. M. da Fonseca.

ITALY: Pink ▷Lambrusco; pink Piemontello, a branded wine, made in Piedmont, which tastes like ▷Asti Spumante, but is the wrong colour!

SPAIN: Pink ▷Cava, for something a little drier and more positively sparkling.

FRANCE: Pink Crémant de Bourgogne, pink Crémant d'Alsace and even pink ▷Champagne, all of which are drier and fully effervescent. Alternatively avoid the bubbles with ▷Cabernet d'Anjou or Rosé d'Anjou.

 ## Médoc

The heart of the Médoc is made up of four villages, St-Estèphe, Pauillac, St-Julien and Margaux. Although these each has its own individual character that the finely tuned palate can recognise, it is possible to detect a broad similarity in the style of the wines of the Médoc. There is an elegance and a finesse about them that does not exist in ▷St-Emilion or Pomerol, while those of the Graves have a certain earthiness, that the French call *goût de terroir*, a taste of the soil. A good Médoc will always have a firm backbone of tannin, which mellows with age, but never entirely disappears. There is a positive structure to the wine, be it a simple appellation Médoc or a classed-growth ▷claret, with elegant cedarwood fruit, flavours reminiscent of pencil shavings and cigar boxes, and the blackcurrants that typify ▷Cabernet Sauvignon.

St-Estèphe is recognised by its element of austerity, while Pauillac is more opulently blackcurrant in flavour and a St-Julien has more elegant pencil shavings. Margaux comes between the two, with a certain richness. The classed-growth clarets, and also *crus bourgeois*, of the Médoc develop more complicated, complex flavours as they age in bottle. For instance a 1988 Pichon Comtesse Lalande will be a sturdy mouthful of tannin, with new oak and balancing blackcurrant fruit, while the 1970 vintage, when it was 20 years old had lost most but not all of its tannin and the oak flavours had mellowed with the blackcurrants into the most delicious glass of wine, slightly spicey, quite full, with lovely cedarwood fruit.

● **Vintages:** 1990, 1989, 1988, 1987, 1986, 1985, 1983, 1982, 1978, 1970.

● **Recommended estates:** Obviously many of the classed growths. The following are my favourites – St-Estèphe; Cos d'Estournel, de Pez, Meyney, les Ormes de Pez.

Pauillac: Grand-Puy-Lacoste, Haut-Bages-Libéral, Lynch-Bages, Pichon–Baron, Pichon–Lalande.

St-Julien: Léoville-Lascases, Léoville Barton, Langoa–Barton, Ducru–Beaucaillou, Beychevelle, Gruaud-Larose, Talbot, St-Pierre, Gloria.

Margaux: Palmer, Rausan-Ségla, d'Angludet.

From other villages: Chasse-Spleen, Cantemerle.

 Taste on:

FRANCE: Other appellations of the Médoc, such as Moulis, Listrac, Haut Médoc, ⊳St-Emilion, ⊳Graves; also ⊳Bergerac, ⊳Buzet, ⊳Cahors, ⊳Madiran.

ITALY: I find a similarity in structure between wines made from the Sangiovese of Tuscany and the Cabernet Sauvignon of the Médoc. A good ⊳Brunello di Montalcino, made purely from Sangiovese, has a similar leanness with a comparable flavour of cedarwood. Both are wines that develop with bottle age, acquiring elegance and subtlety. Try too some of the other pure Sangiovese of Tuscany. These are not wines that conform to the constraints of Italian wine law, and so will be labelled simply *vino da tavola*. Cepparello made by Isole e Olena is one such example; another is Capannelle. Although that does contain a drop of Canaiolo as well as Sangiovese, there is a similarity too in vinification techniques, with the use of new Bordeaux *barriques*.

Then there are the Tuscan Cabernet Sauvignons, of which the most notable example is Sassicaia, which came to prominence in a tasting of Cabernet Sauvignons from around the world, held about 15 years ago. That the winner should have come from Italy was indeed a surprise. The elegance, which is essential with classed-growth claret, is also an important characteristic of Sassicaia. Solaia, Tavernelle and Cabernet di Miralduolo are other pure Tuscan Cabernets.

Finally, Cabernet Sauvignon is often blended with Sangiovese in Tuscany, making an excellent combination of flavour and structure. Try ▷Tignanello, Sammarco, Balifico, Concerto, Grifi and others.

USA: ▷California Cabernet Sauvignon, and also from Long Island, Washington State and Texas.

▷AUSTRALIA: Cabernet Sauvignon.

▷NEW ZEALAND: Te Mata's Coleraine Cabernet Sauvignon.

🍇 Merlot

Merlot is a vital ingredient in the red wines of Bordeaux, especially in ▷St-Emilion and Pomerol, where it is the prime grape variety, along with some Cabernet Franc and Cabernet Sauvignon. It is Merlot that gives Pétrus its ripe, plummy, opulent flavours of cedarwood and spice.

In France it is unusual to find Merlot as a pure varietal, except perhaps in the Midi, where it is one of the grape varieties grown to replace the less exciting flavours of Carignan and Cinsaut. There is a similarity with Cabernet Sauvignon; the colour is as deep, but the flavours are softer, more immediately fruity and chewier and sometimes more vegetal, with less blackcurrant.

This soft, chewy character is particularly noticeable in the Merlots of northeast Italy, of the Veneto and Friuli, which are fruity, easy-to-drink wines, but sometimes of little distinction. They tend to lack tannin and backbone. There is a little Merlot in Tuscany, usually intended for blending with Cabernet Sauvignon.

As for Spain, Miguel Torres in ▷Penedés has recently introduced a pure Merlot, with some ripe, plummy fruit.

There is Merlot all over Eastern Europe, in ▷Yugoslavia, Bulgaria, Romania and Hungary. From Hungary it is a bit earthy, with some ripe berry fruit, while Romanian Merlot is rather coarse with a sweet and sour flavour. In Bulgaria it is often blended with Cabernet Sauvignon.

You can find pure Merlot in California, but more often it is an adjunct of Cabernet Sauvignon, and very successfully so, contributing some ripe, plummy, spicey flavours. It also grows well in Washington State, but not in Oregon.

So far, Merlot has had less appeal in the southern hemisphere. In Australia they prefer to use Shiraz for blending with Cabernet

Sauvignon. There is the occasional example of Merlot in New Zealand and Chile.

 Taste on:

FRANCE: The châteaux of ⊳St-Emilion and Pomerol, notably Pétrus and Ausone. Palmer in the ⊳Médoc also has an unusually high proportion of Merlot in its make-up.

Also the satellites of St-Emilion: estates in the villages of Montagne-St-Emilion, Lussac-St-Emilion, St-Georges-St-Emilion and so on, as well as nearby Lalande de Pomerol, Côtes de Francs, Fronsac and Canon Fronsac.

⊳*Vin de pays* with Merlot on the label, such as Coteaux de l'Ardèche, Hérault and Aude.

ITALY: DOCs such as Collio, Colli Orientali del Friuli, Isonzo, Grave del Friuli.

SPAIN: From ⊳Penedés, Torres Merlot, with ripe, plummy, fruit.

USA: Washington State: Kiona Vineyards, Chinook Wines. California: Newton Vineyards, Duckhorn Vineyards, Rutherford Hill Winery.

CHILE: Errázuriz-Panquehue.

NEW ZEALAND: Less popular than Cabernet Sauvignon, but Esk Valley Merlot is a worthy exception.

🐂 Meursault

For Meursault, also read the other fine white wines of the Côte de Beaune, the southern half of the Côte d'Or, from the villages of Puligny-Montrachet and Chassagne-Montrachet, including the various *grands* and *premiers crus* of these villages, such as Bâtard-Montrachet, les Clavoillons, les Pucelles and most famous of all, le Montrachet, as well as Corton-Charlemagne, from the village of Aloxe-Corton.

There is nothing quite like really fine white Burgundy. It represents the greatest examples of ⊳Chardonnay. These are wines that are kept in oak barrels for several months, and maybe also fermented in oak. They have rich, complex flavours, ripe, buttery, toasted fruit that develops even greater subtlety with age. They are usually quite high in alcohol, and therefore mouthfilling, but not as heavy as some Chardonnays from California or Australia. Good Meursault should always retain the elegance that is the hallmark of fine white burgundy.

* **Vintages:** 1990, 1989, 1988, 1986, 1985, 1982, 1981, 1978.

* **Recommended producers:** From the Côte de Beaune, not just Meursault: Coche-Dury, Guy Roulot, Matrot, Michelot-Buisson, Olivier Leflaive, Ballot-Millot, Blain-Gagnard, Bonneau du Martray, Etienne Sauzet, Chartron et Trebuchet, Yves Boyer, Henri Germain, Jean-Paul Gauffroy, Jean-Noël Gagnard, Simon Bize, Domaine Leflaive, Comte Lafon, François Jobard.

Taste on:

Chardonnay has travelled the world. You will find it in Spain, Italy, California, Australia, New Zealand, Chile, Argentina and Bulgaria, and for most of these wines the producers are looking to Meursault and Montrachet for their inspiration.

SPAIN: Sometimes what we appreciate in Chardonnay is not the actual flavour of the grape but the deliciously toasted taste of the oak barrels. This explains why otherwise competent tasters can mistake other quite dissimilar grapes for Chardonnay for they are confusing fruit with oak. Traditional white ▷Rioja is an obvious taste comparison. Take Marqués de Murrieta or CVNE's Monopole, wines which have spent several months in oak barrels, so that they develop a firm, nutty flavour which can be confused with Chardonnay. I certainly made that mistake as an aspiring Master of Wine.

As well as traditional white Rioja, try Chardonnay from ▷Penedés, from Jean Léon, and also Torres oak-aged Gran Viña Sol, which includes a substantial percentage of Chardonnay along with local varieties.

FRANCE: There is also a similarity between mature white ▷Graves from an estate like Domaine de Chevalier or Château Laville-Haut-Brion. The grape varieties may be quite different but the vinification methods, with the use of oak, are comparable and thereby the structure of the wine, with rich, leafy, mature flavours that may taste remarkably like fine burgundy.

▷Chablis *grands crus* like Les Clos, Vaudésir and Bougros are comparable in weight and richness to the white wines of the Côte de Beaune. The basic difference is a lean streak of acidity, but in a hot year, such as 1986, the difference between Vaudésir and Meursault is less marked.

There is the odd Chardonnay ▷*vin de pays* from the Midi, such as Domaine de St-Martin-la-Garrigue, whose owner planted Chardonnay for the simple reason that he adores white burgundy. He ages his wine in oak, and is aspiring to emulate Meursault.

ITALY: Experiments with Chardonnay are widespread in Tuscany; some ignore oak barrels, so that the wines have more of a resemblance to Chablis, while others are mastering the art of barrel-ageing, and even barrel-fermentation. The relatively recent Predicato del Muscho entails a significant proportion of Chardonnay in the blend and there are numerous pure Chardonnays too, notably Le Grance from Caparzo in Montalcino, I Sistri from Felsina Berardenga in Chianti Classico, Il Cabreo from Ruffino, Il Marzocco from Avignonesi, all aspiring Meursaults, with varying degrees of success. Try too, Cervaro della Sala from Antinori's estate in Orvieto.

In Piedmont, Angelo Gaja has produced a Chardonnay, with some success, sold under the name of Gaia e Rey.

USA: Numerous wineries in California (▷California Chardonnay) are making some deliciously toasted alternatives to Meursault, with elegantly nutty flavours and buttery overtones. Oregon and Washington State also producing some serious Chardonnays, as does New York State, notably in Long Island, from Palmer and Bridgehampton and also from Wagner Vineyards in the Finger Lakes.

AUSTRALIA: Sometimes the flavours of ▷Australian Chardonnay are a little blowsy, with too much tropical fruit and not enough elegance. However some people are getting it right, particularly in the cooler regions.

In the same way that white Graves can be a lateral taste for Meursault, so is ▷Sémillon from Australia. The taste is not the same, but there is a similarity in the feel of the wine, notably in old bottles of Sémillon from the Hunter Valley, that are more often than not labelled Chablis!

CHILE: Some good oak-aged Chardonnays are beginning to appear, notably from Santa Rita, Viña Carmen, Errázuriz-Panquehue and Montes.

▷NEW ZEALAND: Chardonnay.

Minervois ▼

Minervois comes from the foothills of the Massif Central behind the medieval city of Carcassonne. This is another sturdy red wine to go with the wild, arid scenery. There is white and pink Minervois too, but serious Minervois is firmly red, coming from the usual grapes of the south of France, Carignan, Grenache, Cinsaut, as well as some improving Syrah or Mourvèdre, to give extra spice and flavour. Winemaking techniques have improved enormously in this part of France in the last few years, with immense efforts being taken to extract maximum flavour from the grapes. Its success is there to be tasted in the wine. Good Minervois is full-bodied, rich and spicey, with herbal overtones. There is a rugged, meaty quality about it, with a rough backbone of tannin.

• **Vintages:** 1990, 1989, 1988, with little significant vintage variation in this part of France.

• **Recommended producers:** Domaine de Ste-Eulalie, Château de Gourgazaud, Daniel Domergue, Château Fabas, Château de Paraza, Domaine de la Senche, Jacques Maris, Cave Coopérative de Lavinière.

Taste on:
FRANCE: ▷Corbières, ▷Coteaux du Languedoc, especially the districts of Faugères, St-Chinian and La Clape, and ▷Fitou, where the grape varieties are almost identical.

▷Crozes Hermitage and St-Joseph from the Rhône have a similarity to Minervois with a high proportion of Syrah in the blend.

PORTUGAL: ▷Bairrada.

Monbazillac

Monbazillac is the sweet white wine of the Dordogne, coming from vineyards just south of the town of Bergerac. Ideally, climatic conditions are such that the grapes are attacked by noble rot, as in ▷Sauternes and ▷Barsac, but in many years this does not happen and Monbazillac is simply made from overripe grapes. In the past Monbazillac has been spoilt by excesses of sulphur and sugar, but now things are looking up. Good Monbazillac is honeyed and peachy, with some ripe fruit. It should not be cloying, but it will never be quite as subtle nor as concentrated in flavour as Barsac or Sauternes. It is also rather cheaper. It is made from the same grape varieties, Sauvignon, Sémillon and Muscadelle, as the sweet wines of Bordeaux and in the best years can mature into fine old bottles.

● **Vintages:** 1990, 1989, 1988, 1986, 1985, 1983, 1981, 1980, 1978, 1976, 1975.

● **Recommended producers:** Château Treuil de Nailhac, Château La Borderie, Château de Monbazillac, Château Sépty.

Taste on:
FRANCE: The lesser sweet white appellations of Bordeaux, such as Loupiac, St-Croix du Mont, Cadillac and Premières Côtes de Bordeaux.

One estate in the ▷Graves, Château St-Georges, produces sweet wine, contrary to the expectations of the appellation, as the vineyards adjoin those of Sauternes; ▷Sauternes; ▷Barsac; ▷Jurançon *moelleux*.

From the Loire Valley, ▷Coteaux du Layon, Bonnezeaux and Quarts de Chaume, as well as ▷Vouvray *moelleux*.

GERMANY: ▷Auslese is the equivalent degree of ripeness.

CALIFORNIA: Late harvest wines, though they tend to be even sweeter, and often made from Riesling, and so a quite different flavour.

Montilla

Montilla comes from southern Spain, not too far from sherry country. The term *amontillado*, which is commonly used to describe medium sweet ▷sherry, simply means 'in the style of Montilla', which would imply that sherry was imitating Montilla, rather than the other way round. Montilla has acquired a rather dubious reputation as 'a poor man's sherry'. It is cheaper than sherry for the very good reason that it is often unfortified, while sherry always has some brandy added to it. The ageing period for Montilla is also considerably shorter, which also makes the wine less expensive.

Since 1985 Spanish wine law has defined two categories of Montilla, the light, unfortified wines, with no wood-ageing, and the heavier, wood-aged wines, which may or not be fortified. Montilla can be dry, medium or sweet. The use of the terms *fino*, *amontillado* and *oloroso* is restricted to the fortified wines.

Although Montilla can have quite a high natural alcohol level, it does not have that crisp, firm bite of sherry. You can immediately detect the lack of fortifying brandy, so that the wine seems a little flabby in comparison. Dry Montilla has always reminded me of melons, while medium Montilla has something of sherry trifle, with oranges and cinnamon. Cream Montilla is richer and more raisiny.

• **Vintages:** Not sold with a vintage date.

• **Recommended producers:** Alvear, Carbonell, Gracia Hermanos.

 Taste on:
SPAIN: ▷Sherry, with dry for *fino*, medium for *amontillado* and sweet for cream.
▷Málaga.

PORTUGAL: Moscatel de ▷Setúbal.

FRANCE: Rivesaltes.

Moulin-à-Vent

Moulin-à-Vent is one of the ten ▷Beaujolais *crus*, named quite simply after a windmill that stands in the middle of the vineyards. Like all Beaujolais, it is made from the Gamay grape, but of all the Beaujolais *crus*, it has the reputation, which is generally confirmed in the glass, for having more body, guts, flavour and tannin than the others. Usually Moulin-à-Vent is made to last a few years, even as long as 30 in the case of the great vintages, like 1947. Normally however, six to ten years is usually sufficient for it to turn into a wine with a taste more in common with the red burgundies of the Côte d'Or, than neighbouring Beaujolais. Young Moulin-à-Vent has ripe plummy fruit, with some tannin and a bit of acidity. It then goes through an awkward phase when it is neither Beaujolais nor burgundy, and then, if you are patient, it does a chameleon act, developing some of the chocolatey, farmyard flavours of the Côte d'Or.

- **Vintages:** 1991, 1990, 1989, 1988, 1987, 1985, 1983, 1981, 1978, 1976.
- **Recommended producers:** Château de Jacques, la Tour de Bief, Georges Duboeuf's single domaines, Paul Janin.

Taste on:
FRANCE: The other nine Beaujolais *crus*, with apologies for a list: Fleurie, Saint-Amour, Brouilly, Côte de Brouilly, Morgon, Juliénas, Chénas, Chiroubles, and the most recently recognised, Regnié.

▷Volnay and ▷Gevrey-Chambertin from the Côte d'Or.

▷Red wines from the Loire Valley, Bourgueil, St-Nicolas de Bourgueil, ▷Chinon and ▷Saumur-Champigny, with a similar weight and plummy fruit to young Moulin-à-Vent.

Muscadet

I used to have rather negative feelings about Muscadet. When I was studying for the Master of Wine exams, there was a sure way of recognising it, namely by process of elimination. If we had a slightly sour white wine that smelt faintly or even strongly of sulphur and tasted of nothing in particular, then it had to be Muscadet. But that was ten years ago and things have improved dramatically since then as the leading growers have done much to enhance the quality of their wines.

Muscadet comes from the Atlantic end of the Loire Valley, from a grape variety that is also called Muscadet. This large area is divided into three appellations of which the largest and best is Muscadet de Sèvre et Maine. The mention *sur lie* quite often features on the label and means that the wine has been bottled off the fine lees or sediment of the fermentation, so that the merest prickle of carbon dioxide remains in the wine to give it freshness and zest. Sadly, sometimes this is abused by the artificial addition of extra carbon dioxide.

Good Muscadet is firmly dry, with a stoney acidity and lively freshness. It certainly should not have any sulphurous overtones. It is low in alcohol with, unusually for France, a maximum as opposed to a minimum alcohol requirement, of 12.3°, making for quite a delicate wine. A handful of *avant garde* growers are experimenting with wood-ageing for their wine. To my mind this completely deforms the taste of Muscadet for the somewhat ethereal flavours of the grape are completely overwhelmed by the taste of wood.

● **Vintages:** Drink the youngest available. Muscadet is not generally considered to be a wine for keeping, although there are occasional exceptions.

● **Recommended producers:** Sauvion at Château de Cléray, and also their Lauréat label, Chéreau-Carré, Château de Chasseloir, Marquis de Goulaine, Métaireau, Donatien-Bahuaud, Domaine des Dorices, Château la Touche, Guy Bossard, Château la Noë.

 Taste on:
FRANCE: The adjoining VDQS of Gros Plant du Pays Nantais, which is even greener and more acidic than Muscadet can be.

Further along the Loire Valley there is the little-known vineyard area of Cheverny ♥♥ where they grow an even less familiar grape variety, called Romorantin. That made by Francis Huguet has herbal hints on the nose, but the palate is certainly reminiscent of good Muscadet, firm and stoney with a crisp finish.

Bourgogne ▷Aligoté, ▷Côtes de Gascogne, ▷Apremont and Abymes from Savoie.

163

ITALY: The dry white wines of northern Italy tend to be fuller in body. However some also have a similar crispness of flavour, such as Carlo Deltetto's ▷Gavi dei Gavi, with dry, grassy fruit and a hard finish. His Favorita del Piemonte, from an unusual local grape variety that is enjoying something of a revival in popularity, has a dry, stoney character, not unlike a good Muscadet.

SPAIN: The white wines of ▷Rueda in northern Spain, notably Marqués de Riscal Blanco and Marqués de Griñon have a dry, firm acidity, with delicate, stoney fruit, that make an original alternative to Muscadet.

Alella, a DO for white wine, just northeast of Barcelona, can be rather sharp and green, like Muscadet.

PORTUGAL: ▷Vinho Verde, with its crisp acidity.

🍇 Muscat

Muscat has one of the most distinctive flavours of any grape variety, for unlike any of the others, it really does taste of the grape, of those succulent, luscious Italian Moscatel table grapes, with a juicy freshness, sometimes tempered with pithy orange overtones.

There are three main varieties of Muscat, Muscat d'Alexandrie, Muscat *blanc à petits grains* and Muscat Ottonel, which between them make the world's Muscat-flavoured wines. Moscatel is simply another name for Muscat d'Alexandrie, and Muscat Canelli a synonym for Muscat *à petits grains*. There is little obvious difference of taste between the three.

Muscat can be vinified as a table wine, as in ▷Muscat d'Alsace, or fortified by the addition of brandy, as in ▷Muscat de Beaumes-de-Venise or Australian ▷Liqueur Muscat. As a table wine, it may be sweet or dry, while as a fortified wine, it will always be sweet. It is also used for sweet sparkling wine, notably for ▷Asti Spumante.

Muscat in one form or another grows in many different parts of the world, Alsace, the Rhône valley, the south of France, northern Italy, Spain, Portugal, Eastern Europe, Greece, California, Australia and South Africa.

Taste on:

FRANCE: ▷Muscat d'Alsace, ▷Muscat de Beaumes-de-Venise, Muscat de Frontignan, Muscat de Rivesaltes, Clairette de Die Tradition.

ITALY: Goldmuskateller and Rosenmuskateller from the Alto Adige; ▷Asti Spumante; Moscato di Pantelleria, a fortified wine from the tiny island of Pantelleria, which lies between Sicily and north Africa.

SPAIN: ▷Málaga; Moscatel de Valencia.

PORTUGAL: Moscatel de ▷Setúbal; João Pires dry Muscat.

HUNGARY: Hungarian Muscat.

GREECE: Muscat of Samos, Muscat of Lemnos, Muscat of Patras.

AUSTRALIA: ▷Liqueur Muscat, Dry Muscat, Late Harvest Muscat.

USA: California: Moscato d'Oro from Robert Mondavi, Quady's Essensia Orange Muscat.
Washington State: Château Ste. Michelle Muscat Canelli, Cascade Estate Winery Muscat Canelli.

NEW ZEALAND: Matua Valley Late Harvest Muscat.

Muscat d'Alsace

Unlike all the other major wine regions of France, Alsace places more emphasis on the grape variety than on the particular provenance of the grapes. Muscat is one of those grape varieties. It has a very distinctive grapey flavour. Unlike virtually any other wine, Muscat d'Alsace does actually smell and taste of grapes. The nose is immediately reminiscent of ripe Moscatel table grapes from southern Italy, while the palate is drier, with a slight pithy, some say catty, character, tinged with bitter orange peel. It is instantly refreshing and often drunk in Alsace as an aperitif.

Muscat is one of the four grape varieties which may be grown on a *grand cru* site. It is also occasionally used for *Vendange Tardive* (late harvest) and *Sélection de Grains Nobles* (selection of superior overripe grapes) wines.

- **Vintages:** 1990, 1989, 1988; drink as young as possible to retain the fresh, grapey character.

- **Recommended producers:** Kreydenweiss, Zind-Humbrecht, Kuentz-Bas, Becker, Hugel, Trimbach, Domaine Weinbach, Lorentz, Muré.

 Taste on:

FRANCE: ▷Gewürztraminer d'Alsace; the spiciness of Gewürztraminer can sometimes be confused with the grapiness of Muscat. The chances are that if you like one, you will like the other, as they are both packed with lots of positive character. There is nothing ephemeral or wishy-washy about either.

In the south of France, Muscat is most commonly grown to make a sweet dessert wine such as ▷Muscat de Beaumes-de-Venise or Muscat de Rivesaltes. However Muscat de Rivesaltes has not been selling too well lately and instead the grapes have been turned into table wine, for a Vin de Pays Catalan, or Vin de Pays des Pyrenées Orientales cépage Muscat. They retain the characteristic pithy orange flavour of the grape, but lack the elegance and depth of those of Alsace.

ITALY: Goldmuskateller and pink Rosenmuskateller from the Alto Adige.

SPAIN: Torres Vina Esmeralda from ▷Penedés, with two parts Muscat to one part Gewürztraminer.

PORTUGAL: João Pires dry Muscat from ▷Setúbal.

GERMANY: Morio-Muscat on the label indicates a pithy, orange-flavoured, spicey wine, which will probably be sweeter than a Muscat d'Alsace, and also lower in alcohol.

HUNGARY: Muscat with some recognisable varietal flavour.

AUSTRALIA: Brown Brothers Dry Muscat.

ARGENTINA: Torrontes ❦❦, from the country's most northerly vineyards, and also highest in altitude in the province of Salta. This is Argentina's most individual grape variety for it is not a direct import from Europe, but said to be a mutation of Malvoisie, brought from the Canaries in the 1550s. It has a gentle aromatic fragrance, and some of the pithy orange character of Muscat with a little sweetness. Bodegas Etchart and Michel Torino are the best producers.

Muscat de Beaumes-de-Venise

Muscat de Beaumes-de-Venise is the best known of all the fortified Muscat wines of France. Its flavour is very distinctive: once tasted, never forgotten. It makes a delicious dessert wine, with sweet apricots, pithy oranges, honey and toffee, a full-flavoured mouthful, with the weight of the additional alcohol. But sometimes it is just too heavy and there are more delicate, but less well-known examples of Muscat from elsewhere in France.

● **Vintages:** Drink the youngest and freshest available.

● **Recommended producers:** Domaine Durban, Domaine de Coyeux, Jaboulet, the village cooperative.

Taste on:

FRANCE: Muscat de Frontignan ❦❦ from the Mediterranean coast is lighter and more subtle when it comes from Château la Peyrade.

Muscat de St-Jean de Minervois ❦❦, from a little village in the corner of the appellation of ▷Minervois, is often neglected in a line-up of Muscats. Look out for Domaine Barroubio and Domaine Sigé.

Muscat de Rivesaltes comes from a large area in the foothills of the Pyrenees behind Perpignan. The flavours are either lemony and honeyed, or fuller, with the taste of pithy bitter oranges and underlying richness. Domaine de Sarda-Malet favours the delicate, less cloying style, as do Cazes Frères, while that sold under the Arnaud de Villeneuve label is fuller and richer.

Muscat de Lunel, a tiny appellation between Montpellier and Nîmes, and Muscat de Mireval, which adjoins Muscat de Frontignan, are the final two French alternatives.

ITALY: The tiny island of Pantelleria which lies between Sicily and the north African coast is known for its Moscato or Muscat wines. Look for Moscato di Pantelleria ♥♥, not to be confused with Moscato Passito di Pantelleria. *Passito* means that the grapes have been dried after they were picked, so that the taste of the wine is raisiny and reminiscent of ▷port. Plain Moscato di Pantelleria from Marco de Bartoli, the leading producer, has delicious fresh perfumed orange flavours.

SPAIN: Moscatel de Valencia, with some pithy oranges and ripe marmalade and toffee fruit. Likewise Moscatel de Málaga.

GREECE: Muscat of Samos, made from dried grapes and tasting of toffee apples, is more like a liqueur Muscat from Australia, while Muscat of Limnos is fresh and grapey, with the distinctive orange tang.

USA:
California: The small Californian winery of Quady specialises in fortified wines, notably their Essensia Orange Muscat, which is redolent of pithy oranges, but sometimes a little cloying for my taste.

Robert Mondavi's Moscato d'Oro.

Washington State: Muscat Canelli from Château Ste. Michelle and Cascade Estate Winery.

NEW ZEALAND: Matua Valley's Late Harvest Muscat may not be a fortified wine, but it has the similar rich concentrated sweetness.

AUSTRALIA: Late Harvest Muscat, such as Brown Brothers Late Picked Muscat, and even better Orange Muscat and Flora; also Tolleys Late Harvest Muscat.

SOUTH AFRICA: Muscat de Montac.

 Nahe – Schlossböckelheim

The Nahe is one of the smallest wine regions of Germany and a tributary of the Rhine, joining the river at Bingen. Its vineyards are surrounded by those of the Mosel, the Rheinhessen and the Rheingau, and thus they are a melting pot, sharing some of the characteristics of each. You can find the steely, slatey character of the Mosel, some of the honeyed elegance of the Rheingau and a little of the fuller, grassier flavours of the Rheinhessen. As elsewhere on the Rhine, the ▷Riesling grape makes the best wines and in good vintages these mature into wonderful bottles, with apricots and peaches, honey and acidity.

- **Vintages:** 1990, 1989, 1988, 1985, 1983, 1976, 1975, 1971.

- **Recommended producers:** State Domain at Schlossböckelheim, Crusius, Anheuser.

Taste on:
The Bereich of Schlossböckelheim includes the whole of the southern Nahe, while Bereich Kreuznach covers the northern part of the area. Village names not only include Schlossböckelheim, but also Niederhausen, Norheim, Rüdesheim and Bad Kreuznach. The three vineyards of Schlossböckelheim are Kupfergrube, Königsfel and Felsenberg.

The most obvious taste comparisons are with the other wine regions of northern Germany, ▷Bernkastel, ▷Johannisberg, ▷Rheinpfalz-Deidesheim, ▷Nierstein.

Try ▷Kabinett, ▷Spätlese, ▷Auslese, ▷Beerenauslese and ▷Trockenbeerenauslese quality wines from these regions.

▷Riesling d'Alsace and New World Rieslings are usually too heavy and alcoholic, while Riesling Renano from Italy seems to lack the quintessential honeyed quality of German Riesling. However try:

USA: White or Johannisberg Riesling from cooler Oregon.

NEW ZEALAND: Cooks Marlborough Rhine Riesling; Hunters Estate Rhine Riesling; Giesen Dry Riesling.

ᛦ Navarra

Navarra lies immediately north of Rioja on the vineyard map of northern Spain. The DO covers red, white and pink, but the whites are insignificant. Best are the pinks or *rosado*, and young fruity reds made mainly from the Garnacha grape, with an increasing amount of Tempranillo and also Cabernet Sauvignon.

The pinks are dry and delicate, with herbs and raspberries, while the reds are soft and plummy and best drunk young, as Garnacha tends to fade rather quickly. However if they are made from Tempranillo, and even some Cabernet Sauvignon, they have a little more staying power, with some fuller, chewy, spicey blackcurrant fruit.

● **Vintages:** 1991, 1990, 1989, 1988, 1987, 1986, 1985, 1984, 1983, 1982, 1981.

● **Recommended producers:** Bodegas Bardón, Bodegas Ochoa, Chivite, Señorio de Sarria.

Taste on:
RED:
SPAIN: Other red wines from the northern part of the country: 3- or 4-year-old ▷Rioja, but no older; Somontano from Aragon; ▷Toro.

FRANCE: Wines from the south, with a proportion of Garnacha, or Grenache as it is called in France, such as ▷Corbières, ▷Minervois, ▷Coteaux du Languedoc, La Clape.

PINK:

SPAIN: ▷Rioja.

FRANCE: ▷Côtes de Provence, ▷Tavel.

ITALY: Vin Ruspo, the pink wine of Carmignano.

New Zealand Cabernet Sauvignon

New Zealand has established her reputation for white wines, but her reds have also gained in stature over the last three or four vintages, notably ▷Cabernet Sauvignon, which is sometimes blended with ▷Merlot. There are wines being made with good varietal character. They sometimes lack the weight and depth of Cabernet Sauvignon grown in a hotter climate and may be criticised for being a little herbaceous, green and grassy on the palate. However, others have the concentrated ripe blackcurrant flavours, characteristic of well-made Cabernet Sauvignon, with tannin, elegance and some potential for ageing in bottle.

- **Vintages:** 1991, 1990, 1987, 1986, 1985.

- **Recommended producers:** Redwood Valley, Esk Valley, Cooks, Lincoln, Montana, Te Mata, Matua Valley, Vavasour, Villa Maria, Vidals, Brookfields, Kumeu River.

Taste on:
Other cool climate Cabernet Sauvignon:

FRANCE: Cabernet Franc as well as Sauvignon from the Loire Valley such as Bourgueil and ▷Chinon.
  ▷Claret from some of the peripheral areas like Premières Côtes de Bordeaux, Côtes de Francs, Lalande de Pomerol, and even the ▷Médoc.

ITALY: Cabernet from Trentino and Friuli.

USA: Washington State Cabernet Sauvignon, from Columbia Crest Winery, Hogue Cellars, Gordon Brothers Cellars.

❦ New Zealand Chardonnay

New Zealand Chardonnay gets better and better, as the winemakers gain in experience and the vines grow in age. The cool climate of New Zealand helps to avoid some of the intensely tropical fruit flavours of Australia, making for more balanced levels of acidity and a more subtle taste of the grape. Chardonnay is usually kept in oak for a few months and is often fermented in barrel too. There are rich, buttery flavours, with the toasted character that comes from charred barrels, as well as a good level of acidity and an underlying elegance.

● **Vintages:** 1991, 1990, 1989, 1988, 1986.

● **Recommended producers:** Babich with their Irongate Vineyard at Hawkes Bay, Kumeu River, Villa Maria, Matua Valley, Coopers Creek, Cloudy Bay, Te Mata's Elston Chardonnay, Martinborough Vineyards, Neudorf Vineyards, Morton Estate.

 Taste on:
FRANCE: ▷Meursault and Puligny-Montrachet are what New Zealand winemakers are striving to emulate and to some extent they are succeeding; ▷Rully in the Côte Chalonnaise, and maybe *Grand Cru* ▷Chablis.

▷AUSTRALIA: Chardonnay.

USA: Chardonnay from ▷California, Washington State and Long Island.

CHILE: Chardonnay.

ITALY: Chardonnay from Tuscany, classified Predicato del Muschio.

SPAIN: Jean Léon's Chardonnay from Penedés.

❦ New Zealand Pinot Noir

Some of the most successful Pinot Noir outside Burgundy comes from New Zealand. Her cool-climate vineyards, especially Martinborough to

172

the north of Wellington, and those in the South Island such as Canterbury and Central Otago seem to be particularly suitable for this temperamental grape variety, providing a long ripening season, so that delicate flavours are achieved, with the true vegetal character of Pinot Noir and a lovely sweet, chocolatey finish. The handful of producers are still learning how to master this problematic grape variety, determining which are the best clones to plant and how exactly to vinify their grapes. Red wine production here has only begun to gather momentum in the last five years and it would be impossible to find a Pinot Noir from New Zealand older than 1986. However, a handful of committed producers are convinced of the fantastic potential of New Zealand Pinot Noir and the rewards are great.

•   **Vintages:** 1991, 1990, 1989, 1988, 1986.

•   **Recommended producers:** Martinborough Vineyards, Waipara Springs, St Helena.

Taste on:
FRANCE: ▷Gevrey-Chambertin; ▷Volnay; ▷Irancy.

USA: ▷California Pinot Noir.

New Zealand Sauvignon

The development of New Zealand wines is one of the great success stories of the 1980s. It seems incredible, considering the popularity of New Zealand Sauvignon that Sauvignon was first planted in Marlborough, on the South Island, less than twenty years ago and that the very first commercial vintage of Montana's Marlborough Sauvignon was as recent as 1980. Within ten years New Zealand Sauvignon has established itself as one of the most characteristic and typical benchmark examples of that variety, for the cool climate of the Antipodes particularly favours this pungently aromatic grape variety.

There are two distinct styles of New Zealand Sauvignon, depending on whether the wine is vinified with oak or without. The second is the most characteristic, giving pungent green pea and gooseberry flavours on both nose and palate. There is an intense, fresh, crisp acidity, with ripe fruit that makes New Zealand Sauvignon most appealing. Comparisons with the Sauvignons of the Loire Valley are inevitable.

New Zealand Sauvignon has an intensity and concentration, while Loire Sauvignon is lighter, more subtle and less obvious.

In contrast, Sauvignon that has been kept for a few months in oak is less intensely aromatic, but fuller and more buttery. Sometimes you can taste the buttery vanilla flavours of the oak; sometimes there are hints of tropical fruit and generally it is a richer, more mouthfilling wine, sometimes with more in common with Sauvignon from Bordeaux.

● **Vintages:** 1991, 1990, 1989, 1988, 1987, 1986; these are not wines to keep for more than two years, although a recent tasting of Montana Marlborough Sauvignon provided plenty of exceptions to the rule, with the 1980 still showing some lively fruit.

● **Recommended producers:** Cooks, Morton Estate, Selaks, Delegats, Montana, Nobilo, Cloudy Bay, Stoneleigh, Matua Valley, Kumeu River, Brookfields, Hunters.

 Taste on:
FRANCE: Sauvignon from the Loire Valley such as ▷Sauvignon de Touraine, ▷Pouilly-Fumé, ▷Sancerre, Reuilly, Quincy, Menetou-Salon, Sauvignon du Haut Poitou.
▷Graves.

ITALY: Sauvignon from northeast Italy, the Alto Adige, Trentino and Friuli. The DOC Collio gives the most pungent results.

Tuscany, with the classification Predicato del Selvante for Sauvignon. Poggio alle Gazze is one of the best examples of Tuscan Sauvignon.

USA: Sauvignon and Fumé Blanc from ▷California, Washington State and Texas.

AUSTRALIA: Sauvignon and Fumé Blanc, but it is generally nowhere as successful as from across the Tasman Sea.

SOUTH AFRICA: Sauvignon from wineries such as L'Ormarins.

CHILE: Sauvignon from Torres, Canepa.

♈ Nierstein – Rheinhessen

The village of Nierstein epitomises the wines of the Rheinhessen, which is Germany's largest wine region, bordered by the river Rhine in the north and east and the ▷Nahe to the west. The best wines come from the villages of the Rheinfront between Dienheim and Nackenheim with Nierstein at their centre. The Riesling grape has never been quite as important in the Rheinhessen as in the other Rhineland vineyards. In recent years Sylvaner has lost out in importance to Müller-Thurgau and newer varieties like Kerner and Scheurebe.

The wines of the Rheinhessen come between those of the Rheingau (▷Johannisberg) and the ▷Rheinpfalz in weight and flavour. The further south you go in Germany, the fuller the wines become, so while the Rheingau retains a stylish elegance, making the wines of the Rheinpfalz seem almost clumsy in comparison, those of the Rheinhessen bridge the gap between the two. They are softer and grassier, with less elegance, but nonetheless delicious. Kerner gives particularly good results in the Rheinhessen, with pithy, lemony flavours and hints of honey in ▷Spätlese wines. Often, more prosaically, the Rheinhessen is the most common source of ▷Liebfraumilch.

- **Vintages:** 1990, 1989, 1988, 1985, 1983.

- **Recommended producers:** Lingenfelder, Louis Guntrum, Anton Balbach.

Taste on:

GERMANY: The best-known name of the Rheinhessen has to be the ubiquitous Niersteiner Gutes Domtal, which covers a large number of vineyards and villages. There is not much difference betwen it and a Liebfraumilch. Much more distinguished are the single vineyards of Nierstein, with names like Hipping, Pettenthal and Rothenberg, while Spiegelberg, Auflangen and Rehbach are *Grosslagen* or groups of vineyards. Other villages in the Rheinhessen include Nackenheim, Oppenheim, Guntersblum, Bodenheim and Alsheim.

Wines from the villages of ▷Johannisberg, Deidesheim and Schlossböckelheim, ▷Kabinett, ▷Spätlese, ▷Auslese, ▷Beerenauslese and ▷Trockenbeerenauslese quality.

▷Rieslings from California, Oregon, Australia and New Zealand.

175

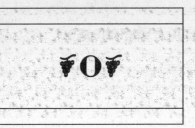

🍇 Oak

Many of the world's fine wines, especially red but also some white wines, spend a few months, or even years, in oak barrels before they are bottled. Some white wines, notably ▷Chardonnay from the Côte d'Or and ▷California, are also fermented in oak. This will have a perceptible effect on the taste of the wine, particularly if the barrels are new. The taste of oak is usually much more obvious in a young wine. In France and the New World they generally use French oak such as Allier, Tronçais, Nevers or Limousin, while American oak is traditionally used in Spain. It is this that gives wines like ▷Rioja a very pronounced vanilla taste.

New oak can immediately be identified by a sweet vanilla bouquet and taste. In the case of white wine, when the barrels have been charred, the wine will have a nutty toasted nose and taste, or if the barrels have been steamed, the flavours may be more buttery. The oak should not over-power the fruit flavours of the wine, though sometimes it does. Its use should be the same as with garlic in cooking, its presence should not immediately be detectable, but the flavour would be that much poorer without it. Small oak barrels, such as the standard Bordeaux *barriques* of 225 litres, have a much greater impact than the large barrels of several hectolitres that are used for ▷Barolo or ▷Brunello di Montalcino.

A wine really needs a certain structure and weight to benefit from oak ageing. If the initial flavours are too light and ephemeral, they are completely overwhelmed by the contact with oak and you are left with what one French winemaker called '*une infusion de chêne*'. In other words the wine tastes as though a tea bag of oak chippings has been dunked in it for so many months or minutes. However, in the right context the influence of an oak barrel adds an extra indefinable something to the wine.

There are wines in which the use of oak is very much more apparent than in others, such as:

Taste on:

FRANCE: Very young classed-growth ▷claret.
Anything with the words *vielli en fut de chêne*, or *cuvée bois*, on the label, which tells you that the wine has been aged in oak barrels, and which may not be a practice normal for the area, for example in ▷Muscadet.
▷Meursault and other fine white burgundy.
▷Gevrey-Chambertin and other fine old burgundy.

SPAIN: ▷Rioja *riserva* and *gran riserva*; ▷Ribera del Duero.

CALIFORNIA: ▷Chardonnay, ▷Cabernet Sauvignon, ▷Fumé Blanc.

AUSTRALIA: ▷Cabernet Sauvignon, ▷Chardonnay, ▷Sémillon.

Organic Wine

Organic describes a style of winemaking rather than a taste of wine. The prevailing preoccupation with healthier living leads us to question the use of chemicals in food production, including wine. A winemaker who follows organic practices in the vineyard uses no chemical weedkillers, insecticides or fertilisers, and works to maintain the natural balance in the soil with humus and manure. In the cellar the use of sulphur dioxide is limited to the absolute minimum and some other substances allowed in conventional winemaking are also forbidden.

An organic wine should be judged by the same standards as any other wine and no allowances should be made for the fact that it is organic. As with other wines, there are badly made organic wines and brilliant ones. One of the problems with organic wine is that there is no universal code of practice, and a multitude of different organisations exist, with slightly differing philosophies. France alone has as many as fourteen different associations involved with organic agriculture, of which about half are concerned with wine, such as Nature et Progrès, Terre et Vie and Demeter. In England organic winemakers follow the principles of the

Soil Association. There are also those winemakers who continue to use the traditional practices of their grandparents, who most years make what could be classed as organic wine, perhaps without realising it. Climate plays its part here for it is much easier to practice organic viticulture in dry, sunny Provence, where the Mistral prevents problems with rot and humidity, than it is in damp, rainy Muscadet.

 Taste on:
Organic winemakers include:

FRANCE: Guy Bossard in Muscadet; Côtes de Provence – Domaine de Richeaume; Domaine des Terres Blanches in the Coteaux d'Aix-en-Provence; ▷Meursault from Jean Javillier; Puligny-Montrachet from Jean-Claude Rateau; Château Jacques Blanc in St-Emilion; Pierre Frick, André Stentz, Eugène Meyer in Alsace; Domaine Font de Michelle in ▷Châteauneuf-du-Pape; André and Jacques Beaufort in Champagne; Jean Musso in the Côte de Beaune; Chateau de Caraguilhes in Corbières; Mas de Daumas Gassac in the Midi.

ITALY: San Vito in Fior di Selva in ▷Chianti; Guerrieri-Rizzardi in the Veneto; Mario Pasolini in Brescia.

NEW ZEALAND: Millton Estate.

AUSTRALIA: Botobolar Vineyard.

ENGLAND: Sedlescombe Vineyard.

🐂 Orvieto

Orvieto, the best white wine of Umbria, comes from vineyards around the hilltop town of the same name. It is made from a mixture of grape varieties, which include Trebbiano, as well as Grechetto and Verdello, which give a little more character. Usually Orvieto is dry (*secco*), though you can also find medium sweet (*abboccato*), which may even come from grapes that have been affected by noble rot. *Classico* describes wines that come from the very heart of the production area.

Dry Orvieto is slightly leafy, slightly nutty, with hints of bananas, a touch of cream and a note of smokiness on the finish. As *abboccato* it becomes fuller, with some honey, peaches and cream, and maybe a hint of the roasted flavour that comes from noble rot. *Abboccato* in Italy equates to the French *moelleux* or German ▷Spätlese, or maybe ▷Auslese.

● **Vintages:** 1990, 1988, 1986, 1985; drink within a year or three of the harvest. *Abboccato* will age a few years more.

● **Recommended producers:** Bigi with its Torricella vineyard, Berberani, Decugnano dei Barbi. Antinori owns Castello della Sala, where it makes wines that do not conform to the DOC regulations, notably dry Cervaro della Sala and sweet Muffato della Sala.

 Taste on:

DRY:
Other white wines of central Italy, such as ▷Frascati, Marino, Torgiano Bianco, Pomino, Bianco Val d'Arbia.

SWEET:
FRANCE: ▷Vouvray *demi sec* or *moelleux*, for *abboccato*; ▷Coteaux du Layon; ▷Jurançon *moelleux*; ▷Monbazillac.

GERMANY: ▷Spätlese, ▷Auslese.

YUGOSLAVIA: Tiger Milk.

 Othello

Othello is the red counterpart of ▷Aphrodite, and is the standard red wine of Cyprus, produced by one of the large island wine cooperatives, Keo. No one grape variety accounts for its flavour, but a mixture of various indigenous grapes like Mavron and Ophthalmo.

The vines grow in the poor, arid foothills of the Troodos Mountains. In summer it is scorchingly hot, and the warmth comes out in the wine. There is a dry, tarry flavour, with hints of spice and warm, stoney flavours, but little tannin.

● **Vintages:** No vintage variation, but drink within a year or three of the harvest, as these are not wines to age.

 Taste on:

CYPRUS: Other Cypriot red branded wines like Othello, with names like Afames and Domaine d'Ahéra.

179

GREECE: Full, earthy red wines like Naoussa and Nemea.

ITALY: Cirò, a full-bodied, warm, earthy wine from Calabria.

FRANCE: There is something a hint Rhônish about Othello, so maybe ▷Côtes du Rhône; ▷Châteauneuf-du-Pape would be flattery. ▷Coteaux du Languedoc, with Faugères, or maybe ▷Fitou.

PORTUGAL: ▷Dão.

SPAIN: ▷Jumilla.

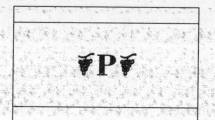

❦ Penedés

For most lovers of Spanish wine, Penedés means Torres, the family who have really put Penedés on the world wine map with an exciting and experimental range of different wines. This is, of course, somewhat unfair to the several other very good producers in the region, such as Jean Léon and Cavas Hill. Penedés is a region where native Spanish grape varieties blend happily with imported varieties from France and Germany, as the Torres range demonstrates so well.

Take whites first. Viña Sol is a dry white made from Parellada, one of the three native white varieties of Penedés. Winemaking techniques have been perfected, to extract the maximum amount of flavour out of this rather neutral grape, so that the resulting wine has a dry, clean flavour, with a crisp, firm finish. Gran Viña Sol contains a substantial dollop of Chardonnay and has been kept in oak for a few months, which gives the wine a certain burgundian flavour. Gran Viña Sol Green Label includes some Sauvignon with the Parellada and is full-flavoured and oaky. Viña Esmeralda, a ▷Muscat and ▷Gewürztraminer blend, has more in common with Alsace than northern Spain, with its bitter orange flavours of Muscat and spicey fruit, while Waltraud, made from ▷Riesling, has the floral character of that variety.

As for red wines, the basic Tres Torres, from traditional grape varieties like Ull de Llebre and Monastrell, is dry and peppery, while Gran Sangre de Toro has a fuller, meatier flavour. Coronas is altogether a smoother style of wine, with vanilla and ripe fruit and a vegetal, burgundian finish. Gran Coronas ❦, with a serious proportion of Cabernet Sauvignon, is a more substantial wine, with an underlying flavour of blackcurrants and firm tannin, while Gran Coronas Black Label, or Mas la Plana as it is now called, is pure Cabernet Sauvignon. The newest in the range is Viña

Las Torres, a pure Merlot, aged in French oak, which is ripe and plummy, with a dry finish.

- **Vintages:** 1991, 1990, 1989, 1988, 1985, 1984, 1983, 1982, 1981,

- **Recommended producers:** Jean Léon for ▷Cabernet Sauvignon and ▷Chardonnay; Marqués de Monistrol for fruity dry whites; Mont Marçal; Cavas Hill.

 Taste on:

Several regions of the world meet in the cellars of Miguel Torres. So if you like his wines try some of the following:

Viña Sol has some of the dry, neutral character of southwest France, so try a white Bordeaux like ▷Entre-Deux-Mers, or ▷Bergerac, Côtes de Duras and some of the rather neutral white wines of central Italy such as ▷Galestro, ▷Orvieto, Bianco Val d'Arbia.

For Gran Viña Sol try ▷Meursault; and also traditional white ▷Rioja; ▷California Chardonnay; ▷Australian Chardonnay.

For Viña Esmeralda try ▷Gewürztraminer d'Alsace and ▷Muscat d'Alsace; Australian Dry Muscat; João Pires dry Muscat from Portugal.

For Waltraud try Australian Riesling from the Barossa Valley; Torres Chilean Riesling.

Tres Torres and Gran Sangre de Toro both have a southern French, Rhônish character, so try ▷Minervois, ▷Corbières, Gigondas and ▷Côtes du Rhône. As for Coronas, I must admit to mistaking it for burgundy in a blind tasting, so try ▷Volnay and ▷Gevrey-Chambertin; also ▷Rioja and ▷Navarra.

For Gran Coronas and Mas la Plana try ▷St-Emilion; ▷California Cabernet Sauvignon; ▷Australian Cabernet Sauvignon.

For the wines of Jean Léon – his Cabernet Sauvignon equates to Gran Coronas and his Chardonnay to Gran Viña Sol so try the wines suggested for these.

🍇 Piat d'Or

Although Piat d'Or can be red, white or pink, for most people, thanks to the telly ads, it is a red wine. There is a rumour that the red version was test-marketed by using ▷Liebfraumilch coloured with cochineal. That may be unfounded, but the fact remains that for a red wine, Piat d'Or is remarkably sweet. If you tasted it with your eyes closed, you would think you were drinking a smooth, medium dry white wine.

The precise origins of Piat d'Or are deliberately vague. All we know is that it comes from somewhere in France, probably from grapes grown in the Midi and from wines blended to a required recipe. If you like your red wine slightly sweet, perhaps you should really be drinking white wine, as there are very few sweet red wines.

 Taste on:

GERMANY: White as well as red wines. Wines labelled ▷Spät-lese, both red and white, if they do not also say ▷*trocken* or ▷*halbtrocken*, will have some residual sweetness.

ITALY: Lagrein Dunkel from the Alto Adige has some soft fruit, without any aggressive edges of tannin. Teroldego Rotaliano from Trentino can have soft, jammy, berry fruit.

EASTERN EUROPE: ▷Cabernet Sauvignon from Yugoslavia which tends to have some underlying sweetness; likewise Pinot Noir from Romania.

CALIFORNIA: Basic red jug wine.

🍇 Pinotage

Pinotage is a South African peculiarity, a curious crossing of Pinot Noir from Burgundy and Cinsaut from the south of France, that was developed there in the 1920s. It is also occasionally to be found in California, New Zealand and Zimbabwe.

Although Pinotage may be seen as a South African original, the flavours are not as exciting as either Shiraz or Cabernet Sauvignon from South Africa. When young it produces some rather chewy, earthy wines, with rubbery overtones, and warm berry fruit. Older bottles can develop into something a little more distinctive and individual, a meaty, spicey mixture with mint and eucalyptus fruit. The danger is that the taste is sometimes diluted by excessively high yields.

● **Vintages:** 1991, 1990, 1989, 1988, 1987, 1986, 1984, 1982, 1980.

- **Recommended producers:** Delheim, Kanonkop, Middelsvlei, Simonsig, Backsberg, Vriesenhof.

Taste on:
SOUTH AFRICA: Other South African reds, like KWV's Roodeberg, which is a blend of Cabernet, Shiraz, Pinotage and others, or Rustenberg's Dry Red, a Cabernet Merlot and Cinsaut blend.

PORTUGAL: Dão.

FRANCE: ▷Bandol, ▷Châteauneuf-du-Pape, ▷Fitou, ▷Côtes du Rhône.

Pinot Blanc d'Alsace

Unlike most other wine-producing regions of France, Alsace gives greater prominence on the label to grape variety than to precise vineyard provenance. Pinot Blanc is not generally given as much attention as the other more distinctive varieties such as ▷Gewürztraminer and ▷Riesling, nor can it produce *grand cru* wines, nor *Vendange Tardive* or *Sélection de Grains Nobles*. Its charm is its immediate appeal of easy drinkability, with lightly grassy, gentle, buttery fruit and good acidity. There is nothing aggressive or hard in its flavour. Often Pinot Blanc includes another very similar grape variety, Pinot Auxerrois. One or two growers pay it a little more attention, such as Jos Meyer, who makes a wine from older vines grown on a *grand cru* site, Domain Ostertag, where they age it in oak, and Marc Kreydenweiss, who makes a Late Harvest wine. However, these are exceptions to the rule and usually Pinot Blanc d'Alsace is a light, fruity wine, with hints of spice, that is often drunk in the region as a very pleasant aperitif.

- **Vintages:** 1990, 1989, 1988; drink the youngest available.

- **Recommended producers:** Jos Meyer, Marc Kreydenweiss, Domaine Ostertag, Hugel, Trimbach, Cave Vinicole de Turckheim, Schlumberger, Marcel Deiss.

Taste on:
FRANCE: Sometimes there is little to distinguish between lighter, unoaked ▷Chardonnay and good Pinot Blanc, so try

▷Mâcon Blanc Villages, and even ▷Chablis, also Chardonnay du Bugey.

GERMANY: Pinot Blanc here is called Weissburgunder and, if fermented dry to make a ▷*trocken* wine, can be similar to that of Alsace. After all, the vineyards of ▷Baden are just across the Rhine, so that a Baden *trocken* 1989 Malterdinger Bienenberg Weissburgunder is virtually indistinguishable from a Pinot Blanc d'Alsace. A Pinot Blanc from Karl Johner in the Kaiserstuhl of Baden, aged in oak for six months, is rich and buttery, with a firm, oaky finish.

ITALY: ▷Pinot Bianco.

YUGOSLAVIA: Pinot Blanc, which is a coarser version of Pinot Blanc d'Alsace.

NEW ZEALAND: St. Helena Pinot Blanc ❦❦, with buttery, grassy fruit.

USA: California: Chalone Vineyards are one of the very few Californian wineries to take any interest in Pinot Blanc. Oregon: Cameron Winery in the Willamette Valley.

❦ Pinot Bianco

North eastern Italy is where Pinot Bianco comes into its own. You find Pinot Blanc on a label in Alsace and Weissburgunder in Germany and Austria, but elsewhere ▷Chardonnay is very much the flavour of the moment. In fact there is quite a lot of confusion between the two grape varieties, particularly as the leaves look very similar and that is the principal way to identify a vine.

The taste can be pretty similar too. Pinot Bianco has a gentle buttery flavour, light and creamy with firm acidity. It has less weight and depth than Chardonnay and certainly responds less well to oak ageing. However it is not difficult to confuse a young Pinot Bianco and a young Chardonnay if they both come from, for example, the Alto Adige. Both have a light buttery taste, with acidity.

Pinot Bianco features in most of the DOCs of north eastern Italy, in the Alto Adige, Trentino and Friuli. Look for Pinot Bianco di Trentino,

Collio, Colli Orientali, Grave del Friuli or from the Alto Adige, where, thanks to historical accidents of boundaries and language, it is also called Südtiroler Weissburgunder.

- **Vintages:** 1990, 1989, 1988; drink within two to four years.

- **Recommended producers:** Abbazia di Rosazzo, Volpe Pasini and Ronco del Gnemiz in Friuli. Tiefenbrunner, Lageder, Hofstätter and Giorgio Grai in Alto Adige. Jermann and Pojer e Sandri in Trentino.

 Taste on:

ITALY: Pinot Bianco from elsewhere in Italy especially in the DOC of Breganze, in the Veneto, where Maculan is the outstanding name. Although it is concentrated in northeast Italy, you also find it as far south as Puglia at Castel del Monte.
 ▷Chardonnay from the Trentino, Alto Adige and Friuli.
 Other Italian DOCs, not necessarily made from Pinot Bianco, but with a comparable light, grassy, creamy flavour, such as Montecarlo ❦❦ and Pomino in Tuscany.

FRANCE: ▷Pinot Blanc d'Alsace.
Pursuing the similarity with Chardonnay: young ▷Chablis and young ▷Mâcon Blanc ❦.

GERMANY: Weissburgunder from ▷Baden.

AUSTRIA: Weissburgunder, also called Pinot Blanc, from George Stiegelmar and Lenz Moser.

❦ Pinot Grigio

Pinot Grigio from Italy may be the same grape variety as ▷Pinot Gris d'Alsace, but it just does not taste the same. Whereas Pinot Gris from Alsace is usually a full-bodied, characterful, spicey wine, Pinot Grigio from Trentino, Friuli and Alto Adige so often tends to be somewhat nondescript and just a hint neutral. It is generally rather light, with a bit of fruit and some acidity, and a hint of spice, if you really look for it. Much, of course, depends on individual producers and vineyards. When properly vinified in the right hands, it does actually have more flavour than Pinot Bianco, and in Italy itself it is rated higher than Pinot Bianco. The DOCs of Collio and Colli Orientali in Friuli make some of the most flavoursome wines; Grave del Friuli tends to be rather neutral.

● **Vintages:** 1990, 1989, 1988, 1987; drink within three or four years.

● **Recommended producers:** Marco Schiopetto, Jermann, Lageder and Russiz Superiore.

 Taste on:

ITALY: Confusingly, as Pinot Gris is called Tokay in Alsace, there is a grape variety that grows extensively in northeastern Italy called Tocai Friuliano, or Tocai Italico in the Veneto, which is no relation at all to Pinot Grigio, but is not dissimilar in taste.
▷Pinot Bianco.
Other Italian dry whites such as ▷Galestro, Bianco di Custoza, Lugana, even ▷Soave for some more flavour.

FRANCE: ▷Pinot Gris d'Alsace, for more impact.

GERMANY: Wines made from Ruländer, though they will be richer and spicier.

HUNGARY: Badacsonyi Pinot Gris.

🐂 Pinot Gris d'Alsace

Unlike all the other important wine regions of France, Alsace pays greater attention on the label to the grape variety than to the vineyard. However as Pinot Gris is one of the four grape varieties in Alsace that is eligible to make *grand cru* wines, as well as *Vendange Tardive* and *Sélection de Grains Nobles*, it does sometimes feature with a vineyard name.

Pinot Gris in Alsace was traditionally called Tokay d'Alsace, but the bureaucrats of the Common Market have determined that it causes confusion with ▷Tokay from Hungary, with which it bears no resemblance whatsoever in taste, and have tried to prevent the use of the term Tokay d'Alsace. Nowadays, labels tend to be a compromise, using both names.

To my tastebuds, Pinot Gris d'Alsace has a spicey character that is not unlike that of Gewürztraminer, except that it is much more subtle and less obvious. If you like one, you will probably like the other, as they are both typical of the quintessential flavours of Alsace. Like Gewürztraminer there is a certain weight and oiliness in the mouth, with a nose that reminds me of mushrooms, or what the French sometimes call *sous bois*, meaning the slightly musty smells of undergrowth in the woods. Sometimes I detect apricots on the palate and sometimes Pinot Gris has a slightly smokey character. In a sweet *Sélection de Grains Nobles* ♥♥♥ Pinot Gris can be a deliciously ripe, mouthfilling wine, with mushrooms and apricots.

- **Vintages:** 1990, 1989, 1988, 1985, 1983, 1981, 1976.

- **Recommended producers:** Domaine Weinbach, Muré, Théo Cattin, Hugel, Trimbach, Léon Beyer, Schlumberger, Marc Kreydenweiss, Jos Meyer, Zind Humbrecht.

 Taste on:

FRANCE: ▷Gewürztraminer d'Alsace.

GERMANY: Pinot Gris is called Ruländer and grown above all in ▷Baden.

ITALY: ▷Pinot Grigio.

HUNGARY: Badacsonyi Pinot Gris, with slightly sweet, mushroomy fruit.

Pinot Noir

Pinot Noir is the grape variety of fine red burgundy. It is at its absolute best in the vineyards of the Côte d'Or, where it can produce some simply sublime flavours, that are delicately velvety, silky smooth, chocolatey and a little vegetal, or maybe even a lot if you believe the line in Anthony Hanson's authoritative book on burgundy that all great burgundy smells of shit. Fine red burgundy can be magic, while bad red burgundy is one of the most disappointing tastes in the wine spectrum.

One of the reasons for this is that Pinot Noir is a temperamental grape variety, difficult to vinify and also reluctant to adapt to other parts of the world. In France it is also the grape variety of red and pink ▷Sancerre and Menetou-Salon and Rouge d'Alsace. You also find it in Saint Pourçain, in the Jura and as a vital part of most ▷Champagne blends. Across the border in Germany it is known as the Spätburgunder and grown in ▷Baden, Württemberg and the Ahr valley, to make rather light, often sweet, pale red wine.

Pinot Noir in northern Italy lacks varietal character and is usually somewhat uninspiring. In England there are two solitary examples, from Bernard Theobald at Westbury and from Thames Valley Vineyard, which deserve marks for trying. In Eastern Europe, ▷Romania is the most successful to date.

▷California Pinot Noir has improved significantly in the last few years. The hot climate does not always lend itself to subtlety and elegance, but there has been more planting in cooler areas like Carneros. There is an element of rivalry with cooler Oregon, which also produces some fine examples of Pinot Noir. In Australia its success is limited to the few cooler vineyard areas, such as the Yarra Valley of Victoria, the Adelaide Hills of South Australia, and Tasmania. The cool climate vineyards of New Zealand – Martinborough and the South Island – offer terrific potential for Pinot Noir, while South Africa has yet to prove itself with this grape variety.

Young Pinot Noir is reminiscent of raspberries, with some underlying fresh acidity. As the wine matures, the flavours develop, filling the mouth, taking on vegetal overtones, or maybe chocolate. The tannin fades and the taste becomes smoother and sweeter. Bad Pinot Noir can be bitter or jammy, burnt or wishy-washy. Good Pinot Noir is unforgettable, both rich and elegant; then it is sublime and unequalled.

 Taste on:

FRANCE: Red burgundy, from ▷Bourgogne Rouge to Romanée Conti, including ▷Irancy, ▷Gevrey-Chambertin ❦❦❦, ▷Volnay ❦❦❦. The name of the grower is as, if not more, important than the name of the vineyard.

From the rest of France try ▷Sancerre Rouge, Menetou-Salon Rouge ❦❦, Rouge d'Alsace, ▷Côtes du Jura Rouge includes Pinot Noir.

GERMANY: Spätburgunder *trocken* from Lingerfelder is one of the most successful examples of real Pinot Noir from Germany; that of Carl Heinz Johner is also good.

AUSTRIA: Pinot Noir from Georg Stiegelmar, with a taste of dry raspberries. The more common Austrian grape, St. Laurent, has a jammy similarity to Pinot Noir.

ITALY: Tondo Nero from Ruffino in Tuscany; Ca' del Bosco's Pinero and Bellavista's Le Casotte from Franciacorta and La Stoppa's Alfeo in the Colli Piacentini of Lombardy. It also features in the DOCs of the Alto Adige, Trentino and Friuli but rarely excites.

USA: ▷California: Acacia, Chalone, Schug Cellars, Robert Mondavi, Au Bon Climat, Saintsbury, Dutton Ranch from the Kistler Estate.
Washington State: Salishan Vineyards, Columbia Winery.
Oregon: Ponzi, Eyrie Vineyard, Bethel Heights.

NEW ZEALAND: Martinborough Vineyards ❦❦, St. Helena, Waipara Springs, Rippon Vineyards.

AUSTRALIA: Bannockburn Vineyard in Geelong, Coldstream Hills, St. Huberts and Tarrawarra Vineyard in the Yarra Valley.

▷ROMANIA: Pinot Noir ❦.

BULGARIA: Curiously the Bulgarian grape Gamza has a simi-larity in taste to Pinot Noir. It is by no means as stylish or elegant, but a young wine from Suhindol has a soft, jammy fruit, with a dry finish, while a ten-year-old Gamza from the same region has a slightly earthy flavour, with overtones of fruitcake, not unlike a rather elderly burgundy.

❦ Port

Port has been called the Englishman's wine, for it was the English merchants of the eighteenth century who did so much to make it the wine that it is today, adding brandy to the young wine, which enabled it to withstand an Atlantic voyage. Port remains a ▷fortified wine, coming from the Douro valley and from a mixure of different grape varieties.

There are several different types of port. Basic port is ruby or tawny or, less commonly, white. Ruby only ever describes a young wine, which is sold after two or three years' ageing in wood, and the same applies to white port. True tawny port ♥♥♥ may be aged for ten, twenty, even forty years in wood, so that it turns a brick orange or tawny colour with age. Cheap tawny on the other hand is usually a blend of ruby and white port.

Most prestigious of all is vintage port. A vintage is not declared every year, but only when the wine is good enough to withstand a long period of ageing in bottle. Alternatives are available. Some shippers produce a single-*quinta* wine, that is from one of their best vineyards, such as Taylor's Quinta de Vargellas, in years that are not good enough for the declaration of a vintage. Another possibility is late-bottled vintage which is, as the name implies, a wine from a single year, that is bottled three or four years later than is usual for a fully fledged vintage port. This is an economical way of producing a vintage-style wine. A wine labelled vintage character (a term which replaces the old crusted port, so-called as it grew a crust or sediment) may be emulating vintage port, but is very much lighter, with less staying power.

As for taste, white port is the least interesting of all. It is light golden in colour and has the faint liquorice nose that is typical of port. The liquorice repeats on the palate, making a slightly sweet, mouthfilling, nutty flavoured wine.

Ruby port is a deep red colour, with a fruity liquorice flavour and a rather spirity, alcoholic finish as the brandy has not yet blended properly. It is usually slightly sweet. Cheap tawny port will be lighter but not dissimilar to ruby in taste, while mature tawny that is at least ten if not twenty years old is quite another taste. It is richly mellow and nutty, redolent of liquid walnuts, very elegant, long and lingering.

As for vintage port, when it is immature, it is very concentrated in flavour with fruit and tannin and spirit. As it ages, it mellows in flavour to become smooth and elegant, with some delicious liquorice fruit that is laced with prunes and spices, and an underlying soft sweetness. Usually, but depending on its age, it has more body than a tawny port of similar years.

Late-bottled vintage port is drunk younger than vintage port, as it has spent more time in wood. It, too, has a concentrated liquorice flavour, but without the weight and staying power of true vintage port. Wines from single *quintas* such as Vargellas, Croft's Quinta da Roeda or Dow's Quinta do Bomfim come between the two in weight and quality, meriting some bottle age, while late-bottled vintage is ready to drink soon after it is bottled. Vintage character port is really only one step up from ruby port.

- **Vintages:** A vintage was generally declared (but not by every port house as it is an individual decision) in 1985, 1983, 1982, 1980, 1977 (the best of the decade), 1975, 1970, 1966, 1963 (the best since 1945), 1960, 1955, 1950, 1948, 1945.

- **Recommended producers:** Churchill, Cockburn, Croft, Dow, Delaforce, Fonseca, Offley, Quinta do Noval, Sandeman, Smith Woodhouse, Taylor, Graham, Warre, Ferreira.

Taste on:

WHITE PORT:
PORTUGAL: Sercial from ▷Madeira.

SPAIN: *Amontillado* rather than *fino* ▷sherry and dry ▷Montilla.

ITALY: Vin Santo ❦❦.

RUBY PORT OR VINTAGE CHARACTER:
FRANCE: *Vin doux naturel* from the south, such as a Rivesaltes called Rimage; young Banyuls from Robert Doutres, with spirity, liquorice fruit.

ITALY: Aleatico di Portoferraio from Elba, with some sweet, plummy perfumed fruit; Sagrantino di Montefalco *passito* ❦❦ from Umbria, made from dried grapes, to give a wine with a sweet port-like flavour, but with a slightly lower degree of alcohol; Valpolicella Recioto Classico, made from partially dried grapes, very rich and raisiny with concentrated liquorice fruit.

GREECE: Mavrodaphne, with sweet, luscious fruit, and overtones of black treacle and toffee.

CALIFORNIA: Quady's Elysium from Black Muscat grapes; Quady's Starboard (double entendre!) Batch 99 Ruby.

TAWNY PORT (ten or twenty year old):
FRANCE: Mature *vin doux naturel* from the south of France, such as Vieux Rivesaltes, old Banyuls and 15-year-old Maury ❦❦.

ITALY: Anghelu Ruju from Sella & Mosca in Sardinia, a fortified wine with a nutty, fruitcake flavour ❦❦.

AUSTRALIA: Galway Pipe from Yalumba, which has some delicious dry walnut fruit; Château Reynella 10-year-old tawny.

VINTAGE PORT: No other wine has quite the stature and style of fine vintage port. The lateral alternatives come under ruby port.

Pouilly-Fuissé

For some reason this appellation of southern Burgundy has become an object of fashion, beset by excessive prices out of proportion to its flavour and quality. Pouilly-Fuissé (not be be confused with ▷Pouilly Fumé from the Loire Valley) is yet another example of ▷Chardonnay. The best can aspire to emulate the wines of the Côte d'Or, probably not ▷Meursault, but certainly lesser villages such as St-Aubin or St-Romain, and also the Côte Chalonnaise and ▷Rully. Alternatively, it can be just a little dull and uninspiring with more in common with the neighbouring plain ▷Mâcon Blanc Villages.

- **Vintages:** 1990, 1989, 1988, 1986, 1985, 1983.

- **Recommended producers:** Château Fuissé, especially the Cuvée Vieilles Vignes, Vincent, Corsin.

Taste on:

FRANCE: ▷Chablis of *premier cru* quality, say a Fourchaume, that is half way between ▷Meursault and ▷Mâcon in style and flavour; ▷Beaujolais Blanc; neighbouring Pouilly-Vinzelles and Pouilly-Loché; ▷Rully, as well as Montagny and other white wines from the Côte Chalonnaise.

ITALY: ▷Vernaccia di San Gimignano, and the other more flavoursome Tuscan whites, such as Pomino and Montecarlo. Also lighter Chardonnay, from Tuscany, such as Capezzana and Avignonesi's Terre di Cortona.

SPAIN: ▷Penedés whites with a touch of Chardonnay, such as Torres' Gran Viña Sol.

NEW ZEALAND: Many New World Chardonnays tend to be heavier and richer, with more buttery and nutty flavours. New

Zealand, with its cooler climate, making for more reticent flavours, may be the possible exception.

🍇 Pouilly Fumé

Pouilly Fumé from the Loire Valley is the twin of ▷Sancerre and likewise known for pungent white wines from the ▷Sauvignon grape. However, unlike Sancerre, it is only ever white. The taste is reminiscent of gooseberries, with an attractive flinty pungency and crisp acidity. The finish is firm and dry.

● **Vintages:** 1990, 1989, 1988. In very hot years such as 1989, Pouilly Fumé tends to be just a little flabby, while in unripe years, it can be somewhat green. Generally it is best to drink the youngest vintage available, as the Sauvignon grape does not have much ageing potential. However the wines of one of the best producers, Château du Nozet, are the exception to the rule, developing softer, more elegant flavours with some bottle age.

● **Recommended producers:** Patrick de Ladoucette at Château du Nozet is generally acknowledged to be one of the best, albeit the most expensive, especially his Baron de L, in this small appellation, whose wines are much in demand, with prices accordingly under considerable pressure. Also Château de Tracy, Didier Dagueneau, Michel Redde, Jean-Claude Guyot, Guy Saget.

 Taste on:
FRANCE: Sauvignon that has not come into contact with oak barrels makes for wines with such a distinctive character that any lateral thoughts are inevitably based upon the same grape variety. The obvious alternatives are the other white wines of what are called the Central Vineyards of the Loire Valley, namely ▷Sancerre, Menetou-Salon, Reuilly and Quincy, for the vineyards are nearby and the grape variety is identical.

NEW ZEALAND: The most characteristic examples of Sauvignon from the New World undoubtedly come from New Zealand. The Sauvignon grape flourishes in the cool climate of these antipodean vineyards, epitomised by Cloudy Bay, or less fashionable and therefore more easily available, Montana Marlborough Sauvignon.

SOUTH AFRICA: The estate of L'Ormarins makes Sauvignon with the refreshing pithiness of the Loire Valley.

CHILE: ▷Chilean Sauvignon from two good producers, Canepa and Torres. Other Chilean Sauvignons have more in common with Bordeaux than with the Loire Valley.

Retsina

Retsina is the most individual of Greek wines, maintaining a centuries-old tradition for adding resin from the Aleppo pine trees to the fermenting wine, as a means of preserving the finished wine. Most retsina comes from Attica.

Retsina is unique. You either love it or hate it. Somehow it epitomises the taste of Greece, with its sharp bite of ginger – others may unkindly prefer to describe it as turpentine – from the resin, which seems to complement the flavours of Greek food so well. Good retsina is light golden in colour, with a hint of amber. It should be fresh and lively, with a very firm attack in the mouth, and never flat and lifeless. The resin dominates the palate to the extent that you can forget that this drink ever originated from grapes.

- **Vintages:** Drink the youngest available.

- **Recommended producers:** Kourtakis, Boutari, Tsantali.

Taste on:
SPAIN: No other country produces anything quite like retsina! But for a similar one-dimensional flavour try traditional oak-aged white ▷Rioja, in which the oak completely dominates the palate, with a firm, dry bite, not so very unlike the effect of the resin in retsina.

FRANCE: ▷Vin Jaune.

▼ Rheinpfalz – Deidesheim

The Rheinpfalz or Palatinate is Germany's largest wine-producing region. Bordering France on the south and southwest, it forms a natural continuation of the vineyards of Alsace and, as in Alsace, the climate is dry and sunny. ▷Riesling is far less important here than in the more northern vineyards of the Rhine, although it is still the prime grape variety on the very best sites. However, you will also find Scheurebe, Kerner, Gewürztraminer, Morio-Muscat and so on, and red varieties such as Portugieser and Spätburgunder, otherwise known as ▷Pinot Noir. ▷*Trocken* and ▷*halbtrocken* wines are also popular, and generally more successful than from further north. Deidesheim is the biggest village of the Rheinpfalz, with vineyards such as Hohenmorgen, Paradiesgarten and Mäushöhle.

The flavours of the Rheinpfalz, thanks to its warm, dry climate, are much richer and fuller than those of the Rheingau or Mosel. The wines have full, ripe flavours, mouthfilling honey and apricots, but lack the steely liveliness of the Mosel or the delicate elegance of the Rheingau. The taste of course varies with grape variety and Prädikat.

- **Vintages:** 1990, 1989, 1988, 1985, 1983, 1976, 1971.

- **Recommended producers:** von Buhl, Basserman-Jordan, Bürklin-Wolf, Deinhard, Fritz-Ritter, Lingenfelder.

Taste on:

GERMANY: The other villages of the Rheinpfalz, such as Ruppertsberg, Bad Durkheim, Kallstadt, Forst and Wachenheim. Some of the most famous vineyards of the Rheinpfalz are in the village of Forst, namely Jesuitengarten, as well as Ungeheuer and Freundstück.

Other regions of Germany: ▷Bernkastel, ▷Nahe-Schlossböckelheim, ▷Johannisberg, ▷Nierstein and ▷Baden.

From all these regions try ▷Kabinett, ▷Spätlese, ▷Auslese, ▷Beerenauslese, ▷Trockenbeerenauslese, ▷*trocken* and ▷*halbtrocken* wines.

FRANCE: ▷Gewürztraminer d'Alsace for Gewürztraminer from the Rheinpfalz; ▷Muscat d'Alsace for Morio-Muscat.

AUSTRIA: The wines of Austria come closer to those of the Rheinpfalz than any other part of Germany. Grape varieties vary, but there is a similarity in ripeness and weight; compare Prädikats, Spätlese with Spätlese and so on.

USA: Riesling and Gewürztraminer from California and Oregon.

AUSTRALIA: Riesling from the Barossa Valley.

NEW ZEALAND: Riesling.

Rias Baixas ₩₩

Rias Baixas is one of the four *Denominación de Origen* (DOs) of Galicia in the northwest of Spain, right next to Portugal. So far the wines are much better known in Spain than abroad, but things may be slowly changing. Galicia is quite the wettest part of Spain, and also the greenest, and so the wines are quite different from those produced anywhere else in the country. It is a region of white wine, with the best coming from the Albariño grape, which gives delicately peachy, perfumed wines, with crisp acidity. They are clean and fresh, fairly low in alcohol and light in the mouth, with hints of peaches and apricots. Sometimes the taste is quite discreet; sometimes more blowsy and obvious.

The adjoining DO of Ribeiro includes red as well as white wine and allows a wider range of grape varieties, including Loureiro and Treixadura for white wine. These make for wines with a firmer, stonier flavour, and a dry finish. The reds still take very much second place, as in ▷Vinho Verde on the other side of the river Minho which separates Spain from Portugal.

● **Vintages:** Drink the youngest available, and always within 18 months of the harvest, as these wines have no ageing potential whatsoever.

● **Recommended producers:** Bodegas Morgadio, Martin Codax, Lagar de Cervera, Dom Bardo.

 Taste on:
PORTUGAL: ▷Vinho Verde.

FRANCE: ▷Muscadet for the stonier flavours of Ribeiro; ▷Côtes de Gascogne; ▷Condrieu, for the Viognier grape has the peachy, apricot characteristics of Albariño, although it is much fuller in the mouth.

ITALY: Arneis, in Piedmont, a DOC named after its grape variety, has a delicate but distinctively peachy flavour.

Ribera del Duero ▼▼

Ribera del Duero is a rising star in the red wine firmament of northern Spain. The name means literally 'banks of the Duero' and the vineyards, lying to the east of the town of Valladolid, are indeed on the banks of that river, which is better known as the Douro, when it crosses the frontier into Portugal. The estate of Vega Sicilia is over 100 years old with a long-established reputation, but other names are now making their mark on the international wine scene, including Viña Pesquera, Bodegas Mauro and Viña Pedrosa.

Tinto Fino is the main grape variety, which is the same as the Tempranillo of ▷Rioja. Wines like Viña Pesquera ▼▼▼ and Viña Pedrosa are made purely from Tinto Fino, while Vega Sicilia ▼▼▼ includes Garnacha and also the Bordelais grape varieties, Cabernet, Merlot and Malbec. A period of ageing in small barrels, either of American or French oak, is also essential and contributes to the stylish impact of the wines. Like Rioja the flavours are a cross between Bordeaux and burgundy. Wines that have spent longer in wood and were lighter in the first place seem more vegetal and burgundian in character, while those with more concentration of flavour have the richness of a fine Pomerol. They have rich, plummy, spicey flavours, with hints of herbs and plenty of cassis, some underlying sweetness from the oak, and a firm backbone of tannin.

- **Vintages:** 1991, 1990, 1989, 1987, 1986, 1985, 1983, 1982, 1981,

- **Recommended producers:** Vega Sicilia – the Unico label is best of all, destined for a tiny part of the production, and only in the best years, while Valbuena in its fifth and eighth year is more accessible. Also Viña Pesquera, Viña Pedrosa, Bodegas Mauro. The wines from the cooperative at Peñafiel can be good, but are a little erratic in quality.

 Taste on:
SPAIN: *Gran reserva* ▷Rioja, with the complexity from oak-ageing and some mature, mellow flavours.

FRANCE: Good Ribera del Duero has the style and stature of fine ▷burgundy or ▷claret. Vina Pedrosa reminds me of an elegant burgundy, with some sweet, vegetal fruit such as ▷Gevrey-Chambertin or ▷Volnay, while Viña Pesquera and Bodegas Mauro lead me to the rich, mouthfilling, plummy, ripe blackcurrant flavours of Pomerol or ▷St-Emilion.

ITALY: Some of the Tuscan blends of Sangiovese and Cabernet Sauvignon that are kept in new oak, such as Sammarco from Castello dei Rampolla, Balifico ▼▼ from Castello di Volpaia, Ca' del Pazzo from Caparzo, and have a spicey richness and a firm backbone of tannin.

CALIFORNIA: ▷California Cabernet Sauvignon, with some rich blackcurrant fruit and sometimes more obvious oak-ageing than classed-growth ▷claret. There is a similarity in style if not in taste.

▼ Riesling

Several different grape varieties include Riesling in their name. There is Welschriesling, or Wälschriesling, which is also called Laskirizling in Yugoslavia, Olaszrizling in Hungary and Riesling Italico in Italy, as well as Grey Riesling and Emerald Riesling, which are Californian peculiarities. However, the one that matters is the Rhine Riesling, which is simply called Riesling in Germany and Alsace and White or Johannisberg Riesling in North America.

This is the grape variety that is responsible for the best wines of both Germany and Alsace. Its taste, unlike any other grape variety except ▷Chenin Blanc, can range from very sweet to bone dry. In Alsace it is usually fermented dry, leaving no residual sugar, while in the best years they also make richer and sweeter *Vendange Tardive* and *Sélection de Grains Nobles*. In Germany Riesling can make ▷*trocken* and ▷*halbtrocken* wines, through to ▷Kabinett, ▷Spätlese, ▷Auslese, ▷Beerenauslese and sweetest of all, ▷Trockenbeerenauslese, as well as ▷Eiswein.

▷Riesling d'Alsace is dry and steely. There is some body and weight, for the wines have more alcohol than their German counterparts, and with age they develop the most delicious slate and petrol overtones, which taste very much nicer than they sound! Across the border in

Germany, the wines are lighter and more honeyed, with delicate flavours of peaches and apricots. An Auslese from a good vintage and a reputable Mosel estate epitomises the flavour of fine German Riesling.

Riesling enjoys the cool climate and long ripening season of the vineyards of the Rhine and therefore has adapted less successfully to the generally warmer climates of the New World. In California they tend to make off-dry Riesling, as well as Late Harvest wines, but these are often heavier and less elegant than their German counterparts. Riesling is grown in Australia too, notably in the Barossa Valley and it has recently begun to enjoy some success in New Zealand.

Taste on:

FRANCE: ▷Riesling d'Alsace, especially *Vendange Tardive* and *Sélection de Grains Nobles* ♥♥♥; Riesling is also a possible ingredient of Crémant d'Alsace.

GERMANY: Not all the wines made from Riesling will say so on the label. If there is no mention of grape variety, but the wine comes from a top estate, then you can assume it is Riesling. The best examples come from ▷Bernkastel in the Mosel and ▷Johannisberg in the Rheingau. Also Schlossböckelheim in the ▷Nahe. ▷Nierstein in the Rheinhessen and Deidesheim in the ▷Rheinpfalz.

Riesling can also feature in German sparkling wine, otherwise known as ▷Sekt, such as Deinhard's Lila Riesling Sekt.

ITALY: Riesling Renano, as Rhine Riesling is called, features in the DOCs of Friuli and the Alto Adige, with some crisp, slatey dry wines. Tiefenbrunner, Jermann and Schiopetto are star producers.

AUSTRIA: Rhine Riesling ♥♥ is much less common than in Germany, but there are some good examples, with peachy fruit and balanced lemony acidity.

USA: California: some good off-dry wines, with more alcohol and body than Rieslings from Germany, and less steely than Riesling from Alsace. Try Freemark Abbey, Joseph Phelps, Trefethen, Château St. Jean, Mark West Vineyards, Firestone and Jekel. Late Harvest wines, made from grapes affected by noble rot, are made most successfully by Joseph Phelps, Château St. Jean and Freemark Abbey.

Oregon: Cooler Oregon has a more suitable climate for producing the delicate Germanic style of Riesling, notably from Knudsen-Erath.

Washington State: For off-dry Rieslings, try Hogue Cellars and Snoqualmie, and sweet Late Harvest Riesling from Arbor Crest Vineyards.

AUSTRALIA: Barossa Valley in South Australia is the best source of Riesling. Yalumba with the Pewsey Vale Vineyard, Petaluma, Henschke and also Plantagenet in Western Australia.

NEW ZEALAND: Fine examples of Riesling ♥♥, both sweet and dry, have appeared in just the last five years or so, such as Weingut Seifried, Dry River, Giesen, Montana and Hunters.

SOUTH AFRICA: Some lovely off-dry Rieslings with the characteristic overtones of paraffin, a hint of honey and some crisp acidity.

CHILE: Torres makes the sole example of South American Riesling, with some petrolly fruit and a sweet finish.

CHINA: Tsingtaõ Riesling is a lone example, and for the moment lacks true varietal character, making more of a talking point than offering a delicious glass of wine.

♥ ## Riesling d'Alsace

Unlike most other wine regions of France, Alsace attributes greater prominence to grape variety than precise provenance on the label, except in the case of the growing number of *grand crus* vineyards. This is the only wine region of France where Riesling is grown and it is generally considered to make some of the best Alsace wines. ▷Gewürztraminer may be the most typical and characteristic, while Riesling provides elegance and style, especially from a *grand cru* vineyard and a talented producer.

Riesling is also the grape variety of the best German wines. However there is a fundamental difference. In Alsace, unlike Germany, it is fermented dry, leaving no trace of residual sweetness, except for the richer *Vendange Tardive* and *Sélection de Grains Nobles* wines. This means that Alsace Riesling is firmly dry to the point of being steely and also higher in alcohol than its German counterparts. When it is young, it has an attractive flowery character, with underlying crisp acidity. With age this becomes more slatey and takes on petrolly overtones. Style varies from producer to producer. Some wines are fuller and more flowery; others are lean and understated, with a steely elegance. Riesling d'Alsace will age beautifully, developing more subtle flavours as it matures. *Vendange Tardive* tends to be rich rather than sweet, ripe rather than honeyed, while *Sélection de Grains Nobles* Riesling is fuller and more luscious in the mouth.

● **Vintages:** 1990, 1989, 1988, 1985, 1983, 1981, 1976.

● **Recommended producers:** Trimbach, especially Clos Ste-Hune and Cuvée Frédéric Emile, Hugel, Domaine Weinbach, Jos Meyer, Zind-Humbrecht, Léon Beyer, Marcel Deiss, Schlumberger, Marc Kreydenweiss, Kuentz-Bas, Domaine Ostertag.

 Taste on:

FRANCE: ▷Sancerre and ▷Pouilly Fumé. The grape variety is quite different, Sauvignon rather than Riesling, but there is a similarity in the fruit and acidity balance in the wine, making it possible to confuse the two as young wines.

GERMANY: The Rieslings of the Mosel ▷Bernkastel may have more in common with Alsace than those of the Rhine, by virtue of their steely acidity. They will be much lighter in alcohol, but with age they take on a similar slatey character, with petrol overtones; some say kerosene!

Also ▷Kabinett as the driest of the Prädikat wines, and also ▷*trocken* and ▷*halbtrocken* wines made from Riesling, notably Schloss Vollrads and wines from other members of the Charta group, which specialise in drier wines, such as Balthasar Ress, Dr Weil, Deinhard.

AUSTRIA: ▷Kabinett wines made from Riesling.

ITALY: Riesling Renano from the Alto Adige and Friuli, made by Tiefenbrunner, Jermann and Schiopetto; also Ribolla

Gialla ♈♈, an unusual grape variety from the Colli Orientali of Friuli, with a perfumed quality and some firm acidity, not unlike Riesling.

USA: California: The weight and alcohol level of a California Riesling has more in common with Alsace than Germany. However the best wines tend to be off-dry, such as Château St. Jean, Joseph Phelps.
Oregon: Knudsen-Erath.
Washington State: Hogue Cellars, Snoqualmie Winery.

AUSTRALIA: Rieslings from the Barossa, Clare and Eden Valleys; Hill-Smith's Old Triangle Riesling is one of the best.

NEW ZEALAND: Montana, Dry River, Giesen and Hunters for dry Riesling.

SOUTH AFRICA: Weisser Riesling.

♈ Rioja

Rioja is the wine that put Spain on the international wine map, providing an introduction to the wines of that coutnry, to the extent that for many of us there is no other Spanish wine. Rioja comes from northern Spain, from vineyards around the town of Logroño, situated on the river Ebro. They are divided into three distinct areas, with different soil and climatic conditions, namely the Rioja Alta, Rioja Baja, and best of all Rioja Alavesa. In fact a good Rioja is often a blend of at least two of these, if not of all three.

The *Denominación* of Rioja covers a wide range of flavours. First of all it can be red, white or pink. Secondly there are four different classifications of age; *sin crianza*, *con crianza*, *reserva* and *gran reserva*. The first describes a young wine, that has not been near an oak barrel, while the other three categories all denote a certain length of time in wood, from a few months to at least three years for a *gran reserva*, or more, depending upon a bodega's house style.

The grape varieties of Rioja have little to do with France, Tempranillo is the Spanish grape variety that gives red Rioja its fruit and flavour. There *may* be an ampelographical link with Pinot Noir, but that is very much open to dispute. Garnacha or Grenache is the other important grape variety, as well as some Mazuelo, otherwise known as Cariñena, or Carignan, and a drop of Graciano, which is tending to disappear from the vineyards. White Rioja comes mainly from the Viura grape.

When I was tasting hard for the Master of Wine exams, about the time that Rioja was just beginning to make an impact on our wine shelves, accepted wisdom said that if we had a red wine that smelt of ▷burgundy and tasted of ▷claret, it had to be a Rioja. A red Rioja that has spent some time in small American oak barrels takes on a very distinctive vanilla nose that is reminiscent of the sweetness of burgundy. But when you taste the wine, it has a structure that is firmer and drier than burgundy, and yet there is an almost imperceptible sweetness about it too, with some vegetal hints. The longer it has been in wood, the more colour it has lost, and the softer the taste has become so that it is all too misleadingly like burgundy, both in taste and appearance, or maybe claret. However, once you have learnt to recognise what is the very distinctive smell of vanilla, which comes from the barrels made of American oak, then you will be able to identify Rioja, or alternatively confuse it with other northern Spanish wines that are also aged in American oak.

Sin crianza red Rioja which has not been aged in wood has a stalky, fruity, spicey flavour about it. It is one of those red wines that is easy to drink, but without any really distinguishing characteristics. It is the oak-ageing that gives Rioja its individuality.

The same may be said of white Rioja, for white Rioja has gone in two directions. The traditional producers such as Marqués de Murrieta and Bodegas Riojanas keep their white wine in oak for a minimum of six months and often for longer. The very first time I tasted a Marqués de Murrieta *reserva blanco*, without seeing the label, I was convinced that it came from ▷Meursault. The stylishly elegant oaky flavour seemed just like the toasted, nutty character that I associate with good white burgundy.

White Rioja that has no wood-ageing is much less interesting. The Viura grape lacks acidity and is pretty short on flavour, which does not augur well for an interesting white wine. Often the most marked characteristic is the aroma of boiled sweets or peardrops that comes from a fermentation at an unnaturally low temperature, which is generally the case with white Rioja. Some *bodegas* manage to achieve a little fruit in their wines too, but you can see why oak barrels were favoured in the first place. The taste is usually clean and fresh, dry but not acid and rather neutral and bland.

•   **Vintages:** 1991, 1990, 1989, 1987, 1986, 1985, 1983, 1982, 1981, 1980, 1976, 1975, 1973, 1970.

•   **Recommended producers:** CVNE, Marqués de Cáceres, Marqués de Riscal, La Rioja Alta, Faustino Martinez, Marqués de Murrieta, Muga, Bodegas Riojanas, with Monte Real and Viña Albina.

 Taste on:
RED *RESERVAS*:
▷Pinot Noir.

SPAIN: Other wines from northern Spain based on Tempranillo and aged in American oak, such as ▷Ribera del Duero, Navarra, ▷Penedés, especially Torres Coronas.

FRANCE: Côte d'Or burgundy, ▷Gevrey-Chambertin, ▷Volnay, ▷St-Emilion and Pomerol.

ITALY: Pomino *rosso* from Tuscany.

RED *SIN CRIANZA*:
SPAIN: Nearby Navarra produces very similar wines; ▷Toro; ▷Valdepeñas.

FRANCE: ▷Côtes du Rhône, ▷Minervois, ▷Corbières.

PORTUGAL: ▷Arruda, ▷Douro.

WHITE *SIN CRIANZA*:
SPAIN: ▷Penedés, ▷Rueda, for a little more flavour.

ITALY: Some of the neutral, dry whites of central Italy, such as ▷Galestro, Bianco Vergine Valdichiana, Bianco Val d'Arbia.

PORTUGAL: ▷Bairrada.

RESERVAS:
FRANCE: ▷Meursault.

GREECE: ▷Retsina.

PINK/ROSADO:
SPAIN: Pink Rioja is generally well made with attractive, fresh raspberry fruit. It is usually quite mouthfilling and not too acidic and is best drunk as young as possible.

SPAIN: Pink from Navarra and ▷Penedés.

ITALY: Vin Ruspo, the pink wine of Carmignano; ▷Bardolino Chiaretto.

FRANCE: ▷Tavel and Lirac; ▷Côtes de Provence; ▷Côtes du Rhône.

☙ Romanian Pinot Noir

Pinot Noir is one of the more exciting varietal examples to come out of Romania, where wine production has hitherto been geared to the sweeter tooth of eastern Europe. Romanian Pinot Noir does have an underlying sweetness, but it comes from the ripe fruit of the grape variety, with a positive chocolatey, vegetal character and soft, ripe fruit and a dry finish. There is a soupy, jammy quality about it, reminiscent of rather clumsy old-style burgundy. Elegant it is not, and it lacks the delicacy of a good ▷Gevrey-Chambertin, but the essential character of the grape variety is certainly there.

- **Vintages:** 1990, 1989, 1988.

- **Recommended producers:** Eastern European anonymity prevails.

Taste on:

HUNGARY: Pinot Noir.

YUGOSLAVIA: Mordi Pinot Noir.

BULGARIA: Mature Gamza, a grape variety peculiar to Bulgaria, has a curiously sweet, vegetal flavour about it, not unlike Pinot Noir.

AUSTRIA: Wines made from St Laurent have a ripe jammy flavour and a soft finish.

AUSTRALIA: This is Pinot Noir from a warm climate. The best however have burgundian elegance.

GERMANY: Spätburgunder from Assmannshausen in the Ahr Valley, for the sweet flavours of Pinot Noir.

FRANCE: ▷Burgundy from old-fashioned producers like Daudet Naudin, rather than the clean, elegant flavours from Clair-Daü or Henri Gouges.

☙ Rueda

Rueda is one of the most characterful white wines of Spain. Ten years ago we had never heard of this dry white from northern Spain and twenty years ago it did not exist at all in the form that we know today, but was an oxidised, fortified, sherry-like wine. It has been transformed by a new generation of winemakers and with investment from outside the region, notably from Marqués de Griñon and Marqués de Riscal. Verdejo is the principal grape variety, which gives a firm, dry, nutty, grassy flavoured wine. Viura is allowed too, as is a drop of Sauvignon for extra pungency. *Superior* on the label indicates a higher percentage of Verdejo, and is worth it for the extra flavour.

Rueda has a full-bodied, grassy flavour. It is dry, without being acidic, with hints of almonds and a slight bitterness on the finish, which comes from the Verdejo grape. Sometimes there is a pithy, stoney freshness about the wine.

• **Vintages:** Drink within two or three years; 1991, 1990, 1989, 1988, 1987.

• **Recommended producers:** Marqués de Griñon, Antonio Sauz, Marqués de Riscal.

Taste on:

SPAIN: Alella, a dry white from just outside Barcelona.

FRANCE: ▷Chablis and ▷Muscadet.

ITALY: ▷Soave.

PORTUGAL: White ▷Douro such as Planalto.

☙ Rully

Rully is one of the four appellations of the Côte Chalonnaise, a small vineyard area that lies to the south of the Côte d'Or in Burgundy. The other appellations are Givry, Montagny and Mercurey. While Rully makes both red and white wine in equal importance, Givry is mainly red, as is Mercurey, while Montagny in contrast is only white.

The red wines of the Côte Chalonnaise are made from Pinot Noir and tend to be a lighter version of ▷Gevrey-Chambertin and ▷Volnay in the Côte d'Or, with some delicious flavours from the right hands.

The white wines again have less punch than the great white wines of the Côte de Beaune, such as ▷Meursault, but with some fine ▷Chardonnay flavours, and more character and depth than ▷Mâcon and even ▷Pouilly-Fuissé.

● **Vintages:** 1990, 1989, 1988, 1986, 1985.

● **Recommended producers:** Domaine de la Folie, Noël-Bouton, Cogny, Dury, Faiveley, Jaffelin, Delorme.

 Taste on:

RED:

FRANCE: The adjoining appellations of Givry and Mercurey; ▷Bourgogne Rouge and Bourgogne Côte Chalonnaise; lighter wines from the Côte d'Or, like St-Romain and St-Aubin; ▷Arbois and red ▷Côtes du Jura; ▷Irancy.

▷NEW ZEALAND: Pinot Noir from Martinborough Vineyards and Waipara Springs.

WHITE:

FRANCE: The adjoining appellation of Montagny; ▷Pouilly-Fuissé; ▷Beaujolais Blanc; ▷Chablis Premier Cru; ▷Bourgogne Blanc and Bourgogne Côte Chalonnaise.

ITALY: ▷Vernaccia di San Gimignano, as well as Montecarlo and Pomino from Tuscany.

NEW ZEALAND: ▷Chardonnay.

 ## Sangiovese di Romagna

The Sangiovese grape is the mainstay of central Italy. The label on the bottle may not say so, but it is the grape variety that is largely responsible for ▷Chianti, ▷Vino Nobile di Montepulciano, ▷Brunello di Montalcino, Carmignano, Torgiano, and numerous other red wines from Tuscany, Umbria, Emilia-Romagna, the Marche and to a lesser extent, Lazio in vineyards around Rome. The flat plains of Romagna are where Sangiovese is at its most prolific and least exciting, so that Sangiovese di Romagna is the Sangiovese grape at its most basic, with its sour-cherry flavour and fruity astringency that is typical of the taste of Italy. It is light in the mouth with a little acidity and a touch of tannin, making it a wine to drink within a couple of years of the vintage. If you order a carafe of house red in an Italian restaurant, the chances are that you will be given Sangiovese di Romagna.

● **Vintages:** Not a wine to keep. 1990, 1988, 1986 and 1985 are the best of recent years.

● **Recommended producers:** Fattoria Paradiso is exceptional, more like Tuscan Sangiovese; Foschi, Nespoli, Casetto dei Mandorli.

Taste on:
ITALY: ▷Chianti, but not Chianti Classico, which would be too heavy; Rosso di Montepulciano, the second wine to ▷Vino Nobile di Montepulciano; ▷Valpolicella; ▷Bardolino; Rosso Conero and Rosso Piceno from the Marche; other Sangiovese-based wines such as Colli Perugini, Rosso delle Colline Lucchesi, Montescudaio.

FRANCE: They say that Nielluccio, the grape variety that is the mainstay of ▷Corsica's Patrimonio is Sangiovese, brought to the island by the Pisans in the Middle Ages, so try Patrimonio for the same cherry fruit and astringency.

☙ St-Emilion

That prolific wine writer and founder of the International Wine & Food Society, André Simon, was once asked if and when he had last mistaken claret for burgundy, to which the reply is reputed to have been 'Not since lunchtime'. It may seem obvious to be able to tell the difference between what are seemingly two vastly contrasting regions, but when you have an elegant St-Emilion alongside a full-bodied burgundy, the distinctions can be all too blurred.

Whereas in the Médoc, ▷Cabernet Sauvignon is the dominant grape variety, in St-Emilion it is the Merlot, which gives the wines a richness that you do not find in the Médoc. There can be a vegetal character that is similar to burgundy, a spiciness and an opulence, with a chocolate sweetness to the finish that you do not find in the Médoc, but which is misleadingly burgundian in character. The clue may be the presence of tannin, which is sometimes more obvious in St-Emilion, and also in the wines of adjoining Pomerol, than in burgundy.

● **Vintages:** 1990, 1989, 1988, 1987, 1986, 1985, 1983, 1982, 1978, 1970.

● **Recommended châteaux:** St-Emilion: Ausone, Canon, Pavie, Magdeleine, La Tour Figeac, Figeac, Tertre-Rôteboeuf.
Pomerol: Bon Pasteur, la Conseillante, Pétrus, Vieux Château Certan, Trotanoy, Lafleur, La Fleur Pétrus, Moulinet, La Tour à Pomerol, Le Pin.

 Taste on:

FRANCE: ▷Médoc; ▷Graves; Lalande de Pomerol; Canon-Fronsac; Fronsac; the satellite appellations of St-Emilion, such as Lussac-St-Emilion, Montagne-St-Emilion and so on.

Full-flavoured red burgundies from the Côte de Nuits, the *grand crus* of villages, like ▷Gevrey-Chambertin.

Some of the richer wines of Provence that include Cabernet Sauvignon in their blend, notably Domaine de Trévallon from

Les Baux in the appellation of Coteaux d'Aix-en-Provence and Château Vignelaure from the same appellation. The richness of flavour makes them more akin to St-Emilion than to the Médoc.

Also from the south of France, not far from Béziers in the hinterland of the Hérault, there is a unique estate, Mas de Daumas Gassac ▼▼▼, where, although Cabernet Sauvignon is the principal grape variety, it is blended with Merlot, Cabernet Franc, Pinot Noir, Syrah, Tannat and Malbec. The wine has been described as the Lafite of the Languedoc, praise which may be fulsome, but the flavours undoubtedly have more in common with St-Emilion than with any of the surrounding estates of the Hérault. Vinification methods are those of a traditional Bordeaux château and the wines have weight, structure and flavour.

SPAIN: ▷Ribera del Duero. The grape variety here is Tempranillo, which has nothing at all to do with Cabernet or Merlot, but the vinification methods have a certain affinity with Bordeaux, so that it would not be impossible to mistake a wine like Pesquera or Vega Sicilia for St-Emilion or Pomerol.

Raimat's Abadia, from the new DO of Coster del Segre also has some of the richness of flavour of a Pomerol.

There are several examples of Cabernet Sauvignon from Spain, including Jean Léon, Marqués de Griñon Tinto and Torres' Mas la Plana, formerly Torres' Gran Coronas Black Label.

ITALY: The wines of Carmignano include an obligatory percentage of Cabernet Sauvignon in their make-up, which fills out the flavour, and results in wines that are less austere than a pure Sangiovese. Tenuta di Capezzana and Fattoria di Ambra are the best estates. Also from Capezzana is another Tuscan answer to St-Emilion, a *vino da tavola* called Ghiaie della Furba, a delicious Cabernet Sauvignon, Cabernet Franc and Merlot blend, with some lovely spicy vegetal fruit.

Also from Tuscany is the up-and-coming estate of Ornellaia, which is close to the coast at Bolgheri adjoining Sassicaia. However they have planted Merlot rather than Cabernet Franc, so that the wines are fuller and richer than those of their neighbour.

Other wines from central Tuscany include Rubesco from Torgiano in Umbria and Morellino di Scansano.

PORTUGAL: Quinta da Bacalhôa is a stunning example of Cabernet Sauvignon and Merlot, with rich blackcurrant fruit, laced with new oak. Also Quinta da Camarate from J. M. da Fonseca, which includes a small amount of Cabernet Sauvignon, has some rich blackcurrant fruit, and a smokey character, not unlike a good St-Emilion.

There are numerous examples of Cabernet Sauvignon from the New World which could easily be confused with wines from Bordeaux. The warmer climates of California and Australia make for riper, richer wines, with flavours more akin to St-Emilion than to the Médoc, but not always. I have had elegant Cabernet Sauvignon from the Napa Valley that would stand undetected in a row of Médoc, but generally the flavours of blackcurrant are more immediate, softer, with a greater initial appeal. They are not reticent wines, as those of the Médoc so often are.

USA: Cabernet Sauvignon from ▷California, Washington, Long Island, Texas.

AUSTRALIA: ▷Cabernet Sauvignon.

▷CHILE: Chile is very much on the learning curve, as wine-making techniques are improving at a rapid pace. Probably the most typical claret lookalike currently coming out of Chile is the best wine from Santa Rita, called Medalla Real. Recent vintages have a rich blackcurrant flavour that is typical of a good *grand cru* of St-Emilion.

SOUTH AFRICA: ▷Cabernet Sauvignon from Delheim, Le Bonheur, Meerlust, Nederburg, Overgaauw.

▷NEW ZEALAND: As winemaking in New Zealand improves apace, with each vintage Cabernet Sauvignon is growing in stature. In warmer years wines from Hawke's Bay have a rich blackcurrant flavour, not unlike St-Emilion. Also Merlot from Esk Valley.

Sancerre

Sancerre is one of the appellations of the area that is commonly called the Central Vineyards of the Loire Valley. It can be red, white or pink, but it is the white version that has put Sancerre on the map, representing as it does, the epitome of the ▷Sauvignon grape. This is where it is at its most elegant, with delicate flavours most often described as gooseberries, while less attractive examples of the Sauvignon grape can have a somewhat coarse taste, with feline overtones. Good Sancerre has a refreshingly crisp acidity, tasting not only of gooseberries, but also of green peas and asparagus, with stoney, flinty undertones. Unfortunately the demands of fashion have made Sancerre expensive.

Red and pink Sancerre are made from ▷Pinot Noir. In all but the very exceptional years the reds are light in colour and body, with delicate raspberry and vegetal flavours, if you are lucky. Pink Sancerre is very delicate, with plenty of crisp acidity and hints of raspberries.

• **Vintages:** Drink the youngest available; good recent vintages are 1990, 1989, 1988, 1987.

• **Recommended producers:** Vacheron, Gitton, Natter, Vatan, Bailly-Reverdy, Crochet, Cotat, Dezat, Thomas.

Taste on:
FRANCE: ▷Pouilly Fumé, the neighbouring appellation, making very similar wines. Differences between the two stem from the winemaker's expertise rather than from any significant variation in soil or climate. The white wines of nearby Reuilly, Quincy and Menetou-Salon all offer less expensive alternatives to Sancerre.

▷Sauvignon de Touraine from further downstream also has a certain similarity to Sancerre. Sometimes the flavour is more markedly pungent; sometimes it is flatter and has more in common with ▷Bordeaux Blanc.

ITALY: Alternatives to Sancerre from elsewhere in the world are inevitably other Sauvignons. It is difficult to imitate that distinctive, crisply pungent fruit, without the benefits of a cool climate. In Tuscany they are still at the learning stage with Sauvignon. Some are rendered clumsy by an excess of oak, so that the best to date is Poggio alle Gazze ♥♥ from the Ornellaia estate in Bolgheri. In northern Italy where Sauvignon features amongst the grape varieties permitted in the DOCs of the Alto Adige and Friuli and where the climate is cooler than in Tuscany, the flavours are more akin to Sancerre. Sauvignon under the Enofriulia or Puiatti label in the DOC of Collio has a firm, pithy flavour reminiscent of green peas. Also try Sauvignon made by Schiopetto and Jermann.

NEW ZEALAND: ▷Sauvignon for some of the most pungent examples outside the Loire Valley.

SOUTH AFRICA: L'Ormarins is one estate making crisp, fruity wine with good varietal character.

CHILE: ▷Sauvignon from Torres and Canepa are crisply pungent, while other Sauvignon from Chile tends to be fuller and fatter and more Bordelais in style. The same goes for Sauvignon from California and Australia.

RED:
FRANCE: ▷Irancy and neighbouring Coulanges-la-Vineuse; also Epineuil, another tiny red appellation near Chablis; Rouge d'Alsace; Bouzy Rouge, the still red wine of Champagne.

PINK:
FRANCE: Marsannay in the Côte d'Or and another pink burgundy, Vin Gris de Pinot Noir from Domaine Dujac; ▷Irancy.

▷ENGLAND: Conghurst in Kent make a refreshingly crisp pink with some dry, peppery fruit ♥♥.

♥ Sassicaia ♥♥♥

Sassicaia was the very first Italian Cabernet Sauvignon. It came to the fore with the 1968 vintage and took the international wine market by storm when it won a competition of comparative Cabernets, including some of the big names from Bordeaux and California. It comes from an estate on the Tuscan coast, south of Pisa, where the Marchese Incisa della Rocchetta (cousin of the Antinoris in Chianti) has planted French grape varieties. The wine is composed of 80 percent Cabernet Sauvignon and 20 percent Cabernet Franc and was the very first Tuscan wine to be aged in small barrels of French oak, as opposed to large barrels of Slavonic oak, which are still used in many parts of Italy. Rigorous standards are maintained and the success of Sassicaia has continued unabated.

To the purist Italophile, Sassicaia is not an Italian wine. The flavours are those of Bordeaux, with the ripe cedarwood and blackcurrant fruit of classed-growth claret, and the subtle flavours that come from a couple of years in oak barrels. Further bottle-ageing enhances the taste, giving it great elegance and style. It has certainly changed many a perception of Italian wine, offering an alternative to the inevitable benchmark of France.

● **Vintages:** 1990, 1988, 1986, 1985, 1983, 1982, 1981.

 Taste on:

ITALY: The adjoining estate is Ornellaia, owned by Ludovico Antinori, who has planted Merlot, rather than Cabernet Franc. However the flavour is very much that of Bordeaux, with ripe, opulent blackcurrant fruit. ▷Tignanello, the wine with which the Antinoris followed Sassicaia is much more Italian in flavour, made mainly from Sangiovese, with approximately 20 percent Cabernet Sauvignon.

Other Tuscan Cabernet Sauvignons include Solaia, Tavarnelle, Sammarco and also Cabernet Sauvignon di Miralduolo from Lungarotti in Umbria.

FRANCE: Classed-growth ▷claret from the ▷Médoc.

SPAIN: Jean Léon Cabernet Sauvignon from ▷Penedés; Marqués de Griñon Cabernet Sauvignon.

USA: ▷California Cabernet Sauvignon.

CHILE: Some of the better ▷Cabernet Sauvignon such as Santa Rita's Medalla Real and Don Maximiano from Errazuriz Panquehue.

☙ Saumur

Saumur can be red, white or pink, still or sparkling. Most frequently it is associated with a sparkling white wine, Saumur Mousseux, made principally from the Chenin Blanc grape, by the same method as champagne. There are strong links between the town of Saumur on the Loire Valley and the Champagne region. Jean Ackerman first introduced the champagne method of making sparkling wine into the Loire Valley at the beginning of the last centry. He married a Mademoiselle Laurance, the daughter of a vineyard owner, and together they created the company of Ackerman-Laurance. Today the well-known Saumur house of Gratien & Meyer owns Alfred Gratien in Champagne, while other champagne houses such as Bollinger and Taittinger own Langlois-Château and Bouvet-Ladubay respectively in Saumur.

Sparkling Saumur may be made in exactly the same way as champagne but it will never taste quite the same, for there is a significant difference in the grape variety. Chenin Blanc has the high acidity and fairly neutral flavour that are desirable in a base for sparkling wine, but never the subtlety achieved in champagne. There can be a honeyed quality that is quite different, combined with much more pronounced acidity. Sometimes sparkling Saumur has a rather dank nose that reminds me of wet dogs or wet wool. However when it is delicately honeyed and fresh, it makes a very acceptable alternative to champagne. Some sparkling pink Saumur is made, and, very occasionally, even red sparkling Saumur.

As for the flat versions of Saumur, the pink and white have a marked resemblance to nearby ▷Anjou, with similar shortcomings in flavour. The pink is sometimes called Cabernet de Saumur. Most interesting is the red wine, made from Cabernet Franc, blended occasionally with some Cabernet Sauvignon, while best of all is a small appellation called Saumur-Champigny, from vineyards around the village of Champigny, south east of Saumur itself. It has a little more substance and weight than simple Saumur rouge, with some ripe red berry fruit, raspberries and cherries, and in the best vintages some tannin, which gives it a few years ageing potential.

- **Vintages:** 1990, 1989, 1988, 1985, 1983, 1982.

- **Recommended producers:** Sparkling Saumur: Gratien & Meyer, Bouvet-Ladubay, Ackerman-Laurance, Langlois-Château.

Usually sold as non-vintage.

Saumur Champigny: Filliatreau, Langlois-Château, Chaintres.

 Taste on:

SPARKLING SAUMUR:

FRANCE: Crémant de la Loire, ▷Vouvray, ▷Anjou, ▷Champagne.

SPAIN: ▷Cava.

GERMANY: ▷Sekt.

ENGLAND: The occasional example of English sparkling wine.

ITALY: Italian spumante made from the Prosecco grape.

SAUMUR CHAMPIGNY:

FRANCE: ▷Anjou, ▷Chinon, Bourgueil and St-Nicolas de Bourgueil; Cabernet du Haut-Poitou.

ITALY: Cabernet from Trentino and Friuli.

NEW ZEALAND: ▷Cabernet Sauvignon, for lighter vintages in cooler years sometimes have a slightly herbaceous quality.

Sauternes

Sauternes is one of the great sweet white wines of the world. It comes from a small enclave in the vineyards of Bordeaux, from around the eponymous village. Good Sauternes is only produced in exceptional years, for its quality depends upon very specific climatic conditions, namely dank misty autumnal mornings followed by blazing sunny afternoons when the grapes are virtually ripe, towards the end of September and early October. If this happens, the ripe grapes develop what is called noble rot, a botrytis or fungus which attacks their skins and dehydrates them, so that all the flavour and sugar in the juice becomes very concentrated, resulting in the most delicious, luscious dessert wines.

I have never forgotten staying in Sauternes as the vintage was starting in 1983. I remember opening my bedroom window about 8 o'clock one morning to find that I could hardly see more than a few yards, so thick was the mist. The atmosphere was laden with moisture, and yet by midday we were sipping an aperitif in the gardens of Château Suduiraut in brilliant warm sunshine, such was the dramatic transformation in temperature. A potentially good vintage could be ruined at the last moment by a heavy rain storm, such are the climatic vagaries that govern the quality of Sauternes, and also neighbouring ▷Barsac.

However, when the weather is kind and conditions are perfect, the result is the most delicious of dessert wines, ripe, honeyed flavours, with hints of apricot, peach, toffee, cream and tropical fruits. There is a richness about Sauternes that fills the mouth with flavour. Unlike sweet German wines, they are relatively high in alcohol and rich in glycerine, with an underlying unctuousness. The effects of the botrytis is detected by a slightly burnt, roasted flavour that the French call *goût de rôti*, which gives the wine a firm bite and prevents it from being cloying and oversweet.

- **Vintages:** 1990, 1989, 1988 (three good vintages in a row is virtually unheard of), 1986, 1983, 1981, 1980, 1976, 1975, 1971, 1970.

- **Recommended producers:** Château d'Yquem is the best, but with a price to match. They say that one vine at d'Yquem produces just one glass of wine. My favourite estates include Châteaux Suduiraut, de Fargues, Caillou, Rieussec, St-Amand, also called la Chartreuse, Gilette, Bastor-Lamontagne. La Tour Blanche is improving.

Taste on :

FRANCE: ▷Barsac; Bonnezeaux; ▷Coteaux du Layon; ▷Gewürztraminer d'Alsace, *Sélection de Grains Nobles*. This is one of the late-picked wines of Alsace, espousing the same principle as in Sauternes, entailing a meticulous selection of berries, as the name implies. Although there is a spiciness about Gewürztraminer that you do not find in the blend of Sauvignon, Sémillon and Muscadelle that makes Sauternes, there is the same rich opulence with the underlying similarity of structure. The feel of the two wines in the mouth is almost identical, especially when they have some bottle-age.

HUNGARY: ▷Tokay, the great sweet wine of Hungary. Old Tokay, with five or six putts (in other words very sweet) develops hints of orange marmalade, as can old Sauternes.

AUSTRALIA: Noble rot is not a common occurrence in the generally hot, dry climate of this continent. However de Bortoli in the Murrumbidgee Irrigation Area of New South Wales is enjoying success with its botrytised Sémillon ▼▼, making some lovely honeyed wines, with a taste of toffee apples.

GERMANY: ▷Trockenbeerenauslese is of similar weight and sweetness, but not of alcohol.

AUSTRIA: Trockenbeerenauslese and Beerenauslese.

ITALY: Torcolato, an intensely sweet dessert wine made by Maculan in Breganze.

▼ Sauvignon blanc

Sauvignon makes deliciously fresh dry white wine, which is at its best in the Loire Valley, in ▷Sancerre and ▷Pouilly Fumé. It is also an important part of the blend of virtually every white wine from Bordeaux, both dry and sweet, as well as the other white wines of southwest France, such as ▷Bergerac and Côtes de Duras. A white Bordeaux made of Sauvignon, with perhaps a little Sémillon, is heavier, flatter and fuller in the mouth and does not have the leanness, liveliness and crisp character of a Sancerre.

In the New World, more often than not, Sauvignon is aged in oak and called Fumé Blanc, which gives it a fuller, richer flavour, with a softer, less obvious varietal character than the unoaked versions of the Loire Valley. While they are typified by gooseberries, with flinty overtones and possibly coarser smells of cats, the Fumé Blanc of the New World has the buttery, vanilla, tropical fruit flavours of new oak. However, too much oak spoils the flavour of the grape.

New Zealand bridges the two styles. You can find both pithy, fresh, unoaked Sauvignon and the riper, richer wines that have been in oak.

Much of the appeal of Sauvignon is its instantly recognisable, easy to drink, refreshing flavours. As a pure varietal wine, it rarely ages well and lacks the subtlety and depth of a ▷Chardonnay or ▷Riesling.

 Taste on:
FRANCE: ▷Sancerre, ▷Pouilly Fumé, Menetou-Salon ▼, Reuilly, Quincy, ▷Sauvignon de Touraine; Vin de Pays du

Jardin de la France and other ▷*vin de pays* from the south of France, marked Sauvignon on the label; Sauvignon de St-Bris; ▷Bordeaux Blanc, ▷Graves, ▷Bergerac, Côtes de Duras, Buzet, ▷Entre-Deux-Mers.

ITALY: Sauvignon from the Alto Adige and Friuli, especially Colli and the Colli Orientali; also in Tuscany, classified as Predicato del Selvante; Avignonesi makes a good example; also Poggio alle Gazze from Ornellaia, and from Castel del Monte in Puglia.

HUNGARY: Sauvignon with some diluted varietal character.

USA: ▷California : both crisp Sauvignon and more often heavier Fumé Blanc.
Washington State: Fumé Blanc from Château Ste Michelle; Sauvignon Blanc from Latah Creek Wines Cellars and Arbor Crest.
Texas: where Cordier of Bordeaux fame is producing a catty, gooseberry-flavoured wine.

AUSTRALIA: Sauvignon here never attains the refreshing pungency of New Zealand. Often oak-matured and called Fumé Blanc. Try Katnook Estate for the fresh, pungent variety; also Taltarni, although they call it Fumé Blanc and Leeuwin Sauvignon Blanc from Margaret River and Shaw & Smith in South Australia; Orlando RF Sauvignon Blanc is overwhelmingly oaky.

▷NEW ZEALAND: Some of the best examples and with more impact than many a French Sauvignon.

SOUTH AFRICA: Try L'Ormarins, Boschendaal, Klein Constantia, Zonnenbloem, Zerenwacht.

🍇 Sauvignon de Touraine

Sauvignon de Touraine is, as the name implies, ▷Sauvignon grown in the province of Touraine in the Loire Valley. As for taste, it comes between the twin appellations of ▷Sancerre and ▷Pouilly Fumé and the Sauvignon of ▷Bordeaux Blanc and ▷Bergerac. Where Sancerre and Pouily Fumé are more elegant and subtle, if the obvious flavours of the Sauvignon grape can ever be described as subtle, Bordeaux Blanc is flatter and more solid. Sauvignon de Touraine can be lightly pithy, with some mouthwatering gooseberry fruit and crisp acidity.

● **Vintages:** Drink the youngest and freshest available: 1990, 1989, 1988.

● **Recommended producers:** Wines from the leading regional cooperative of Oisly et Thésée; Maurice Barbou at Domaine des Corbillières.

 Taste on:
FRANCE: ▷Sancerre and ▷Pouilly Fumé as well as nearby Menetou-Salon, Reuilly and Quincy; Cheverny, a tiny VDQS southwest of Blois, where they grow Sauvignon, amongst other grapes; Sauvignon de St-Bris from close to the vineyards of ▷Chablis in northern Burgundy.

 Schlossböckelheim see Nahe – Schlossböckelheim

 Sekt

Sekt is the common name for sparkling wine made in Germany, which does not necessarily mean that the grapes for it were grown in Germany for more often than not they have come from Italy. For German grapes, as well as German production you have to look for the words Deutscher Sekt on the label. Wines with even more specific information as to their origin, with grape variety and region are better. Most German Sekt is dry and slightly fruity, or occasionally medium dry.

Sekt is very rarely made by the champagne method, but most commonly by the Charmat or tank method, or occasionally the transfer method. Whereas the second fermentation for champagne takes place in the bottle in which the wine is subsequently sold, the tank method means that the second fermentation takes place in a large vat and the wine is bottled under pressure, while the transfer method means that the second fermentation takes place in a bottle, the contents of which are then transferred into a tank for bottling under pressure. One of the obvious differences between the champagne method and the tank method of making sparkling wine lies in the quality of the bubbles. The bubbles in champagne are very small and fine and tenacious, while those of the tank method are large and rather vicious, sometimes attacking your mouth rather fiercely.

- **Vintages:** German Sekt is sold without a vintage.

- **Recommended producers:** Henkel, Kupferberg, Burgeff are sound but unexciting. Deinhard makes one of the best German sparkling wines, Lila Riesling.

Taste on:

FRANCE: A German sparkling wine made principally from Riesling could be mistaken for a Crémant d'Alsace. The high acidity in the wine is also comparable to a Crémant de la Loire.

Wines like Henkel Trocken have more in common with French *vin mousseux* (which translates literally as sparkling wine, and is always made by the tank method) sold under brand names such as Cavalier, Veuve du Vernay, Kriter. The principal taste criterion here is that the wine be clean, fresh, quite dry, with some acidity and slightly fruity, with no defects nor any intrusive characteristics.

SPAIN: ▷Cava.

ENGLAND: Sparkling wines, usually made by the champagne method, from Carr Taylor and Rock Lodge have the flowery character of good German Sekt, as well as some firm acidity.

❦ Setúbal

Setúbal, across the river Tagus from Lisbon, is famous for its Moscatel. The wine can either be called plain Setúbal, or Moscatel de Setúbal, for Moscatel only accounts for about three quarters of the blend, which includes various other white grapes like Bual and Malvasia. Like ▷port and ▷sherry, Setúbal is a fortified wine. The grape skins are left to macerate in the wine for about five months before pressing. The best wines are matured for as long as 20 or 25 years in large oak casks, but recently, however, there has been a move towards producing young vintage wines.

These young wines are fresh and grapey, really tasting of Moscatel grapes, with a spirity finish coming from the added brandy. In contrast, the older wines are much more exciting and complex, rich and toffee-like, with the raisiny taste of Christmas cake and treacle, nuts and caramel, vanilla and bananas.

● **Vintages:** Unimportant.

● **Recommended producers:** J. M. da Fonseca (no relation to the port house) was until very recently the only producer to export its wines. Quinta da São Francisco has since joined the export market.

 Taste on:
YOUNG SETÚBAL:
SPAIN: Moscatel de ▷Málaga and Cream ▷Montilla.

FRANCE: ▷Muscat de Beaumes-de-Venise and other fortified Muscat wines from the south of France, such as Muscat de Frontignan, Muscat de Rivesaltes and Muscat de St-Jean-de-Minervois.

WOOD-AGED SETÚBAL:
PORTUGAL: Bual and Malmsey ▷Madeira.

SPAIN: *Oloroso* ▷sherry and ▷Málaga.

AUSTRALIA: ▷Liqueur Muscat.

CYPRUS: ▷Commandaria.

♉ Sherry

Sherry is the classic aperitif of Spain. It is produced around the towns of Jerez de la Frontera and Sanlúcar de Barrameda near Cadiz in southern Spain. Palomino is the principal grape variety, but that does not contribute so much to the taste as the vinification process, entailing the ageing for several years of different wines in a series of oak barrels, called a *solera* system, as well as the addition of grape brandy, making sherry a fortified wine. All sherry is a blend of several different wines of different years.

You never find a vintage sherry so that any date on a label refers to the year of commencement of a *solera*.

Sherry is the most versatile of wines, covering a broad spectrum of tastes, from absolutely bone-dry, austere *fino* and *manzanilla*, through *amontillado* and *oloroso*, of varying degrees of austerity and sweetness, to the rich, luscious cream sherry. Serve it as an aperitif, as an after-dinner drink or even with some food.

The distinctive taste of *fino* and also *manzanilla* sherry originates from flor, a film of yeast looking just like a veil of cotton wool, that develops on the surface of the wine while it is in cask. *Fino* sherry is very pale golden in colour and tastes bone dry, with a very firm bite and no hint of any sweetness. It is much lighter in body than any *amontillado* or *oloroso* sherry. However it is similar to *manzanilla* sherry. What distinguishes *manzanilla* from *fino* is its particular salty tang, that is said to originate from ageing the wine in close proximity to the sea, in cellars in the port of Sanlúcar de Barrameda. If you compare a *fino* with a *manzanilla* side by side, the *manzanilla* has a positively sea-salty tang, while the *fino* seems slightly softer, indeed almost flabby. However on its own, salty is also an apt description for a *fino* sherry.

The English-speaking world understands the two other principal descriptions of sherry, *amontillado* and *oloroso*, as meaning something rather sweeter than in Jerez itself. In Jerez most sherry, be it *amontillado* or *oloroso*, as well as *fino* and *manzanilla*, is bone dry, while we take *amontillado* to mean medium dry and *oloroso* to equate with a sweet cream sherry. Pale cream sherry (that is the colour of *fino*, but tastes sweet) is something that the Jerezanos do not understand at all.

Most *amontillado* that is exported has a rich, nutty flavour, reminiscent of walnuts and hazelnuts. It is amber in colour, with some underlying mellow sweetness, but not as heavy as a cream sherry. It should be smooth, with no obtrusive acidity, but without the weight of a cream *oloroso* sherry.

In Spanish *oloroso* means fragrant, not pungent like *fino* sherry, but richly aromatic. A cream sherry, often called *oloroso* in Britain, is usually a deep, chocolate-brown colour. It really fills the mouth with the taste of walnuts, toffee, chocolate and raisiny Moscatel grapes, with concentrated sweetness and a luscious richness. If the label should say *oloroso seco*, expect a wine that is austerely dry, but with a firm, nutty flavour of dried walnuts.

• **Vintages:** Irrelevant.

• **Recommended producers:** Antonio Barbadillo, Emilio Lustau for *almacenista* (rare and old) sherries, Valdespino, la Riva, Harveys, Sandeman, Hidalgo, Garvey, Gonzalez Byass, Williams & Humbert. Sometimes brand names are better known than the shippers' names; La Ina rather than Domecq; Tio Pepe rather than Gonzalez Byass.

 Taste on:

FINO AND *MANZANILLA*:
SPAIN: Dry ▷Montilla.

PORTUGAL: Sercial ▷Madeira; white ▷port.

FRANCE: ▷Vin Jaune.

Sherry-style wines are also made in other parts of the world and although attempts have been made to limit the use of the term sherry to the wine of Jerez, Cyprus and also Britain are still allowed it, whereas South Africa has been obliged to abandon it. British sherry however is merely the manufactured product of reconstituted, dehydrated grape must and outside the scope of this book, as it has nothing to do with real wine. Australia does produce some sherry lookalikes, but for the home market.

CYPRUS: Dry sherry.

SOUTH AFRICA: Sherry-style wine, likely to be labelled something like Extra Dry or Pale Dry.

AMONTILLADO:
SPAIN: Medium dry ▷Montilla and Málaga.

PORTUGAL: Verdelho and Bual ▷Madeira.

ITALY: Marsala; Vin Santo; Caluso Passito from Piedmont, made from dried grapes and tasting like sherry trifle.

CYPRUS: Medium sherry.

CREAM *OLOROSO* SHERRY:
SPAIN: Cream ▷Montilla and ▷Málaga.

PORTUGAL: Malmsey ▷Madeira, Moscatel de ▷Setúbal.

ITALY: ▷Marsala.

FRANCE: *Vins doux naturels* from the south; not the ones based on Muscat, but those made from Grenache, which has been aged in large casks for several months, if not years, such as Rivesaltes, Maury, Banyuls and Rasteau.

Vin de paille ▼▼ from the Jura, where they preserve a tradition for this wine, drying the grapes on straw for several weeks, before pressing them to make a sweet dessert wine.

Pineau de Charente, Floc de Gascogne and Ratafia, all of which are made by adding *marc*, the spirit from distilled grape skins, to unfermented juice.

AUSTRALIA: ▷Liqueur Muscat.

CYPRUS: Sweet sherry.

SOUTH AFRICA: A sherry-style with some description like sweet or cream.

▼ **Shiraz** *see* Syrah; Australian Shiraz

▼ **Soave**

Soave is the white wine in the trio of Veneto wines along with red ▷Bardolino and ▷Valpolicella. It comes from a mixture of grape varieties of which Trebbiano is the principal one, while any real flavour originates from Garganega. That is the problem with Soave. Yields have been stretched to such an extent that in so many examples any flavour has completely disappeared, leaving an insipid, diluted, watery taste, with the merest hint of almonds.

But there is real Soave to be found. Look for *Classico* on the label, which tells you that the wine has come from the hilly heart of the region, around the village of Soave. *Superiore* denotes nine months of ageing as well as a minimum alcohol level of 11.5°. Above all it is the name of the producer that really counts.

Real Soave has all sorts of tastes and flavours. It is delicately straw-coloured, with a subtle, grassy nose, and on the palate it has a full, leafy flavour, with a slightly nutty finish. There is acidity, but it is dry, rather than crisp. Wines from named vineyard sites are even better, with a greater concentration of fruit and flavour, so that ordinary Soave just pales into boring insignificance.

As with Valpolicella, there is also a *recioto* ♥♥ version of Soave, a delicate, sweet wine, made from dried grapes. Recioto di Soave can also be fortified, which is rare, and sparkling, but is best as a still wine, with honeyed sweetness and some apricot, marmalade and barley-sugar fruit.

●　　**Vintages:** There is little point in ageing Soave. Drink the youngest available or at least within three or four years of the vintage.

●　　**Recommended producers:** Pieropan and Anselmi are the stars; also Viticola Suavia, Boscaini, Guerrieri Rizzardi, Masi, Tedeschi, Zenato, Santi.

 Taste on:
ITALY: Other white wines from the north like Bianco di Custoza, Lugana, and ▷Gavi dei Gavi; Bianco di Alcamo from Sicily and other dry Sicilian whites, such as Terre di Ginestra.

FRANCE: ▷Chablis.

SPAIN: ▷Rueda.

FOR RECIOTO DI SOAVE:
ITALY: Piccolit; Torcolato.

FRANCE: ▷Barsac and ▷Sauternes; sweet ▷Vouvray.

AUSTRALIA: De Bortoli's botrytis-affected Sémillon; and other late-harvest wines from the New World.

FOR SPARKLING RECIOTO DI SOAVE:
Sweet champagne.

♥ South African Cabernet Sauvignon

Cabernet Sauvignon is the most successful red grape variety in South Africa. Most of it is grown in the slightly cooler vineyards of Stellenbosch and Paarl. Sometimes it is a pure varietal, and sometimes, perhaps more successfully, it is blended with Merlot and even Cabernet Franc. Quality varies. You can find wines with good varietal character, with a taste of cedarwood and blackcurrants, while at other times the flavour is spoilt by an earthy, alcoholic burn and lack of depth. Certainly there is potential for rich, ripe flavours and wines with some staying power.

- **Vintages:** 1991, 1990, 1989, 1988, 1987, 1986, 1984, 1982, 1980, 1974.
- **Recommended producers:** Delheim, La Bonheur, Meerlust, Nederburg, Overgaauw.

Taste on:

SOUTH AFRICA: Blends of Cabernet and Merlot, notably Meerlust's Rubicon, which is 65% Cabernet Sauvignon, 10% Cabernet France and 25% Merlot; Carlonet from Uitkyk, which is mainly Cabernet, but not obvious from the label.

Cabernet Sauvignon from elsewhere in the New World. ▷Chile probably has most in common with South Africa, rather than ▷Australia or ▷California.

FRANCE: ▷Médoc, ▷St-Emilion.

 ## Sparkling Wine

Sparkling wine is a general term to describe a wine containing bubbles of carbon dioxide, which are the result of a second fermentation. A base wine is made in the normal way, and yeast and sugar are added to induce the second fermentation. The yeast feeds off the sugar creating carbon dioxide and also a fine sediment, which needs to be removed. In the case of champagne and other wines made by the champagne method, a complicated process of *remuage*, whereby the sediment is shaken down so that it settles on the cork, and *dégorgement* whereby it is removed from the bottle, is necessary. A simpler process is called the *Charmat* or *cuvé close* method, whereby the second fermentation takes place in a vat and the wine is filtered under pressure to remove the offending sediment. This is used for cheaper sparkling wines like German ▷Sekt, and can be detected as the bubbles are less fine and do not have the staying power of champagne method wines. Alternatively there is the transfer method, which is a mixture of both, in that the second fermentation takes place in the bottle, but then the wine is decanted into a tank for filtration prior to final bottling. It is also possible for carbon dioxide to be injected into a wine, for example ▷Mateus Rosé, but then the pressure is not great enough for it to be truly sparkling and the wine goes flat very quickly indeed.

Taste on:
▷Champagne; ▷Cava; ▷Sekt; ▷Asti Spumante; ▷Lambrusco; ▷Mateus Rosé, ▷Saumur.

☙ Spätlese

Spätlese is the second category of German Prädikat wines. Quite literally it means 'late picked' for the growers are not allowed to harvest the grapes until a full seven days after the start of the vintage for the particular grape variety in the specific region. The delay in picking means that the grapes are riper, with more sugar, so that the resulting wines are usually lightly honeyed, unless they are fermented out to be completely dry as a ▷*trocken* wine. They always have an underlying bite of acidity, but that is often masked by the sweetness. Spätlese is also used in Austrian wine law.

The equivalent in France is *Vendange Tardive*, which you find especially in Alsace, but also occasionally in ▷Jurançon, or anywhere else where the grapes might be harvested later than usual. *Moelleux*, as in ▷Vouvray or ▷Jurançon, indicates a certain degree of sweetness, but nothing too rich. *Abboccato* in Italy, as in ▷Orvieto, describes a medium sweet wine.

In the New World Late Harvest is the customary term on a wine label, indicating a wine that is usually positively sweet, rather than medium dry or medium sweet.

In Germany the Riesling grape makes the finest, most elegant Spätlese wines. From the Mosel valley they will always have an underlying steely acidity, while from the Rhine they will be riper and richer, especially from the Rheinpfalz, while those from Austria are even fuller and more mouthfilling.

Taste on:
GERMANY: Spätlese wines from ▷Bernkastel, ▷Johannisberg, ▷Nierstein, ▷Schlossböckelheim, ▷Deidesheim; also ▷Auslese wines from these districts.

AUSTRIA: Spätlese wines, not only made from Riesling, but also from ▷Grüner Veltliner, ▷Gewürztraminer and so on.

FRANCE: *Vendange Tardive* from ▷Riesling d'Alsace, and also ▷Pinot Gris d'Alsace; ▷Gewürztraminer d'Alsace and much rarer ▷Muscat d'Alsace. *Moelleux* wines from ▷Vouvray, ▷Jurançon.

ITALY: *Abboccato* wines from ▷Orvieto.

USA: Late Harvest wines, especially Riesling from California, Oregon and Washington State.

AUSTRALIA: Late Harvest Riesling, from the Barossa Valley.

NEW ZEALAND: Late Harvest Riesling, and also Muscat.

♆ Steen

Steen is the South African synonym for Chenin Blanc, which has adapted successfully to conditions in the Cape, where the warm climate gives infinitely less acidic grapes than in northern France. The technical expertise, with carefully controlled fermentation, makes for some fresh, grapey, dry white wine. Maybe they are a little neutral in flavour, with less obvious varietal character than Chenin Blanc from the Loire Valley, but often they are more attractive, with less searing acidity than a dry ▷Vouvray or ▷Anjou Blanc. Some Steen is bone dry, with pithy grapefruit flavours, while others are slightly sweet, with an underlying hint of honey. Sometimes Steen is made into a Late Harvest wine, with ripe, honeyed flavours, and varying intensity of sweetness. It is also one of the grape varieties in South Africa's best and rarest dessert wine, Edelkeur, a rich toffee flavoured wine.

- **Vintages:** 1991, 1990, 1988, but drink youngest available.

- **Recommended producers:** KWV, Grünberger, Nederburg.

Taste on:
NEW ZEALAND: Chenin Blanc with some off-dry grapey fruit.

USA: Off-dry Chenin Blanc from California, Washington State and Texas.

FRANCE: ▷Vouvray, Montlouis and ▷Anjou Blanc in riper, less acidic years; ▷Côtes de Gascogne.

ITALY: Some of the rather bland, neutral dry white wines of northern and central Italy such as ▷Galestro, ▷Orvieto.

SPAIN: New-style white ▷Rioja, with no oak-ageing.

🐂 Sweetness

There is an underlying snobbery about sweet wines, and it is not at all the done thing to admit to a sweet tooth. Forget it. Pudding wines are one of the undiscovered delights of wine tasting. I am probably not alone in admitting that the first wine I really enjoyed was pretty sweet, then my tastebuds began to appreciate dry and red wines and finally turned the full circle and returned to lusciously sweet honeyed dessert wines. Try the simple combination of ▷Sauternes and strawberries. The natural ripe sweetness of the strawberries – don't smother them with sugar – complements the honeyed flavours of the wine.

Sauternes is universally recognised as one of the great sweet wines of the world. The production of fine Sauternes, and adjoining ▷Barsac, depends upon very particular climatic conditions to produce what is called noble rot (as opposed to grey rot) or *botrytis cinera*. This is a kind of fungus that attacks the ripe grapes, dehydrating them so that they become shrivelled and almost raisinlike. Noble rot (or *pourriture noble* in French) develops with damp misty mornings, bringing the humidity necessary to encourage the growth of the fungus, which must be followed by brilliant warm autumnal sunshine to dry the grapes. The grape juice becomes rich and concentrated and the resulting wine wonderfully sweet, as the yeast is not able to convert all the sugar into alcohol, leaving much in the wine.

Other wines that depend upon the development of noble rot include the sweet wines of the Loire Valley, such as Bonnezeaux, ▷Coteaux du Layon and Quarts de Chaume, the better German wines from ▷Auslese quality upwards, and similarly Austrian wines. Any Italian wine labelled *muffato nobile* is made from grapes affected with noble rot, and so is sweet ▷Tokay from Hungary. In the best vintages in Alsace they make *Vendange Tardive* and *Sélection de Grains Nobles* from grapes with noble rot.

Terms such as Individual Bunch Selection, Botrytis Bunch Selected, Late Harvest, Botrytis Affected are the terms used in Australia, California, New Zealand and South Africa to indicate a sweet wine.

There are other ways of making sweet wine. In some of the vineyards adjoining Sauternes and Barsac where the development of noble rot is even less certain, they can chaptalise the grape juice and then stop the fermentation by filtration, to leave the desired amount of sweetness in the wine. ▷Monbazillac is usually made like this too, though in an ideal world the grapes are ripe enough not to require chaptalisation and may even develop noble rot.

In ▷Jurançon the grapes are left on the vines well into November in order to allow them to be dried by the prevailing winds from the Pyrenees. *Recioto* from ▷Soave and ▷Valpolicella are also made from dried grapes, which the Italians called *passito*. They are left to dehydrate for a few weeks after they have been picked.

In case of wines like ▷Muscat de Beaumes-de-Venise and other *vins doux naturels*, the fermentation is stopped by adding grape brandy in order to retain the natural sweetness of the Muscat grape. Several other ▷fortified wines are sweet for the same reason.

Taste on:

FRANCE: Bonnezeaux; ▷Vouvray; ▷Jurançon; ▷Sauternes; ▷Barsac; ▷Muscat de Beaumes-de-Venise; ▷Monbazillac; ▷Coteaux du Layon.

GERMANY: ▷Auslese; ▷Beerenauslese; ▷Trockenbeerenauslese; ▷Eiswein.

HUNGARY: ▷Tokay.

▷Riesling.

🍇 Syrah/Shiraz

Syrah and Shiraz are synonymous. Shiraz is what the Australians call the Syrah of France. Popular theory has it that this grape variety originated somewhere in the Middle East, not too far from the town of Shiraz, in what is today southeastern Iran. From there it travelled to the northern Rhône Valley where it makes such powerful, intense wines as ▷Côte Rôtie and ▷Hermitage. Further south it features as part of the blend in ▷Côtes du Rhône and ▷Châteauneuf-du-Pape and is planted throughout

233

Provence and the Midi as a *cépage améliorateur*, an improving grape variety, appreciated for its ability to boost the flavour of less exciting Carignan and Grenache. It can make particularly good ▷*vins de pays*, as a single grape variety, notably in Vin de Pays de l'Ardèche.

Elsewhere in Europe it has been largely ignored, with one successful planting to date in Tuscany, on the Chianti Classico estate of Isole e Olena.

As for the New World, Shiraz accounts for an enormous proportion of the vineyards of Australia, particularly in the Hunter Valley, where it is sometimes called Hermitage. (See entry on ▷Australian Shiraz.)

In California a handful of wineries, dubbed the Rhône Rangers, are producing some very acceptable examples of Syrah, not to be confused with the California Petite Sirah, known as the Durif in France, and no relation.

The flavour is typified by blackcurrant gums, not ripe blackcurrant fruit, but the dry, spicey, peppery flavours of fruit gums, which when mature, develop fuller, meatier flavours, maybe with overtones of rubber or tar. The colour is always deep and intense and the wines are rich and full-bodied, with a high degree of tannin in their youth. In Australia they may also have herbal minty flavours.

 Taste on:

FRANCE: ▷Côte Rôtie, ▷Hermitage, ▷Crozes Hermitage, St-Joseph, ▷Cornas, Vin de Pays de l'Ardèche and other *vins de pays* from the Midi, with the mention of Cépage Syrah on the label.

ITALY: Syrah from Isole e Olena in Tuscany.

▷AUSTRALIA: Shiraz.

CALIFORNIA: Syrah from Joseph Phelps, Ojai, Qupe, Bonny Doon, Kendall-Jackson and Zaca Mesa.

ARGENTINA: Finca Flichman produces a Syrah that is not unlike a light ▷Crozes Hermitage.

SOUTH AFRICA: Shiraz.

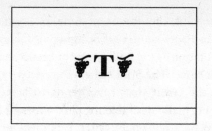

 Tannin

Tannin in wine is detected by the puckering sensation around the tongue and gums. It is identical with the effect obtained from drinking very strong tea and in wine, comes from the skins, pips and maybe stalks of the grapes, and also sometimes from the ▷oak barrels in which the wine may have been kept. It is essential in any young red wine that is destined for a long life. Tannin, as well as ▷acidity, gives a red wine backbone, and prevent it from tasting flabby. As the wine matures, the tannin will diminish, but never completely disappear, so that the taste of the wine softens and mellows. A young wine must have enough ▷fruit to balance the reduction of tannin.

Taste on:

FRANCE: Young ▷claret, ▷Cahors, ▷Côte Rôtie and other wines from ▷Syrah.

ITALY: ▷Barolo and ▷Brunello di Montalcino.

PORTUGAL: Young vintage ▷port, ▷Dão, ▷Bairrada.

USA: Young ▷Cabernet Sauvignon, from ▷California, Washington State, Oregon, Long Island.

AUSTRALIA: Young ▷Cabernet Sauvignon, young ▷Shiraz.

Tavel

For some curious reason, Tavel is an appellation for pink wine alone, in a region that is better suited to producing red wine. It is in the southern

Rhône, northwest of the town of Avignon, which is, above all, ▷Châteauneuf-du-Pape country, if not gutsy ▷Côtes du Rhône. Tavel established a reputation as the leading *rosé* of France, and has been resting on its laurels ever since. The principal grape variety is the rather alcoholic Grenache, with the result that Tavel tends to lack the elegant, fresh fruitiness that is normally desirable for pink wines. It behaves as though it really wants to be a red wine. Often it is more orange than pink in colour and sometimes too heavy and alcoholic, so that it ends up being dull and flabby, without any real fruit. However, if you drink it within a year of the vintage, there is hope. It is still a pretty serious mouthful of wine, no ethereal *rosé*, but quite full-bodied with some strawberry fruit.

● **Vintages:** 1991, 1990, 1989, 1988.

● **Recommended producers:** Aquéria, Genestière, Trinque-vedel, Vieux Moulin, Forcadière.

 Taste on:
FRANCE: The nearby appellation of Lirac; ▷Côtes du Rhône; pink Gigondas and other pink versions of the red wines of the southern Rhône namely Liras, ▷Côtes du Rhône; ▷Côtes de Provence, Coteaux d'Aix-en-Provence, ▷Bandol, Coteaux Varois and Palette rosé.

The pink wine produced by Les Salins du Midi, namely Vin de Pays des Sables du Golfe du Lion, Gris de Gris.

Other pink wines from the south of France, ▷*vins de pays* and ▷Coteaux du Languedoc.

Rosé de Béarn, from the Pyrenees.

SPAIN: Pink wines from the DOs of ▷Rioja, ▷Navarra, ▷Penedés, Léon and ▷Jumilla, which is occasionally pink.

🍇 **Tignanello** ♥♥♥

Tignanello has set the pace for the new wave of Tuscan winemaking over the last two decades. It comes from the internationally popular ▷Cabernet Sauvignon which is blended with the instrinsically Tuscan ▷Sangiovese, in the proportions of one to four, with further international appeal added by 18 months ageing in small French ▷oak *barriques*, rather than the traditional large oak casks of Italy. Its success took even its creators, Antinori, by surprise, and with imitation being the sincerest form of flattery, many other similar *vini da tavola* (which is all Tignanello can ever be, as it conforms to no wine law) have followed in its wake.

In the mid-seventies when Chianti was in the doldrums, Tignanello showed just how good Tuscan wine could be. It is still one of the best super-Tuscans, as these alternative *vini da tavola* are sometimes called; an elegant, stylish wine, reminiscent of good ▷Chianti Classico, if not ▷Brunello di Montalcino, with something of the elegance of a classed-growth ▷claret. Maybe Tignanello is the wine to wean one-track-minded lovers of Bordeaux onto Tuscany, for unlike ▷Sassicaia there is an indefinable Italian quality about it.

● **Vintages:** 1990, 1988, 1985, 1983, 1977.

Taste on:
ITALY: Other so-called super-Tuscan *vini da tavola* such as Cepparello ❦❦, Fontalloro ❦❦, the wines made by Monte-vertine ❦❦, Capannelle ❦❦; ▷Vino Nobile di Montepulciano; ▷Chianti Classico; ▷Brunello di Montalcino; Carmignano, a tiny DOCG, to the west of Florence, that includes a small proportion of Cabernet Sauvignon in the blend with Sangiovese.

FRANCE: Classed-growth ▷Claret, for that is the quality level of Tignanello and the best super-Tuscans, probably St-Julien, Pauillac and Margaux, and maybe also ▷St-Emilion and Pomerol.

SPAIN: ▷Ribera del Duero.

❦ Tokay

Tokay, or Tokaji, to use the Hungarian spelling, is not only Hungary's most individual wine, but one of the world's great dessert wines. It has nothing to do with ▷Pinot Gris-Tokay d'Alsace. That particular confusion of names has something to do with a Baron Schwendi who is supposed to have fought the Turks at Tokay and brought vines back from the area to his estate in Alsace.

Tokay, like many other fine dessert wines, depends upon the grapes being affected with noble rot. There are various degrees of sweetness.

Driest is Tokay Szamorodni, meaning 'as it comes', implying that nothing has been added to the wine, which can be either dry or sweet depending on the proportion of grapes affected by noble rot. Next is Tokay Aszú, the sweetness of which is measured in putts, according to the number of putts of very sweet wine added to the base wine. Three, four or five is normal; six is exceptional. Then there is even sweeter Tokay Aszú Essencia and richest of all Tokay Essence, which is very rare and precious and attributed with life-restoring powers.

Tokay Aszú five putts is what we should look out for, for a deliciously rich, concentrated dessert wine. It is the amber colour of *amontillado* ▷sherry, with a taste of toffee-apples and burnt sugar, with quite a sharp bite of acidity on the finish. It really fills the mouth. Tokay will age for many years, developing a dry, roasted, toffee and treacle flavour, rather like old ▷Sauternes.

• **Vintages:** 1990, 1989, 1988, 1986, 1985, 1983, 1982, 1981, 1979, 1976, 1975, 1974, 1973, 1972, 1971.

• **Recommended producers:** For the moment the State Cellars have the monopoly, but that may change.

 Taste on:
FRANCE: ▷Sauternes and maybe ▷Barsac equal five putts; ▷Coteaux du Layon and Bonnezeaux three putts.

GERMANY: ▷Trockenbeerenauslese equals five putts; ▷Auslese three.

AUSTRIA: ditto.

ITALY: The richness combined with the sharp finish are similar to sweeter forms of Vin Santo from Tuscany, although that is made from dried grapes, rather than grapes affected with botrytis.

SOUTH AFRICA: Edelkeur ▼▼, the country's finest sweet wine.

AUSTRALIA: ▷Liqueur Muscat is a little richer and fuller in the mouth, but there is a comparable sweetness, such as Bailey's Founders' Liqueur Muscat, with wonderful orange marmalade and cinnamon on the palate and a smooth velvety finish.

☙ Toro

Toro is one of the newer *Denominaciónes de Origen* of Spain, created as recently as 1987, for red, white and pink wines, allowing for a classification of *joven, crianza, reserva* and *gran reserva*. However, Toro at its most typical is a red wine, with a year or two's ageing in both barrel and bottle. The principal grape variety is Tinto Fino, the Tempranillo of ▷Rioja, which can be blended with Garnacha (or Grenache), but is best on its own.

When it is young, Toro is quite firmly tannic, but it matures with some ageing in American oak barrels to become softer, with smooth, chewy fruit. Quite spicey, with hints of liquorice and some ripe, plummy fruit, it fills the mouth, but becomes more delicate with age, with some meaty flavours and hints of Bovril.

- **Vintages:** 1991, 1990, 1989, 1986, 1985.

- **Recommended producers:** Bodegas Farina is considered the best, selling their wines under the name of Colegiato (which is aged only in bottle) and Gran Colegiato (which is kept in both barrel and bottle); also Bodegas Luis Mateos with the Vega de Toro label.

Taste on:
SPAIN: Other DOs in northern Spain such as ▷Ribera del Duero, though Toro lacks its elegance; ▷Rioja *con crianza* and *reserva*; ▷Navarra.

FRANCE: Wines from the southern Rhône such as ▷Côtes du Rhône, Côtes du Lubéron and Côtes du Ventoux; wines from the Midi, such as ▷Corbières and ▷Minervois; ▷Bandol; ▷Côtes de Provence and Coteaux d'Aix-en-Provence.

☙ Trebbiano di Romagna

Trebbiano is a constituent of so many Italian white wines, like ▷Soave, ▷Frascati, ▷Orvieto, ▷Galestro, Bianco di Custoza, Lugana and Montecarlo, to name but a few. However, it is in the vineyards of Emilia-Romagna that you find it undiluted by other more interesting varieties and at its dullest and most flavourless. Why include Trebbiano di Romagna in this book at all? Well, it is the mainstay of one and a half and two litre bottles of white wine from Italy. If you ask for a carafe of house white, or *bianco della casa* in an Italian trattoria in London, New York, or Bologna, the chances are that you will be given Trebbiano di Romagna.

You probably will not be that excited by it either. However with luck, if it is well chilled, it will be a perfectly palatable dry white wine, quite innocuous and totally unmemorable. If you taste it, you may find a hint of almonds, a touch of acidity and some fleeting fruit.

Ugni Blanc is the French synonym for Trebbiano and grown not only in the vineyards of the Charente and Gers for distillation into Cognac and Armagnac, but also widely in the south of France, where it contributes to numerous wines like ▷Corbières, ▷Minervois, ▷Côtes du Roussillon, ▷Coteaux du Languedoc and the ▷Côtes de Provence, but never features on the label.

- **Vintages:** Drink the youngest available.

- **Recommended producers:** I do not know of anyone who stakes their reputation on Trebbiano di Romagna.

 Taste on: (more adventurously)
ITALY: Other white wines from central Italy, which include Trebbiano, but other grapes as well, for more flavour, such as Bianco Val d'Arbia, Bianco Vergine Valdichiana, ▷Galestro, Bianco di San Torpè, Est! Est!! Est!!!

▷Soave, and nearby Bianco di Custoza, Lugana, Gambellara.

Trebbiano d'Abruzzo; the only other wine with Trebbiano on the label, which is not made only from Trebbiano, but also from the only slightly less neutral Bombino.

FRANCE: White wines from the south like ▷Côtes du Roussillon, ▷Minervois, ▷Corbières, Picpoul de Pinet in the ▷Coteaux du Languedoc, ▷Côtes de Provence, Coteaux d'Aix-en-Provence, ▷Côtes du Rhône.

🍇 Trocken

Trocken simply means dry and is a relatively new description for German wine. Some German wine producers feel disadvantaged by the underlying implication of sweetness in German wines which they consider makes their wines unsuitable for drinking with a meal. This may be so, but the current fashion for *trocken* wine in Germany does little for the tastebuds. With no residual sugar and the low level of alcohol typical of all German wines, the taste of many *trocken* wines seems skeletal and hollow and completely unbalanced. However, there are exceptions to every generalisation and some producers are achieving some success with the drier wines, particularly those from the more southern vineyards of Germany, with the advantage of grapes that are richer in sugar in the first place, such as Deidesheim in the ▷Rheinpfalz, and especially ▷Baden, where about three quarters of the production is designated *trocken*.

The taste of a good *trocken* depends very much upon the grape variety. Usually it is firmly acidic, but hopefully not sour, light in body, with some dry, grassy fruit, and maybe stoney hints of flavour. A Gewürztraminer *trocken* is not unlike a ▷Gewürztraminer d'Alsace while a Pinot Gris or Ruländer *trocken* may be like a very austere ▷Chablis. I just cannot help thinking that when there are so many other good dry white wines made elsewhere in the world, the Germans would do best to stick to what they are really good at, namely lovely, honeyed, elegant ▷Spätlese and ▷Auslese.

• **Vintages:** The riper years, such as 1990, 1989, 1988, 1985.

• **Recommended producers:** Sichel's Novum, Lingenfelder, Schloss Vollrads, Karl Heinz Johner, Georg Breuer, Weingut Knipser, Schlossgut Diel, Schloss Rheinhartshausen.

 Taste on:
GERMANY: *Trocken* wines from ▷Franconia and ▷Baden; also ▷*halbtrocken* wines.

FRANCE: ▷Muscadet; Gros Plant du Pays Nantais; Coteaux Champenois, the still white wines of Champagne.

▷English wines.

PORTUGAL: ▷Vinho Verde.

 ## Trockenbeerenauslese ♀♀♀

Trockenbeerenauslese is the sweetest category of both German and Austrian Prädikat wines, meaning, literally, a selection of dried berries, or in other words, grapes so affected by noble rot that they have become shrivelled and raisin-like, so that the resulting wines are sublimely rich and luscious and will develop into great bottles with age. Trockenbeer-enauslese wines are only made in the very best years, when the autumn weather gives the desired combination of damp, misty mornings and warm, sunny afternoons to encourage the development of prerequisite noble rot. Quantities are tiny and prices inevitably high.

On the wine labels of the New World the nearest equivalent is Individual Berry Selection. What is not stated is the degree of noble rot but price and presentation are a clue. A very expensive half-bottle is more likely to equate to a TBA, the common abbreviation, than to a ▷Beerenauslese. However, New World wines tend to be higher in alcohol than their German counterparts, thus giving an impression of extra richness.

The best TBAs are made from ▷Riesling in Germany. This grape variety gives the most subtle and complex flavours, ripe and honeyed, lusciously sweet, but never cloying, for it always retains a good balance of acidity to give the wine backbone. Some of the other, newer German grape varieties, such as Kerner, Optima and Huxelrebe attain more easily the required sugar level for TBA, but the underlying flavours lack depth.

●   **Vintages:** 1990, 1989, 1988, 1985, 1983, 1976, 1971, 1959.

 Taste on:

GERMANY: ▷Beerenauslese wines; ▷Eiswein.

AUSTRIA: Trockenbeerenauslese, Ausbruch (an Austrian term, coming between TBA and Beerenauslese) and Beerenauslese wines.

FRANCE: *Sélection de Grains Nobles* Riesling, ▷Gewürztraminer and ▷Pinot Gris from Alsace.
▷Sauternes and ▷Barsac; the underlying fruit flavours may be different, but the degree of sweetness is very similar.
▷Vouvray, Bonnezeaux and Chaume from the Loire Valley; ▷Muscat de Beaume-de-Venise.

ITALY: Torcolato; Recioto di ▷Soave.

CALIFORNIA: Individual Berry Selection Rieslings, from Château St. Jean, Freemark Abbey and Joseph Phelps.

NEW ZEALAND: Late Harvest Rhine Riesling ᵷ from Weingut Seifried's Redwood Valley Estate and Dry River Riesling, Botrytis Bunch Selection.

SOUTH AFRICA: Edelkeur.

Valdepeñas

Valdepeñas is a hilly enclave in the vast plains of La Mancha of central Spain. Back in the 16th century the region was called the Valle de Peñas, or the Valley of Stones, a description which is still appropriate today and gives some idea of the appearance of the vineyards. Although Valdepeñas also produces white and pink wines, it is the red that is making its mark, especially with the considerable recent improvement in winemaking techniques. The best reds come increasingly from the Cencibel grape, which is otherwise known as Tempranillo, as in ▷Rioja. Pure Cencibel aged in oak for a few months offers exciting flavours here, as it does in other parts of Spain. This new style of Valdepeñas is rich, plummy and spicy, with a mellow sweetness and soft chewy fruit.

● **Vintages:** 1991, 1990, 1989, 1988, 1987, 1986, 1984, 1983, 1982, 1978.

● **Recommended producers:** Bodegas Félix Solis, with the brand name Viña Albali, Bodegas Los Llanos. Valdepeñas is where Marqués de Griñon's pure oak-aged Cabernet Sauvignon is produced, but not as a DO wine for it does not conform to the rules. Bodegas Luis Megia, with the brand name Duque de Estrada Reserva.

Taste on:
SPAIN: Other reds based on Tempranillo from ▷Rioja, ▷Ribera del Duero and ▷Toro.
Almansa, a nearby DO where Garnacha and Monastrell are the main grape varieties. However, with comparable climate and soil, there is a similarity in the wines.

FRANCE: The wines of the southern Rhône, such as
▷Châteauneuf-du-Pape, Gigondas, ▷Côtes du Rhône.
▷Corsica.

ᛉ Valpolicella

Valpolicella is one of Italy's best-known wines. It comes from vineyards
northwest of the Romeo and Juliet city of Verona near Lake Garda.
Sadly, it covers a multitude of sins, with a distressingly wide quality
range, resulting from an overextension of the production area and an
excessive increase in yields. At worst it is pale red, boring and insipid.
Look for wines from the traditional heart of the area which will bear the
key word *classico* on the label. This is where the best wines are made.
Even better are the *ripasso* wines when the fermenting juice is put into a
vat of last year's *recioto* (see below) lees, which gives the young wine
much more fruit, flavour, structure and body. A *ripasso* wine is quite
deep in colour, with a nose of ripe plums and cherries. On the palate
there is tannin and plenty of rich cherry fruit, with hints of spice and
liquorice. The taste is rich rather than sweet, with a long finish.
Unfortunately the bureaucracy of the EEC is such that while the word
ripasso is permissible on a *vino da tavola*, such as Campo Fiorin, it is not
allowed on a Valpolicella label, so the poor consumer has no way of
knowing how the wine has been made.

Recioto is another word to look out for on a Valpolicella label. It means
that the wine has been made from grapes that have been left to dry and
dehydrate, so that the juice becomes rich and concentrated. If the sub-
sequent fermentation is stopped before all the sugar has turned into
alcohol, the resulting wine will be rich and sweet. Sometimes it can be
either fortified with brandy or turned into sparkling wine. If on the other
hand it is fermented until it is completely dry, it takes on a different
stature and is called *amarone*. It is rich and concentrated with sour cherries
and plums and a meaty, smokey finish.

- **Vintages:** Basic Valpolicella Classico should be drunk as young
as possible. Recioto della Valpolicella and Amarone: 1990, 1989, 1988,
1986, 1985, 1981.

- **Recommended producers:**
Ripasso styles: Allegrini, Le Ragose, Quintarelli, Serego Alighieri; also
Masi's Campo Fiorin and Tedeschi's Capitel San Rocco, which are sold

as *vino da tavola*; plus Boscaini's Le Canne, Santi's Castello d'Illasi, Bolla's Jago.

Classico: Boscaini, Guerrieri-Rizzardi, Masi, Tedeschi, Zenato.

Amarone: Quintarelli, Allegrini, Le Ragose, Masi, Serègo Alighieri, Tedeschi.

 Taste on:

YOUNG VALPOLICELLA:

ITALY: ▷Bardolino and ▷Dolcetto.

FRANCE: ▷Beaujolais.

RIPASSO STYLE:

FRANCE: Wines of the southern Rhône, ▷Châteauneuf-du-Pape and adjoining Gigondas, Vacqueyras; maybe richer ▷Côtes de Provence and Coteaux d'Aix-en-Provence, particularly from the Coteaux des Baux; ▷Bandol.

RECIOTO:

ITALY: Sagrantino di Montefalco *passito*.

PORTUGAL: ▷Port, maybe of single *quinta* quality, as an after-dinner drink.

FRANCE: Rivesaltes.

AMARONE ❦❦ :

FRANCE: ▷Châteauneuf-du-Pape, ▷Bandol.

▷AUSTRALIA: Shiraz, for a meaty, full-bodied mouthful of wine.

Verdicchio

Verdicchio, or to give this white wine its full name, Verdicchio dei Castelli di Jesi comes from the hills of Marche behind the port of Ancona. The castles of Jesi are the hilltop villages of the region, which look remarkably like ruined castles from afar. *Classico* on the label means the wine has come from the very heart of the vineyard area. The principal grape variety is Verdicchio, which is grown only in this part of Italy. The wine has always been presented in an attention-seeking green, elongated amphora-shaped bottle, which seems to prevent us from taking it at all seriously. However that is our loss, for while it is true that everyday Verdicchio can be just a little bit boring, with rather neutral dry fruit, good Verdicchio, especially from single vineyards, has some real flavour.

The revelation to my tastebuds was Casal di Serra, a single-vineyard wine from Umani Ronchi, which reminded me of ▷Chablis with its leafy fruit and firm acidity. Verdicchio is crisp and fresh, with firm stoney acidity and herbal fruit and hints of green pepper on the palate. The nose is quite fragrant, a little leafy and maybe a touch dusty. Its high level of acidity makes Verdicchio suitable for sparkling wines but these have yet to find their way onto the export market.

• **Vintages:** Drink youngest available.

• **Recommended producers:** With an increasing emphasis on single-vineyard names, or *crus*, it is worth seeking one of these out for extra flavour and quality. Casal di Serra from Umani Ronchi, Le Moie from Fazi-Battaglia, Monte Schiavo's Colle del Sole and Il Pallio, Garofoli's Macrina; also Fratelli Bucci and Zaccagnini.

 Taste on:

ITALY: The neighbouring DOC of Verdicchio di Matelica is rarely seen outside the region, but if you are on holiday on the Italian Adriatic, why not try it? Other wines from central Italy tend to be a little fuller and softer, although Grechetto, a grape variety peculiar to Umbria, may be an exception, with some leafy fruit and firm acidity, if it comes from a good producer like Adanti.

FRANCE: ▷Muscadet; ▷Côtes de Gascogne; ▷Chablis, in exceptional circumstances; ▷Apremont; Vermentino from ▷Corsica and Sardinia has a similar dusty fragrance about it, with firm acidity.

PORTUGAL: ▷Vinho Verde.

 ## Vernaccia di San Gimignano

There are various Vernaccia in Italy, all quite different from each other, covering the taste spectrum with red, white, fortified, sparkling and sweet wines. However, the best-known and most popular is undoubt-edly Vernaccia di San Gimignano, a dry white wine from vineyards around the hilltop town of San Gimignano with the high towers described as Tuscany's answer to Manhattan.

The wine has improved enormously in the last few years, with ques-tioning and talented producers working hard to bring out the hitherto elusive character of the Vernaccia grape. Good Vernaccia di San Gimignano has a dry, nutty, or sometimes leafy quality about it, with hints of butter, not so unlike a ▷Chardonnay. One or two producers are giving their wine some ageing in ▷oak barrels and this does indeed tend to make it taste even more like Chardonnay.

● **Vintages:** 1990, 1989, 1988; drink fairly young, within two or three years of the vintage.

● **Recommended producers:** Poderi Montenidoli; Teruzzi e Puthod, Falchini, San Quirico, Guicciardini Strozzi, Le Colonne, Il Paradiso, Pietrafitta, Pietraserena, La Quercia di Racciano.

 Taste on:

ITALY: Some of the other white wines of central Italy are not so unlike Vernaccia di San Gimignano. The chances are that if you like Vernaccia di San Gimignano, you would also enjoy ▷Orvieto, Montecarlo, Pomino and Montescudaio, wines with a little weight and flavour, which are dry without being acidic.

FRANCE: Some of the more distinctive white wines of the south, such as ▷Cassis and Bellet; ▷Chablis; ▷Mâcon.

Oak-aged Vernaccia di San Gimignano, such as Teruzzi e Puthod's Terre di Tufo has a resemblance to nutty ▷Meursault or ▷Rully.

SPAIN: Oak-aged ▷Rioja, such as Marqués de Murrieta; an oak-aged ▷Penedés.

🐏 Vin de Pays

There are *vins de pays* all over viticultural France, 144 at the last count, covering a multitude of flavours and grape varieties. However, the greatest concentration lies in the south, in the departments of the Hérault and the Aude. It is here that some of the most interesting wines are found, where the greatest amount of experimentation is taking place, using unconventional grape varieties and new methods of vinification. It is, therefore, impossible to categorise *vins de pays* in any way, particularly as the quality range can vary enormously from very simple undistinguished plonk to really stylish, flavoursome wines. One clue to taste of a *vin de pays* will be any mention of a grape variety on the label, such as ▷Merlot, ▷Syrah, ▷Cabernet Sauvignon, ▷Chenin Blanc, ▷Chardonnay, ▷Sauvignon or Marsanne. The most exciting *vins de pays* are produced in regions where there is no corresponding appellation, so that the producer concentrates all his efforts on it alone. The most distinguished example is a Vin de Pays de l'Hérault from Mas de Daumas Gassac, which is in a class of its own, bearing more resemblance to a classed-growth claret or a California Cabernet Sauvignon than a humble *vin de pays*.

In southwest France Vin de Pays des ▷Côtes de Gascogne has come into its own, with the decline in Armagnac sales. Vin de Pays du Jardin de la France covers the whole of the Loire Valley, while Vin de Pays de l'Ile de Beauté describes the island of ▷Corsica. In the Rhône Valley, Vin de Pays de l'Ardèche produces some good Syrah, Gamay and Chardonnay, as do the Coteaux des Baronnies.

● **Vintages:** Vintages are rarely significant. For white wines, drink the youngest available and keep reds no longer than three or four years, except for Mas de Daumas Gassac, which can be left for about ten years.

● **Recommended producers:** *Vins de pays* are often made by local cooperatives rather than individual estates. However, there are several to recommend from the south of France. Mas de Daumas Gassac, Domaine de Limbardie, Domaine du Bosc, Domaine de la Grange Rouge, Domaine de la Fadèze, Domaine de la Gardie, Domaine St-Victor, Domaine des Pourthié, Domaine de Capion, Domaine de l'Arjolle, Domaine St-Martin de la Garrigue, les Salins du Midi, Domaine la Rosière in the Coteaux des Baronnies.

 Taste on:
FRANCE: ▷Côtes du Rhône and ▷Crozes Hermitage for Syrah. Young claret for Cabernet Sauvignon.

▷Sauvignon de Touraine and Sauvignon de St-Bris for Sauvignon.

White ▷Côtes du Rhône and ▷Crozes Hermitage Blanc for Marsanne.

▷Anjou Blanc and dry ▷Vouvray for Chenin Blanc.

▷Mâcon for Chardonnay.

EASTERN EUROPE:

▷Merlot: from Bulgaria or Yugoslavia.

▷Cabernet Sauvignon: from Bulgaria and Yugoslavia.

▷Chardonnay: from Bulgaria, Hungary and Yugoslavia.

Vin jaune ♥♥

Vin Jaune is one of the most original wines of France. It comes from the hilly region of the Jura in eastern France, along the border with Switzerland. The method of making it contradicts most accepted oenological practices, for the wine, made from the little-known Savagnin grape, is left to sit in small oak barrels for a minimum of six years, during which time the barrels are not topped up, but instead exposed to the summer and winter variations of temperature in a cellar that, for this reason, must not be completely below ground. During this ageing period a *flor* or white veil of yeast develops. It is this *flor* that gives Vin Jaune its original flavour. After six years of ageing in cask Vin Jaune has developed into the most distinctively nutty flavoured wine with a firm bite of acidity and almost salty undertones. At first taste it may seem oxidised. You either love it or hate it.

The best Vin Jaune of all comes from the tiny village of Château Chalon, where they make that and nothing else. The three other appellations of the Jura, ▷Arbois, ▷Côtes du Jura and L'Etoile, all include Vin Jaune in their range.

● **Vintages:** 1983, 1982, 1981, 1979, 1978, 1976.

● **Recommended producers:** Jean Macle, Christian Bourdy, Château d'Arlay, Henri Maire, Rollet Frères, Domaine de Montbourgeau, Château de Gréa.

Taste on:

FRANCE: Other white wines from the Jura. While the slightly more conventional white wines of the Côtes du Jura and L'Etoile may not have the weight of Vin Jaune, there is often a similarity in the taste, with the same dry, nutty flavour, that on first mouthful you mistakenly think is oxidised.

SPAIN: The development of *flor* means that a resemblance with *fino* ▷sherry, and also *manzanilla*, is no surprise. Both have that distinctive salty nuttiness, that can be very appealing. However Vin Jaune is a table wine rather than a fortified wine and so is slightly lower in alcohol.

GREECE: ▷Retsina. No, the taste is not the same, but like Vin Jaune, retsina is far removed from the conventional taste of wine. Each has a sharp, distinctive note of flavour that attacks the palate in the same way.

Vinho Verde

The green wine of Portugal can in fact be either red or white. Verde in this instance means young, as opposed to *vinho maduro* which is mature wine. Much more red Vinho Verde is made than white, but more white than red is sold outside Portugal, so outside Portugal Vinho Verde is a light, dry white wine. At least it should be dry, but sometimes more commercial blends of Vinho Verde have had the sharp, acidic edge of youth taken off them, so that they taste slightly sweet and rather soft.

The real thing has a crisp, pithy, lemony, stoney acidity, with apples and apricots on the nose. It is light in alcohol, and if there is a high proportion of Alvarinho in the blend, very fresh, with more apricots and peaches, and without a trace of sweetness. Sometimes there is a tiny prickle of carbon dioxide which adds extra liveliness to the wine. As for red Vinho Verde, this is one of those wines that definitely does not travel. I have enjoyed it in Portugal with a dish of the traditional dried cod, *bacalhau*, but back in London it just did not taste the same, but seemed sour and green. Stick to the white.

- **Vintages:** Drink last year's wine.

- **Recommended producers:** Single *quinta* wines offer more interest and flavour than branded blends: Quinta da Franqueira, Solar das Bouças, Palacio da Brejoeira, Quinta da Aveleda, which is different from plain Aveleda.

Taste on:

SPAIN: The white wines of Galicia, ▷Rias Baixas and Ribeiro are just across the border of the river Minho. Alvariño from Spain is very similar to Alvarinho from Portugal. However, Vinho Verde includes other grape varieties and sometimes has a firm, stonier flavour than the perfumed apricot character of the Alvarinho grape.

FRANCE: ▷Muscadet, ▷Bourgogne Aligoté, ▷Côtes de Gascogne, ▷Apremont.

GERMANY: A dominant feature of Vinho Verde is the lightness in body and alcohol, which it shares with the wines of Germany, particularly those of the Mosel. A ▷Kabinett from ▷Bernkastel may be more flowery in flavour, but will have the same elegance, with some underlying firm, crisp steely acidity.
Try also ▷*trocken* wines.

▷ENGLAND: For wines that are light in alcohol, and dry in character, with delicate fruit.

🍇 Vino Nobile di Montepulciano

Vino Nobile di Montepulciano is a red wine from southern Tuscany, from the hilltop town of Montepulciano. Its noble origins are more than somewhat blurred and no one is quite sure why the wine of Montepulicano was singled out for this epithet in the first place. It went through a period in the doldrums in the 1970s, producing inferior wines that compared with second-rate Chianti, but in the last few years great progress has been made and Vino Nobile di Montepulciano has again become the serious wine it once was. Good Vino Nobile compares with the best of ▷Chianti Classico for the grape varieties are the same, with Sangiovese, locally called Prugnolo, forming the backbone of the wine, with a minimum requirement of two year's ageing in large oak vats. However, from a good producer Vino Nobile can be even richer than Chianti Classico, fuller and plummier, with lovely spicy flavours, and enough tannin to allow it to age for a few years.

● **Vintages:** 1990, 1988, 1985, 1983, 1982, 1981.

• **Recommended producers:** Avignonesi, Poliziano, Boscarelli, Trerose, Rudolf Bindella, Fassati, Le Caggiole di Mezzo.

Taste on:

ITALY: Rosso di Montepulciano, made for the first time in 1989, is a lighter version of Vino Nobile, from the same grape varieties and vineyards, with a very much shorter ageing period.

▷Chianti Classico.

The best Vino Nobile has no white grapes and a negligible amount of Canaiolo, so does not taste so very different from a pure Sangiovese, such as ▷Brunello di Montalcino or some of the pure Sangiovese *vini da tavola* of Chianti.

Rubesco from Lungarotti in Torgiano; Carmignano, a small enclave in Chianti Montalbano, which includes a percentage of ▷Cabernet Sauvignon in its make-up.

FRANCE: ▷Claret, of *cru bourgeois* rather than *cru classé* quality, continuing the relationship between Sangiovese and Cabernet Sauvignon, and between Chianti and claret.

Volnay ♥♥♥

Volnay is taken as an example of the red wines of the Côte de Beaune, the southern half of the Côte d'Or, to differentiate it from the marginally heavier and richer wines of the Côte de Nuits, as illustrated by ▷Gevrey-Chambertin. Volnay is one of the more delicate and elegant wines of the Côte de Beaune. However, that said, much depends upon a producer's individual style. If you like good Volnay, you will also like Vosne-Romanée or Nuits-St-Georges.

As with all the red wines of the Côte d'Or, the grape variety is ▷Pinot Noir. In young wines it has an attractive raspberry-flavoured fruitiness, which develops many subtle and complex flavours as it matures, to take on a smooth, velvety character, sometimes with rich vegetal flavours, and sometimes with a more chocolatey taste. There is just enough tannin to provide backbone and structure. The finish of all good burgundy should be ripe and sweet, not sour and coarse.

There are several first-growth vineyards, such as Cailleret, Bousse d'Or, Les Santenots.

●   **Vintages:** 1990, 1989, 1988, 1985, 1983, 1982, 1978, 1971, 1969, 1966.

●   **Recommended producers:** from all over the Côte de Beaune – Blain-Gagnard, Pousse d'Or, Clerget, Comte Lafon, Marquis d'Angerville, Matrot, Simon Bize, Bernard Morey, Michel Lafarge, Jean-Marc Boillot, Tollot-Beaut, Luc Camus, Domaine Lejeune, Capron Manieux, Domaine Parent.

Taste on:

FRANCE: Other good burgundies of the Côte de Beaune, Aloxe-Corton, Savigny-les-Beaune, Beaune, Pommard, Auxey-Duresses, Santenay and so on. Also the fine burgundies of the Côte de Nuits, such as ▷Gevrey-Chambertin, Morey-St-Denis, Chambolle-Musigny, Vougeot, Vosne-Romanée and Nuits St-Georges.

▷Rully and other red wines of the Côte Chalonnaise, such as Mercurey and Givry.

Pinot Noir remains an elusive grape variety outside Burgundy. Attempts have been made to produce it, with varying success, in California, Oregon, Australia and New Zealand. See ▷Pinot Noir for details.

In Tuscany Pinot Noir has attracted less interest than Cabernet Sauvignon. However, an acceptable example comes from Ruffino, called Tondo del Nero. German and Austrian Spätburgunder just do not achieve the elegance and style of the Côte d'Or, nor does ▷Romanian Pinot Noir.

▼ Vouvray

Vouvray is the most versatile wine of the Loire Valley for it can be firmly dry or richly sweet and all flavours in between. The clue to its taste is on the label, with the words, *sec, demi sec, moelleux* or *doux*. Not only is it a still wine, but it can also be sparkling or *mousseux*, or even just slightly sparkling or *pétillant*.

Vouvray is made from ▷Chenin Blanc, grown around the town of Vouvray on the north bank of the Loire river. Dry Vouvray has a firm, almost green acidity that can be rather harsh, but at the same time it never quite loses the underlying hints of honey that are characteristic of Chenin Blanc. Here I must confess a prejudice. Young Chenin Blanc is one of the wines I find most difficult to appreciate and understand. So often I am disappointed by wines that seem to lack fruit, that have excessive acidity and a nose reminiscent of wet dogs and damp blankets. On the other hand, sweet mature Chenin Blanc is quite another matter. It takes on a completely different character. A young, sweet Vouvray will be deliciously honeyed, with apricots and peaches and cream, but never without that firm backbone of acidity, which enables it to age into a wonderfully complex wine, that may be at its best when it is 40 years old.

Montlouis, the less well-known village on the opposite side of the river, has the same taste spectrum.

● **Vintages:** 1990, 1989, 1988, 1985, 1983, 1982, 1978, 1976, 1975, 1970, 1969, 1959, 1947.

● **Recommended producers:** Foreau, Huet, Poniatowski, Jarry, Brédif, Champalon, Domaine des Aubuisières.

 Taste on:

DRY VOUVRAY:

FRANCE: ▷Anjou Blanc. Other dry Chenin Blanc from the Loire Valley including lesser-known appellations like Jasnières, Savennières, Coulée de Serrant, Coteaux de l'Aubance.
Côtes de St-Mont, from the foothills of the Pyrenees, has some of the honeyed character of Vouvray, with fresh acidity.
Chignin-Bergeron, from the village of Chignin in Savoie, made from the Roussanne grape, with honey and appley acidity.

HUNGARY: Hárslevelü, meaning lime leaf, is a Hungarian grape variety. It gives spice to the flavour of ▷Tokay, and as a varietal wine has the combination of honey and acidity that you find in Vouvray, with a smokey finish.

SOUTH AFRICA: ▷Steen.

SWEET VOUVRAY:

FRANCE: The other sweet appellations of the Loire Valley, namely ▷Coteaux du Layon, Quarts de Chaume, Chaume and Bonnezeaux; also lighter ▷Barsac and ▷Sauternes; ▷Jurançon *moelleux*.

ITALY: ▷Orvieto *abboccato*; Picolit, a sweet wine from Friuli; Torcolato, made by Maculan in Breganze.

SOUTH AFRICA: Late Harvest Steen; Late Harvest wines from elsewhere in the New World.

SPARKLING VOUVRAY:
FRANCE: The other white sparkling wine appellations of the Loire Valley are also made from Chenin Blanc, such as Crémant de la Loire and sparkling ▷Saumur; ▷Champagne; Blanquette de Limoux; ▷Cava;

GERMANY: ▷Sekt.

 # Vranac ❦

Vranac is one of the most original Yugoslav grape varieties, growing in Montenegro and Macedonia, and exported as a varietal wine. It produces full-bodied, robust red wine, with a deep colour, quite high alcohol and with warm fruit that is reminiscent of the southern Rhône Valley. There is a touch of bitterness on the finish, not unlike some southern Italian wines.

● **Vintages:** There is little vintage variation in Yugoslavia; drink within three or four years as Vranac does not age well.

 Taste on:
FRANCE: ▷Côtes du Rhône and nearby appellations such as Gigondas, Côtes du Ventoux and Côtes du Lubéron.

ITALY: Montepulciano d'Abruzzo ❦, not to be confused with ▷Vino Nobile di Montepulciano. In this instance Montepulciano is a grape variety, not a place, and grows in the wild hills of the Abruzzi behind Pescara, to make some warm, earthy, full-bodied red wines, with a slightly bitter finish.

 Yugoslav Merlot

Merlot has rather tended to play second fiddle to Cabernet Sauvignon in so many vineyards all over the world, in France, Italy, Eastern Europe, California and Australia. The one shining exception to this is Château Pétrus in Pomerol, where it accounts for a very substantial part of the blend. Another, less brilliant, example might also be found in Slovenia, along Yugoslavia's Dalmatian coast and in Istria. Merlot tends to flower and ripen earlier than Cabernet Sauvignon and therefore does better in a cooler climate. It has less tannin than Cabernet and in a very hot climate tends to lose acidity and become rather flabby. However, in the right conditions it develops some ripe, plummy fruit with a richness that Cabernet does not seem to achieve in Yugoslavia.

- **Vintages:** 1990, 1989, 1988.

- **Recommended producers:** Not applicable as the wine industry of Eastern Europe is still dominated by anonymous regional cooperatives.

Taste on:

HUNGARY: Here Merlot is confusingly known as Médoc Noir.

BULGARIA: Merlot from various regions, namely, Sakar Merlot. Stambolovo Region, Plovdiv Region.

ITALY: Merlot from the Veneto, Friuli, Trentino, Oltrepò Pavese and Colli Bolognesi.

FRANCE: ▷*Vins de pays* made from Merlot, from the Midi.

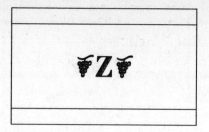

🍇 Zinfandel

Zinfandel is California's most individual wine. It is not produced anywhere else of significance, apart from the odd planting in South Africa and Australia, and no one quite knows where it came from in the first place. Hearsay has it that Agoston Haraszthy, the Hungarian nobleman who did so much for the blossoming Californian wine industry in the middle of the last century, brought numerous vine cuttings back from Europe, including what may have been the Primitivo of southern Italy, which has become the Zinfandel of California.

Zinfandel is above all versatile. It makes all manner of wines from pale pink blush, often labelled white Zinfandel, through fruity ▷Beaujolais lookalikes, medium-weight reds to more heady, alcoholic, tannic wines and finally Zinfandel can be used for fortified wines modelled on ruby ▷port. Californians tend to take it for granted and often ignore its true potential. However, when it is vinified with care and talent, Zinfandel can make some stunningly distinctive wines.

Zinfandel is at its best in the fuller-bodied, mouthfilling wines, that have some ripe berry fruit, with a substantial amount of tannin and meaty, spicey, liquorice flavours, not so very unlike a ▷Syrah. It should have weight and concentration, making a positive impact in the mouth.

- **Vintages:** 1991, 1990, 1989, 1988, 1987, 1986, 1985, 1984, 1983, 1982, 1981, 1980.

- **Recommended producers:** Ridge Vineyards with individual vineyard labels, such as Paso Robles and Geyserville, have paid Zinfandel as much attention as Cabernet Sauvignon; also Frog's Leap Wine Cellars, Lytton Springs, Sutter Home, Kenwood Vineyards, Nalle Cellars.

Taste on:

WHITE ZINFANDEL:
FRANCE: ▷Cabernet d'Anjou and Rosé d'Anjou.

LIGHT RED:
FRANCE: ▷Beaujolais and ▷Coteaux du Languedoc.

ITALY: ▷Dolcetto.

FULL-BODIED RED:
CALIFORNIA: ▷Syrah from wineries like Joseph Phelps, Ojai and Qupe.

FRANCE: Syrah from the Rhône Valley such as ▷Crozes Hermitage, St-Joseph, ▷Cornas.
▷Bandol.

ITALY: Primitivo di Manduria is supposed to be similar to Zinfandel but it rarely travels outside Puglia, so I am unable to substantiate this.
Recioto di ▷Valpolicella.

AUSTRALIA: Cape Mentelle Zinfandel; ▷Shiraz.

LEBANON: ▷Château Musar.

PORTUGAL: Periquita, from J. M. da Fonseca with some spicey, peppery fruit.

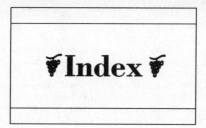

Index

Madeira 145, 147–9, 152, 192, 224, 226
Madiran 46, 53, 58, 80, 94, 149–50, 154
Málaga 84, 145, 148, 149, 150–1, 152, 161,
    165, 224, 226
Marcillac 82
Margaux 153, 237
Marsala 115, 148–9, 151–2, 226
Mas de Daumas Gassac 212, 249
Mateus Rosé 15, 55, 108, 141, 152–3, 230
Mavrud 51
Médoc 22, 48, 53, 55, 56, 57, 59, 80, 83,
    84, 105, 126, 153–5, 156, 171, 211, 216,
    229
Melnik 50–1
Menetou-Salon 11, 133, 174, 189, 194,
    214, 220, 222
Mercurey 208–9, 254
Merlot 7, 22, 49, 51, 55, 57, 59, 79, 83,
    155–6, 171, 249, 250, 257
Meursault 23, 24, 25, 53, 61, 66, 71, 72,
    97, 114, 127, 128, 132, 156–9, 172, 177,
    178, 182, 193, 205, 206, 209, 248
Minervois 16, 19, 86, 89, 91, 92, 98, 99,
    100, 101, 107, 109, 115, 117, 121, 131,
    159–60, 167, 170, 182, 206, 239, 240
Monbazillac 35, 40, 120, 160–1, 179, 233
Montagny 208–9
Montalcino 28, 48, 53
Montepulciano 28, 78, 101, 210, 256
Montilla 84, 149, 151, 161, 192, 224, 226
Montlouis 15, 21, 40, 92, 120, 232
Morago 56, 59
Morellino di Scansano 78
Morgon 36, 162
Moscadello 19, 142
Moscato di Pantelleria 165
Moscato di Strevi 19
Moscato Naturale di Asti 19–20
Mosel 12, 20, 42–3
Moulin á Vent 36, 82, 162
Moulis 154
Mourvèdre 30, 74, 76
Müller-Thurgau 28, 42, 43, 116, 130
Muscadet 11, 13, 17, 44, 90, 112, 121, 129,
    162–4, 177, 198, 208, 241, 247, 252
Muscat 27, 35, 40, 89, 106, 115, 118, 126,
    144, 150, 151, 164–8, 181, 182, 197, 224,
    231, 233, 241, 242, 259

Nahe-Schlossböckelheim see
    Schlossböckelheim
Navarra 101, 170–1, 182, 206, 207, 236,
    239
Nebbiolo 31, 33–4
New Zealand 36, 56, 72, 80, 123, 125,
    136, 165, 170–4, 183, 243
Nierstein 21, 39, 110, 136, 139, 143, 144,
    169, 175, 197, 201, 230
Nuits St Georges 61, 254

Oak 176–7, 235

Olasrizling 142, 144
Organic wine 177–8
Orvieto 21, 36, 93, 117, 120, 121, 138,
    178–9, 182, 230, 231, 232, 239, 248, 256
Othello 102, 107, 179–80

Palette 30, 64, 75, 76, 105, 128, 236
Pantelleria 168
Passe-tout-grain 52, 146
Pauillac 153, 237
Penedés 73, 80, 100, 99, 101, 113, 121,
    126, 144, 155, 156, 157, 166, 172, 181–2,
    193, 206, 207, 216, 236, 248
Periquita 18, 28, 100, 259
Pessac-Léognan 63, 64, 126
Piat d'Or 182–3
Piccolit 36, 93, 138, 228, 256
Pinotage 183–4
Pinot Bianco 185–6
Pinot Blanc 11, 28, 29, 50, 66, 67, 112,
    116, 129, 146–7, 184–6
Pinot Grigio 187–8
Pinot Gris 11, 28, 29, 40, 67, 116, 121,
    129, 130, 186–8, 231, 237, 242
Pinot Noir 9, 17, 18, 29, 52, 54, 61–2, 68,
    76, 122, 123, 133, 172–3, 188–90, 197,
    206, 207, 209, 214, 253, 254
Poggio alle Gazze 215
Pomerol 22, 84, 123, 155, 156, 200, 206,
    211, 237
Pomino 206
Pommard 17, 123, 254
Port 104, 108, 148, 168, 190–3, 223, 235,
    246
Pouilly-Fuissé 52, 53, 72, 147, 193–4, 209
Pouilly-Fumé 11, 62, 81, 174, 194–5, 203,
    214, 220, 222
Priorato 76, 87

Quarts de Chaume 35, 40, 76, 160, 232,
    255
Quincy 174, 194, 214, 220, 222
Quinta de Bacalhôa 18, 22, 56, 213

Regnié 162
Retsina 196, 206, 251
Reuilly 133, 174, 194, 214, 220, 222
Rheingau 135–6, 143, 175
Reinhessen 169, 175
Rheinpfalz-Deidesheim see Deidesheim
Rias Baixas 11, 86, 198–9, 252
Ribera del Duero 22, 59, 114, 123, 177,
    199–200, 206, 212, 237, 239, 244
Riesling 7, 9, 11, 20, 29, 40, 42, 43, 130,
    135, 139–40, 142, 144, 169, 170, 175,
    181, 184, 197, 198, 200–4, 220, 231, 233,
    242
Rioja 50, 81, 99, 101, 123, 157, 170, 171,
    177, 182, 196, 199, 204–7, 232, 236, 239,
    244, 248